ADS TO
ICONS

More praise for *Ads to Icons*

"A very timely and important contribution as the communications industry and all those within it face up to the challenges of the multimedia, digital age which is most certainly now upon us."

John Bartle, Co-Founder, Bartle Bogle Hegarty

"The concept of 'pulling' versus 'pushing' communications is a revelation. And like most great concepts, I'll be using it over and over again."

Steve Stretton, Co-founder and Creative Head, Archibald Ingall Stretton

"Advertising is no longer the complacent, formulaic industry it once was. Creatively, it has become a wild frontier and *Ads to Icons* is its first guidebook."

Shaun McIlrath, Creative Director, Hurrell and Dawson

"How do brands continue to build equity in a world where there's a global case of attention deficit disorder? This book provides inspiration by telling stories of what the brand leaders are doing as changes in the media landscape become ever more relentless."

Ajaz Ahmed, Co-founder, AKQA

"While the press is talking constantly about the death of advertising, here is a book that will help students and practitioners alike realize it is far from true. Indeed, advertising is in rude health. The opportunities that modern technology affords agencies and clients are making creative possibilities endless and commercial success reachable. If you need great examples of how direct, digital, events, product, TV, print and mobile campaigns have worked to help clients grow their businesses, then *Ads to Icons* is a reference book you should have close to hand."

Elliot Moss, Managing Director, Leagas Delaney London

"We all know about the perspiration needed to achieve success, but inspiration and creative brilliance in advertising can transform a brand. This book illustrates some brilliant examples of this inspiration across a whole range of different media."

Miles Templeman, Director General, The Institute of Directors

ADS TO ICONS

How Advertising Succeeds in a Multimedia Age

Paul Springer

KOGAN PAGE

London and Philadelphia

First published in Great Britain and the United States in 2007 by Kogan Page Limited

120 Pentonville Road
London N1 9JN
United Kingdom
www.kogan-page.co.uk

525 South 4th Street, #241
Philadelphia PA 19147
USA

© Paul Springer, 2007

The right of Paul Springer to be identified as the author of this work has been asserted by him in accordance with the Copyright, Designs and Patents Act 1988.

ISBN-10   0 7494 4936 5
ISBN-13   978 0 7494 4936 0

British Library Cataloguing-in-Publication Data

A CIP record for this book is available from the British Library.

Library of Congress Cataloging-in-Publication Data

Springer, Paul.
    Ads to icons : how advertising succeeds in a multimedia age / Paul Springer.
        p. cm.
    Includes bibliographical references and index.
    ISBN-13: 978-0-7494-4936-0
    ISBN-10: 0-7494-4936-5
1. Advertising–Case studies. 2. Advertising campaigns–Case studies. I. Title.
    HF54823.S76 2007
    659.1'13--dc22

                                    2007001963

Typeset by Saxon Graphics Ltd, Derby
Printed and bound in Great Britain by Cambrian Printers Ltd, Aberystwyth, Wales

Dedicated to Doreen R Springer
… with sincere thanks to Andrea Springer, for supporting me throughout

Contents

Acknowledgements

Producing a book like this is never a one-person task and I have many people to thank for advice along the way, most notably my text, image and contact crunchers – Phil Johnson, Reg Winfield, Andrea Springer, Corrine Ellsworth, Irene Hoffman, Yan An, Marcus Wood, Vicki Turner, the MA Advertising students at Bucks University, and my very connected advisers, Suzie Shore (Getty Images), Olivier Rabenschlag, Steven Walls, Craig Ellson, Malc Poynton, Wu Xiaobo (Ping Cheng Advertising Co Ltd), China Advertising Association in Beijing, Zhang Yip Ping (Beijing Normal University), Jon Buckley and Stuart Archibald (Archibald Ingall Stretton, London), Cat Campbell and Jo Wallace (Quiet Storm, UK), Tim Allnutt (Naked Communications), Ajaz Ahmed (AKQA), Jane Austin (Austin O'Brien) and Julie Wright (Bucks University).

I would like to thank some key people for the good advice I received around the world: Xavier Adam, Tim Allnutt, John Bartle, Tom Bazeley, Gavin Bell, Thomas Beug, Cordell Burke, Jessica Bush, Mel Carson, Liz Childerley, Mark Collier, Jen Coupland, David Droga, Matt Eccles, Pierre Humeau, Simon Kershaw, Andy Law, Lorelei Mathias, Vibica McCoy, Shaun McIlrath, Gordon McMillan and team at Brand Republic UK, John Merrifield, Diana Nasello, Lisa Needham, Ng Tian It, Wendy Nicholl-Clark, Carol Ong, Malc Poynton, Nick Presley, Lino Ribolla, Alexander Shevelevich, Ed Shore, Peter Slater, Carolyn Tao, Damon Taylor, Vicki Trehaeven, Marcus Vinton, Delia Wen at CAA Sunshine Institution, Uri Wolter, Peter York, Zhang Yiping, Frank Yu and staff of Ping Cheng Advertising Co. Ltd, Guangzhou.

I owe a dept of gratitude to the creative directors, planners, producers, marketing directors, brand managers, legal people and many others with job titles I'd never heard of before this book, who have helped me on the way – and of course, all those quoted within.

I would particularly like to thank my employers, Buckinghamshire University, for giving me time and support during the production of this project, particularly my colleagues in the Faculty of Creativity and Culture who have chipped in with many neat observations on the way.

Finally, I'd like to thank my publishers Helen Kogan, Pauline Goodwin and the team at Kogan Page for their full support throughout the journey.

What *Ads to Icons* is about

Ads to Icons is about recent developments in the media-drenched age, where so many channels, public spaces and personal technologies carry advertising that it's hard for any messages to register. This book shows how advertising can still rise above the noise and clutter of mass communication to make people take notice. The fundamental argument that runs throughout the book is that advertising has been regenerated and transformed. Campaigns no longer need to just aim for attention; they can get customers to want more from *ads* in order to revere the *icons* they've created.

To prove the point, 50 unique approaches to advertising are illustrated. The reasons behind their successes are highlighted and analysis is given to show the contribution they have made to the development of advertising. The cases are supported by chapters that illustrate how the climate in which advertising operates has become appropriate to the new methods shown.

Examples of the world's best advertising campaigns are highlighted to reveal how they have made ads into cultural icons. Through tactical, carefully targeted campaigns, in an age of media saturation, advertisers have decided to grow beyond their traditional boundaries. Just when you thought you knew every advertising trick in the book, they can find ways to make you desire new products – *and* everything they stand for...

Overview

Chapters 1–6

Fifty cases of 'benchmark' advertising

I argue that each example in chapters 1–6 has made people identify, engage with and remain loyal to brands.

One could argue at length whether the selected 50 projects are the 'best', but the examples selected were either the first of their kind or have become the most renowned for their approach. They are certainly the *main* examples associated with the methods used. Some are famously high profile while others are quietly functional. All can claim to have moved the brands they promote towards something more iconic than advertising would, ordinarily, be expected to achieve.

In other publications all 50 would be described as unconventional – they are not your regular television or cinema commercials, billboards or press advertisements. Instead they realize original ways of engaging – and have proved to be commercially successful!

Chapters 7–10

Four contexts to reposition advertising

Chapters 7–10 provide a context for multimedia campaigns featured. Chapter 7 examines the potential of digital (*'new'*) media for advertising and reveals the tactics advertisers are using to win customers online. The new jobs in advertising that emerged through recent changes are profiled in chapter 8. Chapter 9 shows how advertising used a combination of new communication channels, analysis techniques and customer data in getting closer to customers, while chapter 10 reviews the 'bigger picture' by questioning where the boundaries of advertising now lie. The text concludes by demonstrating, once and for all, that advertising can now help its subjects occupy a culturally iconic position in the popular imagination.

Reflection on global advertising

Examples are drawn from 13 countries around the world, although many that are global campaigns stem from the UK or the United States. This raises the issue that 'world advertising' has often been taken to mean Western – US and European, the community of old capitalist economies. This is problematic in that the old order (first world, late-capitalist, in their second generation of commercial culture) is presently being challenged by newer capitalist economies in terms of volume, adspend and influence. The largest-spending economies on advertising – the United States, Germany, Italy, Japan and the UK – are being overtaken by China,

India and Arabic nations, while advertising produced in Brazil and Singapore is becoming increasingly influential. The material in this book has been assembled against the backdrop of this change, although, surprisingly, the newer forces in world advertising currently tend to look to be influenced by the older Western models. This will undoubtedly change in the near future, and as more new economies produce leading-edge campaigns, they will feature on this book's website, www.adstoicons.com.

Ten features and practical benefits

Shows the best examples of advertising promotion in different media

Charts mapping the modern mass-media landscape and mapping the timescales for cases

Diagrams showing how the case studies fit within a media mix

Outlines of how the campaigns were constructed, offered as future working models

Summary of 'essentials' at the end of sections

Professional profiles highlighting new roles in advertising

Updated industry profile revealing the issues driving creative advertising industries globally

Definitions of industry jargon and buzz words used

Global reach: examples drawn from 13 countries including the United States, China, the UK, Singapore and Germany. Contains examples from emerging advertising economies

Fifty case studies plus more examples in 10 chapters

How to use this book

Ads to Icons brings together 50 advertising projects from around the world that have moved advertising on from its conventional approaches. The book explores why they are benchmarks and what they offer for others seeking to promote beyond the widely regarded boundaries of advertising.

The text is designed to be used in a number of ways:

- *Dip in, find out* the best uses of each medium by looking at the best examples (chapters 1–6).
- *Read and reflect on issues* behind media choices in the contextual chapters, which profile innovative global works and the new media landscapes (introduction and chapters 7–10).
- *Browse* the case studies, and understand the thinking behind the innovative approaches taken.
- *Review* advertising tips in the case summaries.
- *Home in on the 'Essentials'* as the lessons to be learnt from each case study.

The book has been constructed in two parts:

Cases   Chapters 1–6 review 50 cases of new and iconic advertising from around the world and offer profiles, analysis, details of creative direction and a list of essential tips that can be taken from the case studies. These are designed to be dipped into. Each chapter has its own introduction.

Context   In chapters 7–10 the book shifts from review to analysis, to provide a context for integrated multimedia advertising. This includes an assessment of digitization in advertising, new jobs profiles, how advertisers target individual consumers and a reassessment of advertising boundaries. These provide a backdrop to the case studies and provide food for thought.

Logic of the structure

As well as the split into *case* and *context* sections, chapters are organized to trace developments from fixed to fluid formats; from direct offline tactics using established media (chapter 1 – Rethinking mass media) through to guerrilla and ambient approaches, which have opened up the range of advertising opportunities (chapter 2 – Widening formats and chapter 3 – Events-driven). The book then considers how advertising has affected the consumption experience (chapter 4 – Shaping product experiences) and the benchmarks of online advertising (chapter 5 – Digital persuasion and chapter 6 – Online spaces) as advertising moves towards more customer-integrated formats.

In the final section of this book, a discussion is mounted in which chapter 7 projects the significance of new personal and interactive media for advertising. Chapter 8 outlines the current roles within the advertising profession that have emerged as a consequence of new approaches to advertising while chapter 9 maps out key stages that show how advertisers have got closer to customers with their advertising. Finally, chapter 10 reviews all of this in light of the advertising industry, reappraising where advertising stops… and marketing begins.

Use of language

I have tried to avoid using jargon. Where specific terms commonly used in advertising feature in this text they are italicized. You will find them explained in a glossary of terms at the back of this book. In addition, the book's website, *www.adstoicons.com,* contains a larger glossary of terms.

The book's website: *<adstoicons.com>*

The material in this book is a snapshot of this moment in advertising, and is part of a fluid period of change. The book's website [adstoicons.com] will be updating the discussion and key cases as this fascinating phase in global communications develops. The website also contains other features such as an expanded (ongoing) glossary of terms used by industry professionals. You will find new terms, descriptions (and some jargon) first on this site!

Introduction

Background

- Essential argument: better methods are not necessarily more effective.
- Whoever said 'the ad is dead' is wrong.
- Not so 'New Media' advertising.
- What the digital age has done for advertising.
- *Digital and direct advertising benchmarks (timeline tables).*
- Effectiveness, mood marketing and the communications mix.
- 'The line' in advertising.
- Ethics of being unconventional.
- Big ideas come from advertising.
- *Range of media options (table).*
- Summary.

This section introduces some of the background issues that underpin the case studies in the next six chapters. Many of the issues briefly outlined in this introduction are discussed in greater detail later in this book. The purpose here is to explain why the situation is right for fresh approaches to advertising – and to dispel a few myths about the changes taking place.

Essential argument: better methods are not necessarily more effective

Advertising is represented in this book as being in a state of change for a number of reasons:

- The growth of digital technology led to more communication channels, so there are more opportunities to reach customers. However, so far this has mostly taken the form of *junk mail* and unwanted text messages.
- The development of online communications means that more customers can be addressed individually. Therefore adverts can be tailored to customers' preferences. However, advertising in this mode often takes the form of *spam*.
- Five decades on from the Madison Avenue, New York models of mass-media advertising, customers have grown up in a commercial environment. They are savvy enough to spot when they're being sold to, so that most adverts pass them by.
- So much of the urban landscape in cities is wrapped in 'communication messages' that the visual noise prevents conventional adverts from registering. Even on a one-to-one level, resistance to cold calling is still the norm.

The problems listed above should no longer concern advertisers. Advertising agencies can now access through digital channels such detailed customer data knowledge that, theoretically, they should be able to get closer to customers. However, more targeted information does not automatically mean that advertising is more effective. Despite increased investment in digital communications and a better understanding of how products appeal to customers, there is still widespread failure to understand and employ the potential of information on offer. So on the one hand, advertising has reached saturation point because there is too much of it, and advertisers have more information than they know what to do with. On the other hand, advertisers have the capacity to tailor messages to their target market, individually. There is even the potential to measure effectiveness more accurately.

Whoever said 'the ad is dead' is wrong

Reports of advertising's demise have been greatly exaggerated. A whole stream of branding and PR books have proclaimed the *fall of advertising and the rise of PR*, yet the revenues for *media advertising* – press ads, billboards, TV, film and radio commercials – still represent by far the largest slice of gross global ad spend.

So, let's resolve a few myths about media advertising right now:

- *Digital media such as the internet and database marketing spell the end of advertising.* No. Direct marketing can target ideal customers – and *prospects* – by name and

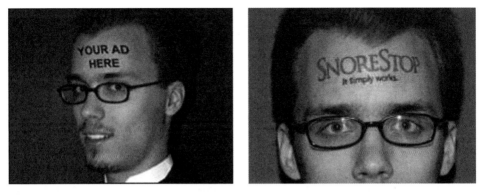

In 2005 American student Andrew Fisher received over 100 genuine bids on eBay when he auctioned his forehead as a billboard. Fisher's 'ad space' was a non-permanent tattoo on his forehead for one month. The stunt attracted global media coverage worth far more in publicity than the winning bid of $27,375 paid by medical company SnoreStop. The stunt was successful in getting media attention, but was the attention appropriate for the product?

> spending habits, but it doesn't make people want to change brands. In other words, broadcast channels are best at launching (or '*bursting*') new products into the public's consciousness.

- *TV commercials and billboards don't sell products any more.* True, but that's not the point. Adverts rarely result in direct sales, but they make products and services relevant. They give viewers a flavour of what they are about. Mass-media adverts like billboards and commercials are an introduction: you need to know something exists before you can decide if it's for you.

- *Using mass media is a blunt way to sell things.* Yes, but it still has capacity to reach masses. At its peak, a prime-time commercial in the United States is still seen by 88,000,000 people (during *Super Bowl 2005*) and 14,500,000 in the UK (for a Sunday morning Rugby World Cup Final in 2003). China's state television network, *China Central Television (CCTV)*, can command an audience of over 1 billion people. No other form of mass communication comes close to this level of customer reach.

- *You need to use old-style mass-media advertising to carry 'the big idea'.* This is partially true, but now media advertising is part of a much wider range of advertising activity. Campaigns may lead with high-profile advertising to raise awareness, but the art of selling may well be invested in other targeted activities.

- *Advertising through new media just uses old techniques.* This is partially true, although methods such as product placement and product comparisons need to be adapted to their format. Other methods such as product endorsement have not made the transition so well. *Brand ambassadors* (spokespeople) in the way that Tiger Woods is for *Buick* and Michael Jordan was for *Nike* no longer inspire the levels of trust they once did (see chapter 9).

To the public, commercials may seem much the same now as they were in 1990. Commercial television channels still have ad breaks, where there are still 30-

second commercials featuring product shots and slogans. TV is still able to create a powerful, coherent voice for a product. Commercials still create a buzz beyond the advertising slot. A US product ad featuring Brad Pitt during *Super Bowl 2005* generated publicity in the popular press days after it was broadcast. *Super Bowl* commercial spots are so coveted that 30-second slots in 2006 broadcasts went for $2.4 million. In the UK a commercial for *Lynx* deodorant attracted free daytime TV editorial space, enough in fact to propel the ad's soundtrack to the top of the UK singles chart. Such examples highlight the fact that commercials still have the largest audience reach, and can make a subject relevant on a mass scale.

Yet as anyone who has worked in the industry through the last 10 years would know, advertising isn't what it used to be. That's not to say it's worse, just a lot different. Unfortunately, there are only a few 'special moments' (such as sports tournaments) that can generate mass viewing, so programme makers have developed their own. Recently the conclusions to reality TV shows attracted mass audiences on a regular basis, but not on the scale of the late 1980s. This has become a recurring challenge for programme makers, who now need to drive ratings to generate that all-important ad revenue.

Media advertising is still effective, then, but has had to review its methods since the mid-1990s.

Not so 'New Media' advertising

Advertising techniques have already been established through digital channels – as chapters 6–10 illustrate. *SMS text* messaging (commonly used in China by e-commerce companies), e-mail (used in the United States by medical suppliers), *blipverts* (used in the UK as programme reminders) and even handles on petrol pumps (digitally rendered and used by car manufacturers in Britain) are now formats frequently used by advertisers, so the term 'new media' is not really representative any more.

Consumers are now equipped to check the claims of advertising campaigns online, through authorized material put out by brands and through unauthorized channels such as *social network* sites. So the link between a customer seeing an advertisement and the experience of consuming a product needs to be a seamless transition (see examples in chapter 4). Digital advertising has often been employed as the 'glue' in this process (as cases in chapters 5 and 6 illustrate). Viewers can check the claims of advertising and find further product information at their own time of choosing. They can also act on impulse to advertisements online, in a way that they cannot necessarily respond immediately to a television commercial (see chapter 9).

It does what it says on the tin

More so with digital advertising, there has to be a *truth* in the message that customers can identify with, for the strategy to strike a chord. If a campaign over-claims or is found to be flawed, the product would have been better served had the customer had not seen it in the first place. A bad personal experience with a product could well develop into a negative *product testimony*. Therefore an advertisement's claim must match people's product experiences (examples of campaigns that misfired can be found in chapter 9).

One could argue that linking product experiences to advertising is the way forward: several campaigns featured in chapters 3 and 4 mix online and offline methods to involve customers in core brand campaign messages. An old Maori saying explains this strategy well:

> **Tell me and I'll forget. Show me and I might recall. Involve me and I'll remember**

What the digital age has done for advertising

Digitization has made an old dog learn new tricks. The old dog – developed advertising industries in trade capitals (New York, Chicago, London, Munich, Tokyo, Milan and Shanghai) – learnt the new tricks offered by digital communications and adapted their old methods to new media (see chapter 1). Since the 1990s advertising industries have been going through the teething process of adapting to a digital age. Mergers and flexible working models characterized the 1990s in advertising, as established agencies grappled with the rapid influx of online media available. Video cassette recorders (VCR) and later live digital viewing (Sky+ and TiVo) enabled viewers to edit their own viewing. As with consumers' freedom to click and view on the internet, technology has conspired to make disruptive advertising less effective.

As advertisers looked for new ways of making an impact, they expanded beyond established media and into everyday urban landscapes, which have been redeveloped as advertising platforms. You only have to enter the subways of Hong Kong and see the posters and ad messages moulded around structural columns, escalator steps and handrails, on walkways and around subway trains to know the truth of this.

> **Today customers operate seamlessly across multiple channels, moving from awareness to purchase to advocacy at their own pace. And they expect their brands to do the same.**
> **(Euro RSCG 4D)**

This 'any space goes' outlook permeated through to the newer types of ad agency. Yet few established advertising agencies are experimenting with digital advertising and most are instead adopting a 'wait and see' approach.

In London even busking has been reshaped as an advertising platform. Buskers audition to become one of the *Carling Live!* performers in designated areas at the bottom of escalators and subway steps. This is often referred to as ambient advertising. This project ties in with other *Carling Live!* events, which include open-air concerts and sponsored music venues. (See chapter 2.)

Effectiveness, mood marketing and the communications mix

> **I know that half of my advertising budget is wasted. But I'm not sure which half.**
> **(Lord Leverhulme)**

Advertising that mixes several approaches at any one time employs what is often referred to as *the communications mix*. The approach has a number of distinct advantages but most significant is that more 'touch points' can be created between the message and the customer. By homing in on the places where customers are likely to be or are likely to look, awareness can be raised in the targeted audience, so campaigns will seem relevant to the audience that matters most, when it matters most.

Going beyond orthodox advertising media and into the spaces where *prospects* will be ensures that the right audience can be reached in the right tone, at a time when the message is relevant. A *media-neutral* approach to advertising (see later in this section) can integrate a product into the fabric of its intended customers' lives – before any purchase has been made. The aim is to ensure that the advertised

Digital advertising timeline

	Facilitators & watersheds	Benchmarks
	Google buys *YouTube*	*Orange* e-mail prompt for TV commercial (UK)
2 0 0 6	**Microsoft adCenter** **MySpace and Google tie-up** Boom in communications mix/ mash-ups Boom in online advertisement **ITV drama *Dubplate* (C4, UK)**	*match.com* first live broadcast advert, on *ITV3* (Monkey, UK) *Mentos/Diet Coke* user generated mash-up (US) **ch. 9** *Marc Ecko* 'Still tree' viral (Droga5, US) **ch. 5** *Hasbro* Monopoly live! (OMK/DDB, UK) **ch. 6** *Verizon* Beatbox Mixer (R/GA Interactive, US) **ch. 5**
2 0 0 5	**iPod Nano** **Microsoft adCenter flexible ad format** ch. 1 **Revver user-generated framework** ch. 1 **YouTube video share** ch. 1 **Google Earth**	O_2 communications mix retention scheme (AIS + others, UK) **ch. 4** *Sony Ericsson K750* 'Take your best shot' interactive interest site (Dare, UK) **ch. 6** *Orbitz The Gamer* (US) *Sony Ericsson D750* '5 seconds...' video/web/ TV mash-up (b+d, Germany) **ch. 4** *Singapore Airlines* Boarding Pass Privileges Scheme (Singapore) **ch. 6** *Axe Lynx* Axefeather site (BBH/Dare, UK) **ch. 6** *Audi A3* 'Art of the H3ist' online/offline launch (McKinney-Silver, US) **ch. 5** *Loctite* Super Bonder site (DDB, Brazil) **ch. 6**
2 0 0 5	**Web 2.0 coined, describing participatory web** **Boom in blogging activity** **Netscape scales down operation** **MMS (Multimedia txt message)**	*Back Dormitory Boys'* viral <www.backdormitoryboys.com> (China) **ch. 9** *Dove Unilever* Campaign for Natural Beauty social web network (O&M global) **ch. 6** *Pot Noodle* (CHI in-house, UK) *Orange Playlist* interactive TV programming (Initial, UK) **ch. 3** *J Sainsbury* Direct Smile (Hewlett Packard/TBWA\ London, UK) **ch. 9** *Amex* Adventures of Seinfeld & Spiderman webisodes (O&M/Digitas, US) **ch. 6** *Burger King* Subservient Chicken site (CP+B, US) **ch. 5**

Digital advertising timeline *continued*

	Facilitators & watersheds	Benchmarks
2 0 0 3	*Google AdSense* paid-for advertising **ch. 1** *MySpace* social site **ch. 1** SMS Txt Msg boom – e-business (China) *Sky+* (UK) **Hewlett Packard 'Direct Smile' platform**	*Wrangler Jeep Rubicon/Tomb Raider* Trial of Life advergame (Terminal Reality, US) **ch. 5** *Land Rover* information exchange <findyouraq.com> (Y&R/RKCR, global) *Volvo V50* website <http://demo.fb.se/e/v50/site/> SMS text messaging for automotive products (China) *Ford Mondeo* iTV microsite (O&M, UK) **ch. 1** *Sega* ESPN NFL Football 2K4 'Beta-7' launch (Wieden + Kennedy, US) **ch. 5**
2 0 0 2	**3G phones** *Apple* launches *iPod* *WiFi Tin Cans* <www.turnpoint.net/wireless/cantennagowto.html> **Blue Casting (via Bluetooth)**	*Tokyo Plastics* advertising/sales site <tokyoplastic.com> *Star Wars Kid* viral <www.ebaumsworld.com/starwarskidv.html> *AOL* online banners (Lean Mean Fighting Machine, UK) **ch. 9** *Mini Adventure* cross-media campaign (UK) *NEC* Ecotonoha website <www.ecotonoha.com>
2 0 0 1	Blog site boom Growth of *Hi-Res* 9/11: online market crashes *Apple iPod* *Wikipedia* (L Sanger & J Wales) Advergames appear online SMS Txt boom (UK) **TiVo interactive TV (US)**	*Sony PlayStation XBOX* viral <playmore.com> (Dare, Global) *Budweiser Whasssssup* viral ad with Superheroes (DDB Tribal, US) *DTM Race Driver* TVC in-game advertising (Energy Source, China) **ch. 5** *Nike Run London* site (AKQA, UK) **ch. 4** *Suicide Girls* pop site <www.suicidegirls.com> *Cadbury's* TXT 'n' WIN, on-pack/SMS/phone mash-up (Triangle, UK) **ch. 2**
2 0 0 0	Interactive TV shows: Survivor, Reality TV *I'm a Celebrity* & *Big Brother* *Friends Reunited* (f. S&J Pankhurst) **Claire Swain's rude e-mail circulated worldwide**	*Nike*-branded social network site *Nike* in-store interactive digital events (worldwide) **ch. 9**
1 9 9 9	*Microsoft Windows 2000* *Apple iMac* 'Think different' campaign Collapse of *boo.com* (UK) Txt msg boom **J Maeda publication** *maeda@maeda* **Millennium bug scare**	*Levi's* Sta-Prest Flat Eric web virals (BBH, UK) **ch. 2** *Nike iD* online <www.nikeid.com>

Digital advertising timeline *continued*

	Facilitators & watersheds	Benchmarks
1998	*Napster & MP3* *Google search engine* *G4 Mac & Microsoft PowerPoint* **Application programming Interfaces (APIs)** ***LiveJournal* (F B Fitzpatrick) Mac** *Canal+ buy Euro digital networks* **Talmud Project, MIT media lab (F D Small)**	First site for broadband <heavy.com> *Sony PlayStation* game *Grand Theft Auto* (GTA) launched on PC *Amex* viral advertising (O&M, global) *Mastercard's* 'Priceless' tag adopted online, **ch. 5**
1997	Mpeg **Asynchronous JavaScript & XML (AJAX)** Dot com boom Branded website phenomenon	
1996	*Yahoo!* *Macromedia Flash 1.0* *Web syndication* – gateway to *blogs* Rich text format **Global internet boom (first world)**	*Hewlett Packard* first rich media ad banner in digital game *Pong* (Red Sky Interactive, US) *Nike Town* opens (New York, US)
1995	*Hotmail* (F J Smith & S Bhatia) email *eBay* online trading site (f. P Omidyar & J Skoll) *Sim City* *Craigslist* (US, F C Newmark) *Amazon* online store Online pay-per-view (pornography industry) *Microsoft Windows 95* **1994** Netscape **1993** CD ROM, V Chip **1993** WiReD magazine **1991** IMDb.com (Internet Movie Database) founded **1991** BSkyB (UK) – 100 satellite channels **1991** Windows 3.0 **1984** Apple Mac **1983** Microsoft Word **1981** IBM's 1ˢᵗ PC **1979** Philips CD format	First online advertisement – *AT&T* banner (US) *1994* – hotwired.com first digital banner, US *1993* – *Land Rover Adventures* data base profiling (Craik Jones WMV, UK) **ch. 2** *1993* – *Tesco Clubcard* trialled (Evans Hunt Scott/Dunn Humby, UK) *1992* – Dec: first commercial Short Message Service (SMS) sent (to a *Vodafone*) *1991* – Aug: world wide web (f. Tim Berners-Lee, Queens Coll., Oxford U) *1989* – *Procter & Gamble* first iTV interactive advertising in the US *1982* – "☺" invented (www.cs.cmu.edu/~sef/Orig-Smiley.htm)

Compiled by: Paul Springer with Suzie Shore, Stephen Walls and Garry Sharpen

Direct advertising timeline

	Facilitators & watersheds	Benchmarks
2 0 0 7		
2 0 0 6		*IKEA* 'Everyday Fabulous' outdoor flash installations (IKEA/Deutsch, US & Japan) **ch. 3**
2 0 0 5		*Nike 90 Swift* football vending machines (Kinetic, Singapore) **ch. 2** *Audi A3* 'Art of the H3ist' online/offline launch (McKinney-Silver, US) **ch. 5**
2 0 0 4	**Andrew Fisher's forehead as adspace on *eBay***	*Singapore Fair Trade* stickered oranges (DDB Global, Singapore) *Singapore Cancer Society* lung ashtrays (Dentsu Young & Rubicam, Singapore) **ch. 3** *Lance Armstrong Foundation/Nike Livestrong* Bands (US/global) **ch. 3**
2 0 0 3	**In-store supermarket screens**	*Lego* environmentally blended billboards (O&M, Chile) **ch. 1** *Britvic Tango* Gotan family & Big Drench Roulette events (HHCL/Triangle/CHI, UK) *Johannesburg/First National Bank* cooling towers project (FCB 361, South Africa) **ch. 2** *Sibirsky Bereg Beerka* advertising tagged beer commercials (KRYN/Starcom, Belarus) **ch. 1** *Carling Live London Underground* buskers (Vizeum/Kinetic, UK) **ch. 2** *Polska Telefonia Cyfrowa* launch of *Heyah* (Polska & OMD, Poland) **ch. 4** *Médicos sin Fronteras* posters, offline and online (McCann Erickson, Spain) **ch. 2** *Lips Enterprises/Zippo* cab roof mounts (McCann Erickson, Singapore) **ch. 2**
2 0 0 2		*Mattel 100% Hot Wheels* small ads in *Auto Trader* (David&Goliath, US) **ch. 1** *adidas* vertical football billboard (TBWA\Japan) **ch. 3** *Marlboro Motel* (Tequila, UK) **ch. 3** *Mini Cooper* Mini Adventures (WCRS, UK) *COMME des GARÇONS* Guerrilla stores (in-house, fashion capitols) **ch. 3**

Digital advertising timeline *continued*

	Facilitators & watersheds	Benchmarks
2 0 0 1	First guerrilla stores	*Virgin* V Festivals *Skoda* 'Live with it…' direct mailers (AIS, UK) **ch. 4** *Britart.com* street captions (Mother, UK) *Nike Run London* 10k events (AKQA, UK) **ch. 4**
2 0 0 0	Advertising on subway steps, London	*Levi's Sta-Prest Flat Eric* soft toy launched **ch. 2** *FHM* Parliament projection (Cunning Stunts, UK) **ch. 4**
1 9 9 9		John West Salmon viral advert (UK); later a TV commercial
1 9 9 8		*Apple iMac* 'Think Different' Campaign (Chiat Day, US/global) Levi's *giant jeans* trailers around London & New York
1 9 9 7		*Siemens S10* mole phones cab drivers as brand ambassadors (Impact FCA!, UK) **ch. 4** *Britvic* Gotan Doll (HCL+P, UK)
1 9 9 6	*Pepsi* **Chart Show**	*Cadbury's Coronation Street* programme sponsorship (Triangle, UK) **ch. 1**
1 9 9 5		*1993 – Land Rover* Adventures (Craik Jones WMV, UK) **ch. 2** *1993 – Tesco* Clubcard (EHS, UK)

Compiled by: Paul Springer with Suzie Shore and Garry Sharpen

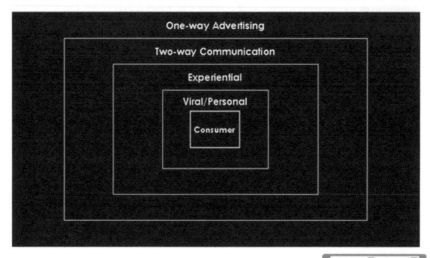

Wrapping the Consumer in Layers

One-way Advertising

Two-way Communication

Experiential

Viral/Personal

Consumer

[naked]

Wrapping the Consumer in Layers

Cab/Sat		Commercial TV				Press		Magazines
	Loyalty Schemes	Direct Mail					Competitions	
		Instore POS	Event Sponsorship	Cause Related	Store Card			
Internet Advertising	Advertorials/ Expert	Prog/Content Creation	SMS/Mobile		Art Galleries/ Exhibits Sponsorship		Vouchers	London Underground
		Editorial			On Pack Comps.			
			Guerrilla					
Commercial Radio	DR Press	Internet Content	Consumer Lifestyle Entertainment		Consumer Trade Shows		Member Schemes	Poster Exposure
		DR Radio		DR TV				
		Cinema		Ambient Outdoor				

[naked]

In defining appropriate consumer 'touch points' for a campaign, the well-known planning group *Naked Communications* use a '4d model' to map potential opportunities for interaction between the consumer and the product/brand. This is then mapped on to the span of media available (source: *Naked Communications*, 2006).

product springs to mind when a purchase choice is being made. If a message that reminds customers of a TV ad is placed, say by chocolate bars, it is more likely that earlier thoughts about the ad and the chocolate bar will come into play, and adjust the customer's intended purchase, thus effecting what's called *repertoire buying*. This is most common in the market for *fast-moving consumer goods* (FMCGs, see glossary).

> As consumers seek to avoid advertising, integration of creative messages into content will continue to develop until we embrace the game of 'engage the consumer' with gusto. (Marc Mendoza, MPG)

In recent years, marketers and advertising agencies have become fascinated by the potential for shaping advertising around the moods and behavioural patterns of likely customers. However, while better information is now available on customers, knowing what customers do or prefer is not the same as affecting their (ever-shifting) buying habits.

In fact, advertising's effect on sales has been so 'hit or miss' that many companies have sought out more reliable ways of increasing profit margins (see *Imagining new formats* in chapter 1). This has led to claims by the likes of former *Coca-Cola* Chief Marketing Officer Sergio Zyman that we've reached the end of advertising as we know it: creative advertising has been called upon to be more accountable because other modes of promotion are. Marketing texts proclaim 'mood marketing' to be more of a science, planners have claimed that the urban environment is now a '360 degree brandscape' (for instance, Hallberg, 1995), while design firms have developed specialisms in 'product-user experience'. Design and research units of *Philips* (Eindhoven), *Imagination*, *IDEO* (both London), *Sony Ericsson* (in Sweden, Japan, China, the United States and UK) and *Apple* (California) have specialist divisions that consider the relationship between product communication and product experience.

Other names for the *communications mix*

Marketing driven	Planning driven	Creatively driven
Mood marketing	360 degree advertising	product-user experience
Experiential marketing	multimedia advertising	
Mind messages		

In other words, different disciplines claim to have more effective methods of getting customers to bond with products, brands and services. Advertising needs to tap into these disciplines if it is to maintain its currency as *the* most effective means of managing awareness.

Advertising has battled back by reshaping its strategic approach. Advertising planning firm *Naked Inside* developed a 'Four circles process' where tangible information about products, *prospects*, brand cultures and aspirations are assessed. This has proved a useful way to establish principles of a communications strategy.

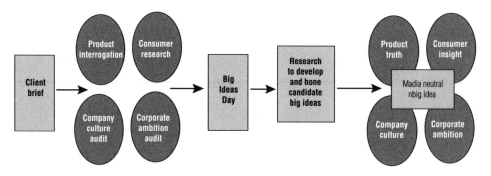

Four Circles Process is *Naked Inside's* method of ensuring each area of a client brief is addressed. Staff visit the client's factories and talk to their staff. In getting to know the product, they research around the target consumer and set up focus groups to understand the company culture and assess how it's seen. They also interview management to see what their customer's idea of 'success' looks like.

'The line' explained

Above-the-line advertising is…
Media advertising
TV commercials
Cinema adverts
Press adverts
Billboard posters
Mass media advertising

17.5% commission
threshold

Thru the line advertising is…
Media neutral

Multimedia advertising,
including online integrated
(Above & Below) approach

Below-the-line advertising is…
Direct advertising
Magazine inserts
Advertorials
Direct mail
Ambient advertising
One-to-one/business-to business

'The line' in advertising

For the most familiar forms of promotion, *media advertising* (which comprises television, cinema and radio commercials, press ads and billboard posters), advertising agencies can charge in excess of 17.5 per cent commission. This commission threshold is often referred to as *the line*.

This threshold became increasingly significant during the 1990s in the United States and UK. Ad agency planners and account handlers, who were used to dealing only with media advertising, avoided *below-the-line* work. They tended to farm out work such as direct mail, or give it to junior advertising teams and charge a nominal fee. Ad agencies were reluctant to take on such work because they could not charge as much, so the 17.5 per cent commission became a measure of whether agencies would be willing to take the work on. Smaller advertising jobs did not require advertisers' existing mass-media facilities and did not draw the scale of revenue required to maintain advertisers' overheads. Consequently, junior advertising staff began to specialize in direct advertising and went on to start their own 'below the line' firms, taking the work being passed over by the larger agencies. Ironically, many companies also chose to shift large portions of their budget from *media* to *direct* advertising because it offered better returns.

The commission system had protected advertising agencies from inflation and rising media costs, which were in effect being passed on to clients. However, in 1992 US and UK clients changed this by demanding reduced rates averaging between 4 and 8 per cent. This was hotly contested in the industry press at the time. In the wake of a global recession, several leading agencies buckled under the pressure. As soon as some agencies reduced their commission levels the system was effectively broken and full-service agencies lost their authority. Mass-media advertising agencies responded by attempting to diversify, having learnt that by producing work above and below the line their employability increased. More agencies started taking on jobs such as leaflets, flyers and magazine inserts and work normally done by marketing firms, such as targeted letters *one-to-one* from companies to individual consumers (see chapter 8). The transition from *above-the-line* to *media neutral* was not smooth in US or European agencies. Richard Huntington, a planning director at *HHCL/Red Cell United* UK, remarked that there were 'the ostriches who bury their heads in the sand and insist nothing fundamental is going to change. Then there were the lemmings, leaping off the cliff shouting "content, content, it's all about branded content"' (Bannister, 2005). The latter continued to push the old media formats, in the hope that famous advertising might be confused with value for money.

Some advertising groups in the UK set up their own 'below the line' departments. For instance, *Bartle Bogle Hegarty* set up *Limbo*; *Lowe Howard Spink* set up *Lowe Direct*; *Ogilvy & Mather* set up *Ogilvy Direct*; *Saatchi & Saatchi* set up *Saatchi Direct*; *Publicis* developed *Publicis Dialog*. Media holding groups such as *Omnicrom*, *Publicis*, *WPP* and *Havas* acquired successful below-the-line advertising firms.

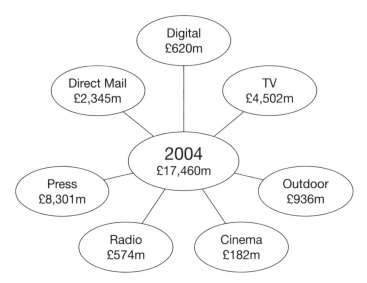

Advertisers' media options in 2005.

Media advertising agencies such as *Grey Worldwide* and *M&C Saatchi* (UK) also bought below-the-line firms and re-branded them as satellite partners.

This is when the distinction between the roles of advertising and marketing started to blur.

Ethics of being unconventional

By taking advertisements out of their usual broadcast frames and placing them in everyday environments, concerns have been raised that they should not be allowed where they cannot be avoided – on escalator risers, walkways, wrapping buildings

In urban and rural areas, the landscape is increasingly wrapped in advertising messages. It is more likely that lack of impact rather than legislation will halt its growth.

or even wrapping broadcast news. The level of intrusion could be extended to digital media – e-mail, landline and mobile phones. For digital communication, opt-in/out legislation has had to be rapidly drawn up in different countries, with cross-national regulatory bodies rapidly establishing precedents for future practices (see *Regulatory environments*, chapter 1). At present, advertisers can get away with far more online than through broadcast channels, although this is in the process of being redressed in Asia, North America and Europe.

Internationally, industry and government regulators are being tested to adjudicate the wave of new media. In France and Norway, for example, bans have been imposed on SMS messages, but they are allowed in China, the United States and the UK. Laws have been introduced in China to regulate e-messaging, while operator licence sales for telecommunications have been more tightly regulated in France, Italy and the UK.

Part of the dilemma that self-regulation has created is that contentious cases tend to be newsworthy, which in itself makes being censored a viable 'medium': within capitalist societies, all aspects of the everyday are understood to 'communicate', so potentially anything could work as a commercial. The landscape for modern advertising is therefore a complex one, where most spaces – physical or virtual, online and offline – could be deemed a potential advertising platform.

Big ideas come from advertising

Has advertising encroached on other forms of promotion, or has marketing fully absorbed advertising? As in any new era, defining who leads and who follows is a bit of a 'chicken and egg' conundrum. Inevitably perhaps, outlooks on this issue will be shaped by which perspective best serves your interests. The dynamic between advertising, marketing and public relations is considered at greater length in chapter 10.

Most advertising agencies now purport to go beyond their usual remit and seek to create 'big ideas', intended to go beyond the immediate promotion of a product to produce the total communication solution. Many pronounce this on their website:

'One idea at work. One way of looking at things. One spirit – the one idea.' *aislondon.co.uk*

'Big strategic ideas lay the foundation for brand growth.' *bbh.com*

'In the business of communication, the idea is king.' *tribalddb.com*

'We need to create ideas that people want to spend more time with.' *jwt.com*

'We create ideas that inspire enduring belief.' *leoburnett.com*

'We believe… in the power of ideas to transform our clients' businesses, brands and reputations.' *saatchi.com*

'… to develop a big inclusive idea which works hard across numerous communication levels.' *Loweworldwide.com*

'We believe that brilliant ideas can achieve extraordinary results.' *ddb.com*

'New ideas are our lifeblood, and we constantly strive for creativity in everything we do (apart from our accounting!).' *newmediamaze.com* (online marketing/PR)

Many in advertising point to a British example, *FCUK*, which ran between 2000 and 2005 for *French Connection*, as an example of an advertising-centred 'creative idea' that transformed the presence and market share of a fashion chain. Taking on the 'bigger picture' of developing communication strategies means that advertising agencies would like to get involved at product design stage. Yet in practice, production companies that use advertising are keen not to over-commit to one advertising agency. They prefer to be the guardians of their own brand and like agencies to pitch for tender.

For instance, back in 1999, the *Apple Corporation* famously opted to use the features of their new *iMac* as the driver for their promotional material. Ad agencies were charged with using the look of the iMac as a visual hook and selling proposition, so that media campaigns around the world settled on a similar 'product as star' tactic. *Apple's* promotional success was mostly down to managing their communications strategy from source – an approach previously used with success by *Coca-Cola*, *Gap* and *Benetton*.

The blurring of distinction between advertising, marketing and design has led to situations where different types of creative firm have pitched for the same work. In 2003 the men's fashion label *Van Heusen* tendered work for brand development and received pitches from a marketing firm, a top-ten-listed media advertising agency, an integrated advertising agency, a PR firm and a design agency. All were deemed capable of delivering on the brief. The client had to decide which type of approach would provide the best 'fit' [sic]. Jon Ingall of *Archibald Ingall Stretton* – one of the agencies pitching – observed that 'we see this more and more where the mix of agencies pitching covers a wider range of skills'.

Essentially what we see now is products, spaces and events more often becoming extensions of advertising campaigns. Some of the prime examples of this feature in chapters 3 and 4, where purpose-built environments, participatory activities and even fashion accessories have been constructed to raise awareness of a particular product, brand or cause. Such types of promotion could conceivably be generated by advertising, marketing or public relations firms: the decision tends to be based on where a project sits within the bigger promotional scheme.

What we can see then is that the climate is right for advertising to use a communication mix. In an age where more media are capable of being used to carry advertising and where advertisers are required to work harder for customers' attention,

Three ways of making advertising work in a multimedia age: captioning the landscape for *Britart.com* (see chapter 3); in-game advertising, which used virtual space as adspace for *DTM* (see chapter 5); and a live digital game of *Monopoly*, played out online and acted out offline and incorporating material generated by those taking part (see chapter 6).

Range of media options: the following have been used as advertising platforms

Television & press	Ambient (outdoor & indoor)	Digital
• Idents/ sponsorship • Programme creations • Interactive (txt or phone line supported) • Teletext • Cinema ads • Advertorials • Editorials • Branded titles • Inserts • Competitions • Direct mail • Sample mounts: CD/DVD • Cause-related • Direct response (TV, radio & press) • TV station (Audi) • Product placement • Optical – blipverts, interstitial station logos, sponsorship bumpers	• Subway escalators, hand rails, columns and flooring • Carpark barriers • Pavements/curbs • Transvision: screens in stations, on buildings & tube escalators • In-store TV • Shopping trolleys • appropriated spaces: exhibitions, retail space, parks, street 'happenings' • Cab drivers • Buses • Taxis • Posters • Outdoor billboards • Bus shelters • Blimps (balloons tethered or free-flying) • Aircraft towing banners • Neon signs on top of buildings • Laser light projections onto buildings • River barges • Graffiti/'copy-left' stencil • Buskers • Sponsored events • Cut-outs • In-store point of sale • Wobblers, card cut-outs, floor transfers • On-pack • Face-to-face (on street, at doorstep) • Environment 'wraps' • Vans/board vans • Decked-out cars • Pavement artists • Appropriations: dust on car, air fresheners • Guerrilla (unpaid)	• Wireless – SMS WAP & PDA • Drag 'n' drop ads (AOL) • Banners • Virals: MPGs, QuickTime movies • Web links/downloads • Web sites – personal and product/brand • Interactive links • Telephone 'hotlines' • E-mail, personalized and mass-distribution • Blog sites; business, culture/personal, political • MMS: Multimedia text • Bluecasting: Bluetooth • Pop-ups • Search engines and navigation structures • Information sites – sponsored review and product info sites • Podcasts • Search engines • Member schemes • Store cards • Events • Loyalty schemes • Exclusive support services (lounges) • Away-days • Targeted promotions & vouchers • Direct mail pieces (millions of different formats) • Telemarketing (inbound & outbound) • Custom published magazines (Visa, Amex, supermarkets, electrical stores, etc)

we can see a new era emerging for global advertising. The campaigns in the following sections go some way to showing what operations in the new *communications-mixed* advertising environment will be like.

Summary

Multimedia advertising	A connected mix of promotional approaches – mass and personalized media
Has marketing/PR replaced advertising?	No. The boundaries between disciplines are now less clear, and different types of promotional practice compete for the same work
The line	A commission threshold that is often charged to produce high-cost mass media. The term has now come to distinguish old from new media
Above-the-line	Mass-media, mass-audience approach, including TV, press & billboard ads
Thru-the-line	An integrated approach of mass and personalized media
Below-the-line	Direct advertising, direct mail, online and other targeted one-to-one media
Strategic communications	Campaign planning can be carried out by advertising, marketing, PR and planning firms, depending on what drives for the idea for the strategic plan
Who now does the marketing, PR and advertising bits?	It depends on whether you're launching a new product or simply raising awareness. Advertisers, marketers, PR, data analyst experts can all claim to be specialists in delivering the total communication solution
What's digital done for advertising?	Digital has allowed advertisers to reach customers in new ways. It has allowed advertisers to create interactive catalogues, set up customer support and set up information channels and has introduced the possibility of company-to-customer dialogue

PART 1

Cases

1 Rethinking mass media

This chapter considers the advertising scene from three perspectives: it addresses how old formats have been revitalized, how new channels offer fresh opportunities and how regulatory bodies are meeting the changing state of advertising.

Rethinking old formats

The first section features cases that have redesigned established formats. These include 'hard copy' formats – making the billboard format eye-catching (*Lego*) and using the 'small ad' format differently (*Mattel*) – and television formats – commercial breaks (*Sibirsky Bereg*), programme sponsorship (*Cadbury's*) and interactive television (*Ford*).

Imagining new formats

The second section reviews more recent advertising methods online. This includes the use of search listing (*Google*), niche timeslots (*Microsoft*), social networks (*MySpace*), video sharing (*YouTube*) and user-generated entertainment (*Revver*).

Regulatory environments

The third section considers the regulatory environment for advertising by reviewing a cross-section of industry and government regulatory bodies from the United States, Japan, the UK, China and a cross-European regulatory body.

Cases featured...

Rethinking old formats
Sibirsky Bereg Beerka delivering to beer – connected with other advertisements in a commercial break

Ford Mondeo interactive – pushed the potential of cable and satellite viewing by using an interactive format

Cadbury's Coronation Street sponsorship – the long-term development of a brand through association

Mattel 100% Hot Wheels 'small ads' – tested preconceptions of small-ad readers in a niche market

Lego billboards – blended posterscapes

Imagining new formats
MySpace – personal web space

YouTube – video upload and share

Revver – user-generated, advertising tagged material

Google AdSense – Search platform

Microsoft adCenter – niche positioned advertising

Regulatory bodies
BBB – USA, an industry-based pressure group

JARO – Japan, the national advertising regulatory authority

Ofcom – UK, office of the communications regulator that monitors and arbitrates broadcast advertising

CAA – China, regulatory body upholding integrity of communications for industry and government

EASA – Pan-European, a body that arbitrates between national regulatory bodies across Europe

Suggested reading

Battelle, John (2005) *The Search: How Google and its rivals rewrote the rules of business and transformed our culture*, Nicholas Brealey, London

Handy, Charles (2001) *The Elephant and the Flea*, Hutchinson, London

Heath, Joseph and Potter, Andrew (2005) *The Rebel Sell: How the counterculture became consumer culture*, Capstone, Sussex

RETHINKING MASS MEDIA 1:
RETHINKING OLD FORMATS

Sibirsky Bereg Beerka 'Buffer' Commercials

Product:	*Sibirsky Bereg* bar snacks, *Beerka* sub-brand
Target market:	men, 18–24 years old, Russia
Agency/country:	Kryn/Starcom, Belarus
Planning/production time:	12 months
Reach:	over 60 million viewers
Length of customer engagement:	20-second slots
Brief:	reinforce *Beerka's* positioning as the right snack to accompany beer
Budget:	undisclosed
Lifespan:	4 months (June–September 2004)
Benchmark:	fresh use of TV commercial format, media placement

The strategy for *Sibirsky Beerka* relied on juxtaposition with beer advertising.

Project background

The launch of a bar snack in Russia during 2004 involved an innovative approach to using the television commercial format. The advertisers aimed to distinguish a new brand, *Beerka*, from other snacks by associating it with drinking beer, but did not want the campaign confused with drinks advertisements. So the advertising agency *Kryn* bought 20-second advertising slots immediately following beer commercials for a four-month period on one of Russia's leading commercial channels and ran an advertisement to connect drinking beer in a bar with the snack.

The simple idea immediately gave the new product a market presence and soon made it the snack to have in Russian bars.

		03				04									
Timeline	S	O	N	D	J	F	M	A	M	J	J	A	S	O
Concept development	■	■	■	■										
Completed project launch				☼	☼									
Online activity							☺	☺	☺	☺	☺	☺		
Additional promotion					◎	◎	◎	◎						
Media exposure										--	--	--	--	
Hits (millions)				0.5	1	3	5		6	8			10	

Sibirsky Bereg, which is a well-established manufacturer of Eastern European snack foods (with over 20 per cent of the snack market), is famed for creating new pockets in the mass market. *Beerka*, a salted fish and meat offering, was initially launched as a mass-market beer snack, not a bar snack only. However, they felt that traditional snack food did not match beer well and proposed *Beerka* to bars and beer producers as a special snack. The consequence was that *Beerka* had a widespread presence in retail grocery stores trading beer and in bars as well. This made it ripe for its strategic positioning in commercials as the snack to have with beer. An agreement had already been reached to make it available in Russian bars. The campaign's hook line *Beerka. Delivering to beer!* reflected the product's positioning and reinforced it. Men were targeted as the main consumers of beer and beer snacks in a bar environment, so the campaign aimed to convey that drinking beer was a better experience with beer snacks – after a sip of beer you want to have a snack, and after having a snack you want another sip of beer...

Profile: campaign strategy

Snack food producers *Sibirsky Bereg* were keen to establish their snacks for a male adult audience, whereas most snacks were aimed at younger audiences. The snacks were salty and had a strong flavour, so the connection with bars and beer drinking was envisaged from the outset. However, the market was notoriously difficult to break into without an existing presence. Drawing on brands that were already synonymous in existing Russian bars gave *Beerka* a ready-made platform that inferred an endorsement from brands that beer drinkers would know and trust. So the promotional campaign in bars, where the product was in the right environment, was supported by the main campaign on television.

Preliminary negotiations with Russia's main beverage brands were significant in ensuring that the campaign worked across the range of brands simultaneously. Negotiations emphasized the need to maintain balance between rival beer brands, and the campaign treated preceding commercials with parity by ensuring that *Beerka's* advertisements were a generic parody of beer commercials. As a form of *third party association* the campaign was positioned as being beneficial to the drinks industry by raising the presence of bar culture in the commercial break.

Prior to launch, an extended lead-in time was required for media specialists to negotiate buying commercial break slots well in advance. They also needed to negotiate with media buyers at other advertising agencies to check their scheduling. In other words, the agency *Kryn* had to conduct exhaustive research on advertising space positioning in the beer market, which involved negotiating with the individual drinks producers and holding companies.

The campaign also included outdoor advertising, which exploited the Russian and Belarusian roadside billboard format of displaying posters in pairs. *Sibirsky Bereg Beerka* posters were simply juxtaposed with images promoting beer. *Beerka's* website included a bar-themed web *blog* and posting board featuring images of pin-ups and bar pranks, so a bar room ambience was developed around the product online.

As a way of 'bursting' the product onto the market, the technique proved extremely effective, helping *Sibersky Bereg* to make *Beerka* one of Russia's leading snack brands within four months, during the run of the campaign, to the extent that the seafood snack market segment is almost as big as the potato crisp market in value.

Creative direction

The commercials used a tone of humour synonymous with beer commercials in Europe. The narrative device is also familiar to beer commercials: in each of the six *Beerka* commercials a male central character is featured watching television. At the moment he is about to drink his beer the events on the screen burst into life in his living room. The casting and exaggerated storyline provided a treatment that was clearly consistent with beer advertising.

Much of the campaign's success was to do with its planning and media-buying strategy. *Sibirsky's* plan was to encourage open and friendly interaction with partners in the drinks industry. This enabled *Beerka's* positioning as a non-competitor with beer commercials in an advertising break.

In terms of planning, the campaign challenged an assumed television advertising convention. In some countries advertising breaks usually involve brands competing with one another in an effort to grab viewers' attention (having competing brands in the same commercial break is relatively recent in the UK). *Beerka's* launch strategy challenged the assumption that all brands during commercial breaks are in competition. Preceding beer commercials served to set the context for *Beerka*. In return, *Beerka's* 'add-ons' helped make commercial breaks memorable for beer commercials. *Beerka's* scheme of looping in beer brands raised the profile of the genre on Russian television. It was in the interests of beer producers, as advocates of beer brands, to support *Beerka's* interconnected campaign.

Review

Television commercials were launched simultaneously with the press and billboard ads within the campaign. Juxtaposed billboards appeared in cities and on roadsides.

The tone and treatment of *Sibirsky Bereg Beerka* commercials were consistent with those of Russian beer commercials, so they appeared to naturally follow on.

- The positioning of the 20-second commercials was of greater significance than the content of the advertisements because they made the connection between drinking beer and eating snacks.
- The campaign used a classic *third party association* strategy to set up the project. By making it in the mutual interests of beer producers to go along with the promotion, *Beerka* benefited by being the only beer snack involved.
- Although the media used were conventional, a buzz was created by using the format in an imaginative way, which made commercial breaks appear less predictable to viewers.
- The launch campaign enabled *Beerka* to become the market leader in the beer snacks category of the Russian market after only four months. Awareness of the brand across Russia and Belarus was 35%, and their share of the beer snacks market reached 11%.

Integrated mix

proportion of budget

- Commercials
- Online
- Ambient

proportion of campaign

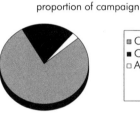

- Commercials
- Online
- Ambient

Essentials

1. Re-examine the 'rules' of advertising and assess whether they can be renegotiated.
2. Consider the other stakeholders – who else benefits from challenging existing formats?
3. It is worth acknowledging which medium is the main driver for a campaign. Other platforms can be used to reinforce the buzz independently.

For links see www.adstoicons.com.

Ford Mondeo interactive commercial

Product:	Ford Mondeo
Target market:	29–35 male, young family car market
Agency/city:	Ogilvy & Mather, London
Planning/production time:	6 weeks, from concept to production
Reach:	UK, 5 million viewers with satellite television handsets
Length of customer engagement:	30 seconds–5 minutes
Brief:	communicate how the 1,500 improvements to the new-look *Ford Mondeo* are greater than the sum of their parts. Encourage viewers to order a brochure or request a test-drive
Budget:	approximately £50,000 to produce the microsite
Lifespan:	September–December 2003
Benchmark:	interactive television commercial advertising

Ford Mondeo television commercial in 2003; an interactive link was added for viewers who pushed the red button on their digital TV remote-control handsets.

Project background

In March 2003 *Ogilvy & Mather* launched the first interactive television commercial in Europe. The advertisement, launched in a prime-time slot on *Sky One*, Britain's largest satellite channel, invited cable and satellite viewers to discover more by pressing the 'red' button on their remote control handsets. By pressing the red button viewers were transferred to a digital 'microsite' that provided product information and the opportunity to order a catalogue from *Ford*. For *Ford*, this created a situation where viewers could become self-selecting prospects, simply by clicking a button during their commercial.

Timeline	02 O	N	D	03 J	F	M	A	M	J	J	A	S	O	N	D
Concept development								■	■	■					
Completed project											■	■			
Launch												☼			
Span												☺	☺	☺	☺
Media exposure												◙	◙	◙	◙
Hits (interactive, 10,000s)												10	20		35.7

Ford had made over 1,500 improvements to the *Ford Mondeo* and needed to demonstrate to its audience that these refinements added up to more than the sum of their parts. The car also had a new positioning – *one of the safest places to be*. Like the *Mondeo*, a microsite was a safer and less crowded space to address interested viewers directly.

As a feeder to the microsite, the commercial started like a 1950s animation overlaid onto real film footage. It featured cat and mouse cartoon characters Tom and Jerry in a chase scene, where Jerry the mouse seeks refuge in the safety of a *Ford Mondeo*. In the top right of the screen, a small red symbol appeared throughout, inviting viewers to press the 'red' button.

In contrast to the frenetic commercial that dramatized *Mondeo's* positioning, viewers were transported to a safe place to admire the new-look refinements to *Mondeo*. The tone was more serious and product oriented: after the hook of the commercial, the microsite operated as pre-showroom salesperson.

Access to the *Ford* microsite was free to satellite and digital viewers and did not require additional hardware or upgrades for access. At any time during the TV commercial, viewers could press the red button on their remote control to launch the interactive content. The sites uploaded options enabling viewers to click through more 'extended advertisement' content, at their own pace. Extended information included details of changes to the interior and exterior of the *Mondeo*, and allowed the viewer to order a brochure and even book a test drive – far more than could be achieved through a 30-second commercial.

Once on the microsite, *O&M* could monitor usage by tracking the rate of *click-throughs* from the interactive menu. The site provided fresh customer data through catalogue requests, for which prospects would have to provide contact details. The microsite therefore created the chance of building customer relationships.

The conversion rate from viewers to *prospects* was significantly more than for previous *Mondeo* campaigns – 357,000 individuals interacted with the ad, and over 3,500 brochures were requested and 1,203 test drives booked. The cost was esti-mated at just 6 pence per 30 seconds of each *prospect's* time.

Profile: interactive television commercials

Ford Mondeo's campaign was the most prominent example of the interactive televi-sion (iTV) medium and heralded the start of a genre made possible by the advent of digital satellite and cable television. The first interactive commercials were aired in the United States during 1998 while the first in the UK was for *Procter & Gamble Pantene* shampoo (2001) through the *Cable & Wireless* network, where pressing the red button gave viewers advice on shampoo for different types of hair and offered them free mailed samples.

The layered approach of iTV enabled advertisers to elaborate on product bene-fits for interested viewers without having to create a general buzz, because viewers had already registered interest.

This first wave of interactive advertising held advantages over television commer-cials, in that it was not subject to the time constraints of television commercials. They did not need to establish a narrative format and could get straight into details with an interested viewing audience; they could also distinguish interested viewers and target markets by region or customer type. The method had other advantages too: it provided fresh data on interested *prospects* in terms of size of interest and created an opportunity to incentivize a customer niche that had registered interest.

Creative direction

As part of the creative brief, the microsite's art direction was designed to match the car's craftsmanship. It did not need to extend the commercial's storyline because it was dealing more directly with interested customers, getting them to take a closer look at the new *Mondeo's* refinements.

The microsite's purpose was therefore direct and functional in directing viewers towards recording interest. The sub-channel allowed people to respond to the advertisement immediately on impulse. Where the commercial stoked interest, the microsite provided the tools to make direct contact. The *call to action* was therefore immediate, as interest could be followed up in an instant.

Review

The *Ford Mondeo* interactive commercial featured in the national press as an innovation in the week leading up to its first airing. Therefore anticipation had been created, and the brand had benefited by being seen to pioneer this type of digital advertising.

> The **Ford Mondeo iTV defined what a best-in-class interactive car-buying experience should be: it allowed users to know more about the car, see its features and benefits in detail and order a brochure, all from the comfort of their armchair. It even enabled users to book a test-drive, linking the online experience with the one in real life.**
>
> **(The commercial's Creative Director, Lino Ribolla, now Senior at OgilvyInteractive, New York)**

- The *Mondeo* campaign was among the first to flex the potential of some 10 million UK homes with cable or satellite connections. The level of interaction was basic – people were rewarded for following the link with more footage, and the chance to get more product information.
- The red button opened the potential for supplementary content and generated *click-through* data. This allowed the advertiser to measure the microsite's effectiveness without relying on the broadcaster to provide statistics.
- The response rate was initially high during the first wave of interactive commercials on both sides of the Atlantic. During 2000 in the United States it was estimated that over 23% who clicked the red button were willing to take further action – either by following up on an offer or by requesting further information (source: *RespondTV*). The response rate has decreased as 'enhanced commercials' have become more of a broadcast norm.

Ford Mondeo's interactive advertisements distinguished potential *prospects* from curious viewers.

Ford Mondeo interactive television pages: viewers clicked through options using their remote handsets.

Integrated mix

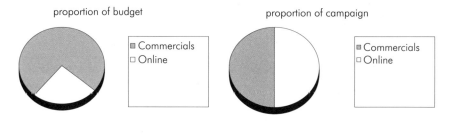

proportion of budget

☑ Commercials
☐ Online

proportion of campaign

☑ Commercials
☐ Online

Essentials

1. Interactive commercials allow viewers to respond on impulse.
2. Interactive links can address niche markets by region or social demographics.
3. Quantitative data can be collated from *click-throughs*, while qualitative data on prospects can be generated if viewers demonstrate a willingness for involvement.

For links see www.adstoicons.com.

Mattel 100% Hot Wheels Classified Small Ads

Product:	**Mattel 100% Hot Wheels miniature car models**
Target market:	specialist collectors
Agency/city:	*DavidandGoliath*, Los Angeles
Planning/production time:	2 months
Reach:	300,000
Length of customer engagement:	placed weekly magazine
Brief:	extend the campaign headline *Almost Too Real* to let people know how realistic-looking the miniature cars appear
Budget:	$40 each small ad
Lifespan:	one month, 2003
Benchmark:	rethinking placement and use of established media

(These ads for 1/18 scale Hotwheels were placed next to actual car listings in 'Auto Trader')

One of a series of press advertisements taken out in *Auto Trader USA*, advertising *100% Hot Wheels* classic sports car miniatures alongside the full-size models.

Project background

The market for *Mattel 100% Hot Wheels* model cars is small but their customer base tends to be loyal. *Mattel* aimed to extend their customer base with the proposition that their top-of-the-range miniatures were *almost too real*, so the agency *DavidandGoliath* targeted the most likely specialist interest group, classic car fanatics, because they too tended to be devoted to their hobby. They took out a series of small ads in the classified section of *Auto Trader*, and had the advertisements for *Mattel's* model cars placed next to adverts for the full-size versions. Readers were able to judge how close the collectable miniatures were to the originals.

Timeline	02 S	O	N	D	03 J	F	M	A	M	J	J	A	S	O	N
Concept development					■	■									
Launch						☼									
Online activity							☺	☺	☺	☺	☺	☺			
Additional promotion				◙	◙	◙	◙								
Media exposure							--	--	--	--	--	--	--	--	--
Hits (millions)							1	5	10		20				50

The placement of the small ads was significant in that it gave *100% Hot Wheels* distinction by being the only 'accessory' in the car section of *Auto Trader*. For a major campaign the advertisement slots were very cheap – $40 each – and succeeded in attracting unpaid-for write-ups in the US auto trade press. The press, attracted by the unusual positioning, was credited with increasing demand.

Profile: strategic insight

The *100% Hot Wheels* range is marketed not as toys but as collectables for adults. The readership of *Auto Trader* was ideal in that they could be assumed to take classic cars seriously. It could also be assumed that serious readers of *Auto Trader's* small ads had a disposable income that was large enough not to baulk at the $25 each for *100% Hot Wheels* premium scale model cars.

Creative direction

The tagline '*Almost too real*' cued the idea that the miniature cars could be confused with the slightly bigger, more expensive real thing.

The design of the small ads was true to the format commonly used in the magazine. In re-creating the three-quarter-angle car image to scale with full-size versions, the camera was mounted close to the floor. A miniature-scale piece of flooring was used to get the background in proportion to the miniature car.

In mixing images of miniature models with images of the real thing, the advertisers were effectively setting up a graphic product demonstration, inviting readers to compare images and spot the miniature without reading the small print.

The result was an image and body text that appeared authentic and conventional in its reconstruction of the small-ad style, until the price and website address gave clues to the illusion.

Review

The small ads were placed without prior notice, and *Auto Trader* received the images and copy in the manner that their other small ads were received. Part of the skill in the stunt was in getting the advertisements past the experts.

> **What do you get when you position Hot Wheels cars net to the real thing? A huge hit.**
> **(Agency DavidandGoliath's website www.dngla.com)**

- Because the print adverts were unusually placed, they broke through the clutter of seemingly identical classified small ads.
- The copy does not attempt to hoax the reader. Instead it simply demonstrates a knowledge of the classic car market by using the right parlance of *Auto Trader* small ads. The 'reveal' of the web address offers a link to finds out more on the product's website. As a concise advertisement it offers a taster of the way the miniatures are meant to be viewed, after having demonstrated their credibility by mixing with the 'real ads' effectively.
- The campaign was helped by boldly targeting a new but slightly related market.
- The tone of the campaign managed to make a serious and witty point. The serious message was how realistic the models looked, while the placement in *Auto Trader* ensured the small ads would exclusively reach an adult market. The message's wit was in passing off miniatures as full-size versions. The message conveyed was 'if you can't afford the full-size versions, buy the miniatures'.

Integrated mix

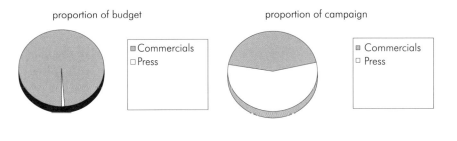

proportion of budget

▣ Commercials
□ Press

proportion of campaign

▣ Commercials
□ Press

Essentials

1. A campaign strategy can be distinct by simply being out of context. *100% Hot Wheels* mixed in with genuine advertising is memorable for daring to be different.
2. To make the illusion work, the copy and image needed to be extremely well crafted, otherwise the *almost too real* message would have been undermined.
3. The advertisements contain a clear *call to action* by pointing readers to follow up interest on the *100% Hot Wheels* website.

For links see www.adstoicons.com.

Cadbury's Coronation Street Idents

Product:	**Cadbury's** **Confectionery Range**
Target market:	1 million television viewers, *ITV1* (repeated *ITV2*)
Agency/city:	*Triangle Communications*, London
Planning/production time:	6 months
Reach:	UK mass audience (terrestrial, cable and satellite broadcast)
Length of customer engagement:	10 seconds: 4 programmed around each 25-minute episode, 3 evenings a week
Brief:	to reinforce chocolate as a comfort break, like watching TV
Budget:	initially £200,000: 2006–08 deal estimated to be worth £20m
Lifespan:	started 1996, to 2008 (under 2006 agreement)
Benchmark:	programme sponsorship *idents*

The front-end frame of *Cadbury's idents*, which featured at the beginning and end of each segment of the television soap opera *Coronation Street*.

Project background

Coronation Street is the longest-running soap opera on television in Britain and still regularly attracts the highest weekly viewing figures on commercial television. It is broadcast in a prime-time slot, usually between 7:30 and 8:30 pm three evenings a week and contains the most sought-after and expensive commercial spaces in British broadcast schedules. The branding is placed before, during and after the show.

Cadbury's sponsorship is lucrative for programme makers and has proved highly effective in connecting the activities of watching *Coronation Street* and eating *Cadbury's* chocolate among both confectioners and the programme's target audience – the lower to mid-range (predominantly female) demographic.

Timeline	96 S	O	N	D	97 J	F	M	A	M	J	J	A	S	O
Concept development	■	■	■	■										
Completed project				☼										
Launch					☼									
Word-of-mouth/blogging					☺	☺	☺	☺	☺					
Additional promotion					◙	◙	◙	◙	◙					
Media exposure				--	--		--			--	--	--		
Hits (millions)				0.5	1	3	5		6		8			30

Cadbury's initial sponsorship in 1996 was a means of positioning *Cadbury's* chocolate brands as close as possible to the main draw – *Coronation Street* – without appearing among the other brands competing in an advertising break. What's more, they would receive four slots within 30 minutes spanning the periods before, during and after the show. The deal allowed *Cadbury* 10-second slots immediately preceding and following *Coronation Street's* credit sequences. Over the course of the sponsorship, *Cadbury's* has also used the buffers as a vehicle to launch new products and for seasonal promotions.

The choice of programme was particularly appropriate for the confectionery brand. *Coronation Street's* viewing figures and audience profile were ideal for the producer of *FMCGs*, where a high volume and rapid turnover were essential. The *idents* that were developed also served to forge connections between watching television and eating chocolate; both were readily associated with moments of relaxation, escapism and having a break from domestic chores. Product and programme shared the same target demographic – C1, C2, D and E – which is a broad cross-section of the British population still reachable as a homogeneous mass. So the reach and relevance of the show were a perfect match for the confectioners.

Profile: programme sponsorship

As television commercials have established themselves as a consistent mass-reach platform used for over half a century, they have come to present problems for prime-time television advertisers. The use of product placement in television programmes is restricted under broadcasting laws in most countries, and commercial breaks are customarily used by viewers as viewing breaks during popular programmes. Yet television commercials have historically been the best platform for promoting fast-moving consumer goods, because they make products relevant by putting them in the viewer's mind and tend to influence people's choice when faced with making a selection (called *repertoire buying*).

Cadbury's sponsorship of *Coronation Street* was the first of its kind in the UK and is the most widely recognized programme sponsorship on British television. In 2006 the sponsorship was the most expensive broadcast agreement outside the United States, and the continuous sponsorship has forged a connection in the minds of viewers between two of Britain's best-known names.

The biggest advantage for *Cadbury* was that they were guaranteed the 'last and first word' in every ad break before, during and after *Coronation Street*. This meant that they served as *buffers* for the show, cueing up the audience in time for the programme content. At a time when the threat of viewers avoiding ad breaks was a major concern for the industry, by flicking channels or recording the show and fast-forwarding through ad breaks, *idents* were used by viewers to identify programme content from commercials. Therefore *idents* were a mid-way point between programmes and commercial breaks.

Creative direction

To reinforce the connection between the programme and the chocolate range, integrated advertisers *Triangle Communications* opted for a tone and treatment that echoed the programme's flavour; animators *Aardman* (creators of Oscar-winning characters Wallace and Grommit) were appointed to produce new characters that echoed the community spirit and warm wit of the show. Consequently, both brands benefited from the treatment because the light-hearted send-up reaffirmed the show's charm and warmth.

The characters created by *Aardman* were full-figured and rounded, relating back to the show's heritage. Significantly, all the characters and the street setting featured in the *idents* were coloured brown to reinforce the connection with chocolate.

Review

News of the sponsorship first featured in the business and media sections of the national newspapers (not the programme's main target demographic). Otherwise little pre-publicity was required for the sponsorship to be effective. The first series of *idents* were brand salient to establish the connection between confectioners and the programme.

> **Cadbury is a national institution, and that's why we sponsor
> Coronation Street, the nation's favourite soap.
> (Cadbury's marketing)**

The styling of the *idents* reflected the added value *Cadbury's* received from sponsoring *Coronation Street*. It was entertaining, down to earth, familiar and ritualistic – an ideal environment to associate eating confectionery.

- The tone and treatment of *Cadbury's idents* established a connection with the long-established spirit of the programme. The campaign targeted the programme's heritage rather than its contemporary storylines as a means to establish a cross-over of identities in the *third party association* platform.
- The broad appeal and frequency of the show made it an ideal platform for a mass-produced FMCG.
- Aspects of the programme's personality – its sense of community, familiarity and its mix of characters – made it an appropriate match for a producer with a range of product identities to maintain in the public eye.
- The vignettes in *Cadbury's idents* featured snippets of conversation that aped dialogue from the show. The *endline, relax with Cadbury's Caramel*, became familiar as the feeder to the show's opening credits.

Integrated mix

proportion of campaign

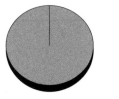

▣ Commercials

Essentials

1. More than commercials, programme sponsorship links the identities of the programme and sponsoring brand in the manner of a *third party association*.
2. If you plan on programme sponsorship as an advertising vehicle, it is important to make sure that the existing personality of the platform is appropriate for both parties.
3. *Idents* can be the most expensive advertising platform, so it is worth considering how the platform will contribute to a long-term television-driven advertising strategy.

For links see www.adstoicons.com.

Lego Posterscapes

Product:	Silfa and Lego
Target market:	Santiago residents and commuters, Chile
Agency/city:	*Ogilvy & Mather*, Santiago
Planning/production time:	4 months
Reach:	estimated 500,000 live/up to 10 million as images worldwide (online)
Length of customer engagement:	varies
Brief:	bring *Lego* to life
Budget:	undisclosed
Lifespan:	1 month as a poster in 2005, still circulating on the internet in image form
Benchmark:	ambient impact, offline and online

The giant poster for *Lego*, which made chunks of the everyday environment appear as if they were constructed from *Lego*. This was one of three spots that were so successful as images that they were widely circulated across the internet.

Project background

While the effectiveness of conventional media such as posters is often doubted, modern poster technology enabled this visual illusion promoting *Lego* to be constructed. Not only did the poster blend in and make a powerful environmental illusion, it was also widely circulated on the internet as the sort of image that made people ask, *'is it for real'*?

Timeline	04				05										
	S	O	N	D	J	F	M	A	M	J	J	A	S	O	N
Concept development			■	■	■	■	■								
'Live' poster run + digital image distribution						☼	◉								
Word-of-mouth/blogging							☺	☺	☺	☺	☺	☺	☺	☺	
Media exposure							--	--	--	--	--	--	--	--	--
Hits (100,000s)							5	10			20				50

The project existed in two formats. The first was a stunt in Santiago, where the illusion relied on blending in with a landscape people were familiar with, and catching people out with the image of missing *Lego* bricks as pedestrians and drivers passed by. The defining *Lego* references were deliberately understated in the poster design so that they would blend with the environment to make the illusion work at a glance.

The poster covering the side of a building was said to have caused drivers to brake suddenly in the streets, as did the railway bridge poster, although there were no reported accidents. The office poster would only have been seen by people entering the building. The illusion worked best when people were closer to the buildings.

An unintentional feature of the campaign was that the images were widely exported in digital format through world advertising review sites and entertainment sites. It was the type of 'have you seen...' image frequently tagged and sent via e-mail. To an international audience the images were like a typical international cityscape. They featured at least one person in shot to give a sense of scale. As *Lego* is marketed globally, the reference would have been easily understood.

Creative direction

Locations were chosen because they looked like everyday cityscapes. The apparent transformation of ordinary buildings into *Lego* constructions is quite startling and provokes one to double-check. This was achieved by designing the poster images around the chosen locations. Details such as the lines of the building blocks and the colour and texture of the covered areas were matched on the posters. A non-permanent adhesive was used to fix the poster prints directly onto the surface of the building.

With each poster the panels seamlessly align with their environment, with the exception of an area where one *Lego* brick is missing. This is where the defining *Lego* pimples can be seen. What makes the illusion most striking is that the 'frame' of the poster is not close to the missing brick: in fact the 'exposed' *Lego* section takes up less than 20 per cent of the poster's surface area. Therefore it is difficult to distinguish where the two-dimensional poster ends from the side of the building. The scale of the illusion made it capture people's imagination in both ambient landscape and image format.

Review

The poster was printed in sections and was assembled late one evening and early the following morning, so that it would have appeared that the Lego building had shot up overnight.

> **The campaign was primarily designed as outdoor pieces. The proliferation of them on the web has been more of a consequence than an initial objective.**
> **(Spokesperson, O&M Santiago)**

- The project draws on the idea that many children first learnt about construction through *Lego*. Therefore the real-life *Lego* building is a witty and evocative reference that many around the world would have understood (even though the campaign was initially intended for the Chilean market).
- The stunt relies on viewers noticing the small 'missing brick', which is a small part of the poster. However, the illusion relies on the 'negative' poster space blending into its mounting as a backdrop. The big impact relies on a subtle graphic trick for the stunt to work.
- The images circulated over the web provide just enough context for the illusion to work. They are not heavily populated areas and would otherwise be banal snapshots of the everyday. The photographer's briefing therefore helps the image to set up the illusion very effectively in the photographs.

A *Lego* poster installation on an office block in Santiago, Chile. Note the efforts by the poster's designers to blend in with the style of the architecture.

Integrated mix

proportion of campaign

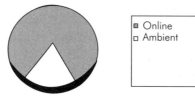

▣ Online
▢ Ambient

Essentials

1. The technologies of modern digital printing material allow for imaginative 'off-board' advertising possibilities. For these to work, however, permission needs to be negotiated with the local authorities first.
2. To make a stunt of this kind work, the illusion needs to be designed in full. It is the way the space around the 'missing brick' blends into the environment that makes it work.
3. As an advert the poster operates in an ambient way. That is, viewers are required to read the visual play and relate it to their pre-knowledge and earlier experiences of the brand.

For links see www.adstoicons.com.

RETHINKING MASS MEDIA 2: IMAGINING NEW FORMATS

This section reviews key shapers of the online advertising environment. In particular, it considers what impact video streaming, personal web space and *user-generated content* will have on advertising.

The global advertising industries are expected to spend $1.9 billion on social-networking sites in 2010 according to *eMarketer* (*Adage.com*). This represents a relatively small proportion of all future online advertising spend, although it's widely considered that advertising online is still in its early stages.

> **To see online advertising, imagine being able to watch 'must see' video clips wherever, whenever. The only payback is, you have to watch an ad first.**

The examples featured in this section

The five main examples featured are in fact advertising infrastructures that have been created as ready-made solutions for digital advertising. They have all become established networking centres and as such are considered *mediums* – not messengers. This distinction is important because, unlike brand sites, they are considered to be non-partisan and are bases that people trust as an intermediary. For instance, trading platforms like *Amazon* and *eBay* have established rules that all users work to. Penalties for breaking the codes – such as bad 'star' reviews on *eBay* and blacklisting on *Amazon* – have proven successful deterrents. Therefore they have established infrastructures that have become a 'given' in online business.

> Fifty-six per cent of online ad spend is on search listings. (Mel Carson, *Microsoft adCenter* Community Manager, Europe)

Like *Amazon* and *eBay*, the five examples in this chapter are established as neutral trading platforms. They also have particular significance for advertising. Because of their high volume of internet traffic they lend themselves to advertising. The site managers were smart enough to anticipate this and devised ways to make their sites advertising-friendly but controlled, so that viewers do not feel that advertising gets in the way. They are:

Cases featured...

MySpace – the world's largest social network, with personal web space, blogs and interest groups

YouTube – the most established digital video upload and share site, attracting work-break web *snackers*

Revver – contained user-generated, advertising tagged material

Google AdSense – the largest word-search advertising platform, reworked as an advertising service

Microsoft adCenter – the largest digital network system has flexible ad space and niche positioning.

Social network

MySpace

Founded:	2003, USA
By:	Tom Anderson and Chris DeWolfe, bought by *News International Corporation* in 2005
Audience:	broadly European and American, 16–35-year-olds
Address:	myspace.com

Future view: model for the online social networking phenomenon

MySpace was (in 2006) the largest platform for social networking, where web users were given internet space as their personal platform to enter into an internet community of their choosing. In 2006 it was described by *Reuters* as the 'biggest online teen hangout', accounting for over nearly 4.5 per cent of all US internet traffic.

For advertisers, personal online spaces are capable of attracting high-volume web traffic and these are the sites that advertisers are keen to target (Lindstrom, 2005). *MySpace* is ranked in the top five most popular English-speaking websites by *Wikipedia* and will generate $180 million in advertising revenue during 2006 in the United States alone, according to online analysts *eMarketer* (1.7 per cent of the $16.7 billion spent on US online advertising in 2006, estimated to hit 6.3 per cent by 2010).

As a funded advertising structure

At present *MySpace's* core advertising revenue derives from standard disruption formats – banners and buttons mostly. Some commentators have suggested that this more traditional form of online advertising does not sit well with the uncommercial ethos of *MySpace* (Sweney, 2006). Yet for the most part the citing of most adverts to each personal web page seems well matched. Compared to when viewing *virals* or digital videos, viewers spend longer viewing pages in *MySpace* (estimated to be approximately 30 minutes per visit).

As the platform has grown, *MySpace* has managed to negotiate a legal issue regarding the ownership of materials posted on its site: until 2006 subscribers had to sign the rights of use over to the site, but *MySpace* reassured its users by amending this to avoid claiming ownership rights, thus allowing subscribers freedom to create and retain ownership of their work. This was significant in maintaining the site's freedom of use. It is not from web users but from advertisers following the web traffic that the site seeks to earn revenue.

Platforms that were being developed in 2006 include branded pages, increased targeting methods on personal profiles and a search-listing system in conjunction with leading search engine providers.

What it means for advertising

If companies can go even deeper to develop marketing efforts that fully embrace the one-to-one-to-many nature of social networks, ad revenues will soar... The underlying concept will influence the way advertising is done in all media, not just online. (DA Williamson, 2006)

MySpace is the largest provider of social network space and, with *News Corp's* backing, has a vast array of other traditional media platforms to draw on for support as it expands as the main platform of its kind. It is already the main source for *viral seeders* to investigate *early adopters*. It is even a music-selling platform for unsigned pop acts.

In terms of developing the space as an advertising mass medium, *MySpace* has the scale of audience to dictate the design and shape of formats that advertisers will have to follow. Its methods are likely to spill into other online channels.

Video platform

YouTube.com

Launched:	2005, United States
By:	Chad Hurley, Steve Chen and Jawed Karim
Audience:	video *snackers*, sharers and creators online
Address:	youtube.com

Future view: a model for sharing digital video

> Broadcast yourself on *YouTube*.
> Watch – instantly find millions of fast streaming videos
> Upload – quickly upload and videos in almost any video format
> Share – easily share your videos with family, friends or co-workers
> (homepage, www.youtube.com)

In 2006 so many people were viewing and sending digital video that it became a recognized mainstream 'medium'. It also became clear that the format had advertising potential. *YouTube* is a centre for consumer-generated videos and its website allows viewers to view, upload and share videos posted by other users. In other words, members of the public can upload their videos to *YouTube* and download others from the site.

YouTube is rated as one of the fastest-growing websites, streaming approximately 100 million videos a day in 2006 (Bambi Francisco, *MarketWatch*).

As a funded advertising structure

As *YouTube* banks videos created by its users, the site is able to avoid current copyright issues. Its rules allow only video creators (or copyright holders) to upload their material onto the site, which helps *YouTube* avoid liability. However, the verdict of the ongoing court cases between *EMI* and *Universal* and music-sharing service *Napster's* former financial backers, which started in 2000, may have consequences for free-to-view video distribution. *YouTube* has had broadcasters asking for the removal of clips, but this is a less frequent occurrence as they have become more widely known.

As traffic to the website has grown, many major networks that have had clips featured on *YouTube* have come to regard this as useful exposure rather than copyright infringement, which aids *YouTube's* emerging prominence as an acknowledged neutral platform.

As the site has grown, *YouTube's* owners have refined its operations. On most pages they have set a 10-minute limit on the length of videos. *YouTube* now also features official contracted 'channels' for major broadcasters to preview clips and showcase tasters of forthcoming shows. Income from broadcast networks is therefore another of its funding avenues. Its income base derives from publishers and producers keen to distribute video and who need *YouTube's* technology and reach to share it fast and cheap. The website does not therefore need pop-ups or banner advertisements to fund itself.

Like *Amazon*, *YouTube* has a rating scheme and layout that shows the number of hits, contains reviews and has further URL links. It even has a web community and competitions where people submit video entries.

What it means for advertising

> It's random. It doesn't have an agenda, it's not about necessarily making money or necessarily about promoting a certain viewpoint. There are people on this channel who are combing their hair, dancing, fighting with their friends... it's totally random. ('janjee', US video *'YouTube is history'* on *YouTube*)

YouTube claimed market leadership by establishing itself before the boom in the number of people spending time watching videos online. While media firms were figuring how best to capture the video market, *YouTube* was catering for the demand and gaining credibility, *word-of-mouth*, as an easy-to-use site.

Video advertising accounted for only 2 per cent of online advertising in 2005 (according to *eMarketer*) but this is clearly a platform with boom potential. Following *YouTube's* buyout by *Google* in 2006, it is likely that *Google's* organizational systems will help shape *YouTube's* growing archive stock, which presents opportunities for video producers to bid for prime listing. As one of the first to provide a system for video exchange on a website, *YouTube's* operational model will be among the first to define the basic format that others will use.

Video distribution

Revver

Launched: 1995, United States
By: Ian Clarke, Oliver Luckett and Steven Starr
Audience: video creators and *mash-up* exponents
Address: revver.com

Future view: model for tagging adverts and sharing profits

Until 2005 advertisers had hardly woken up to how popular webcams and digital video were with internet users. Sites that hold *user-generated content* figured out how their spaces worked as a commercial operation before advertisers. *Revver's* site enables video providers to make money from their uploads, based on the number of hits their work receives.

Revver is a site with a fast-growing volume of traffic – mostly 10-minute-break internet surfers, known as '*snackers*'. Part of its popularity is due to the operational model *Revver's* site developers have constructed – which has far-reaching significance for advertisers: each digital video uploaded free of charge contains an advertisement. The reward for watching an advertisement is to get the video for free. Revenue earned from *tagged* advertising is split 50/50 between the site and the videos provider – members of the public who submit material.

As a funded advertising structure

Revverize your videos. Share them with the world. Make money. (*Revver.com* website)

Revver describe revenue generated by advertisement tagging as *RevTags*. A short advertisement is tagged to the end before it is posted on the site and is inseparable from the downloadable content. Advertisers pay per click, so the more popular the video, the more it costs advertisers.

Revver is among the first online companies to give amateur video producers the opportunity to profit from their work, and the model is becoming a commonly accepted financing model by site and content providers alike. *Revver's* biggest hit to date has been the *Diet Coke and Mentos Experiment* video, posted in 2006. Within four months both *Revver* and the video's producers had earned well over $5,000 each from the 50/50 revenue-split from tagged advertising after the video had been seen over 800,000 times. It is estimated that the video had been seen over 6 million times by the end of 2006.

The tagged advertisements tend to be end-frame still shots – a bit like television commercials but with a significantly longer time on screen as they are the final freeze-frame shot. The tagged adverts usually contain a link and are cut off when the viewer clicks out of the video.

What it means for advertising:

Four quick reasons to use *Revver*

1. The deal is simple: advertisers' money is split 50/50 between the video's author and *Revver*. If there's an affiliate involved (for example: a site that posts or links to your video) they get 20%, and the rest is split 50/50.
2. We use *Creative Commons* licenses in most cases.
3. Signing up is quick and easy. Uploading videos is drag & drop.
4. Our website has tens of thousands of viewers. Your video will be posted there, and if it gets high ratings, more people will watch it. The more people that watch it, the more clicks the advertisement will get and the more money the video will generate.

(*Revver* site)

Revver offers a unique opportunity to earn revenue from user-generated content. The tagging system has proven effective because the volume of exposure is proportionate to the cost of advertising. It is difficult to guarantee the exact scale of exposure that videos get, but advertisements are swapped to ensure that advertisers get the number of hits they have paid for.

The content does not relate to the advertising message, which could be perhaps be seen as a disadvantage, but the advertisements are more welcome than television commercials because, as an end frame, they do not disrupt viewing. The *RevTag* system therefore offers a means to make *user-generated content* viable for advertising. Already advertisers have used the format innovatively, linking URLs to other web-based content.

Ad links

Google AdSense

Founded:	2003, United States
By:	Rex Wong (originally called *Applied Semantics*), sold to *Google* in 2005
Audience:	video viewers, sharers and creators
Address:	www.google.com/adsense

Future view: model for sourcing content and ranking significance

The potential reach of advertising through *Google* is huge. In the UK alone, 70 per cent of internet users use *Google* as their primary search tool (*Timesonline*). In the past *Google* have negotiated advertisers' unpaid attempts to manipulate *click-through* ratings and move up the automatic listing. Then *Google* capitalized on their popularity by allowing companies to pay for prime listing. Now *Google* have extended their position as a 'neutral' internet portal by developing a stand-alone advertising platform.

    Google AdSense is a system where people sell space on their websites to *Google*-registered advertisers. *Google* provide the material and links and by featuring *Google*-managed search links, website owners earn revenue by feeding traffic to paid-for advertising sites. The advertiser–site matches are managed by *Google's AdSense* set-up.

As a funded advertising structure

Google is able to draw on the capabilities of its search engine to ensure that relevant subjects are advertised on each *Google*-sponsored site. Sponsored sites receive relevant image and URL word-link text, which is determined by *Google's* search profiling data. The system still relies on key words to hook with sponsored links: *Google* checks to ensure that advertisers use descriptively accurate key terms. Websites are also able to sign up to *Google's* international search-advertising platform *AdWords*, set up by *Google* in 2000 and still one of its major sources of advertising revenue. *AdSense* is more adaptable to newer formats of advertising such as video, which allows for *third party* hook-ups with broadcasters. As an advertising platform it requires brevity of communication – website owners are required to summarize link sites in concise search phrases. As a system for connecting commercial activity with everyday websites and content the model is the most convenient currently available.

As the *AdSense* funding mechanism has developed, *Google* has remodelled its payment model from a percentage 'per click' to a system that measures the income generated by each lead.

What it means for advertising

Discover your website's full advertising potential.
(*Google AdSense* banner, home page)

Google receive approximately 70 per cent of the world's search traffic, so their presence as an advertising platform is very significant.

At the heart of *Google's* advertising service is its search technology, which, through a range of business tie-ups, is being extended to other platforms such as *MySpace*. The significance for websites looking to generate income is that their prose will operate as key terms, so online copy will increasingly be written with as many strongly themed, open-ended hooks as possible to increase earning opportunities.

Google have introduced measures to prevent the use of overstated or misleading key words. As *Google* now have methods to prevent 'click fraud', fake *blogs* and other scams designed to get websites higher up the results rankings, they have a resilient and transferable advertising system that can be extended through other web activities. Many sites have been designed to maximize income from *AdSense*. They are typically text based to allow for more sponsored links. Many independent reviews claim *AdSense* offers good returns for search-based website advertising, and their search infrastructure is so large that many brands have started to rationalize their branding to a single word, which makes it clearer for customers to anticipate what may lie at the end of a link click. Like *Google*, rich-text search systems such as the classified advertising site *Craigslist* (United States) have potential to be used further afield (although *Craigslist* serves mostly online communities in the United States).

Tracking effectiveness

Microsoft adCenter

Launched:	2005 (France and the United States), 2006 (UK, northern and mainland Europe)
By:	*Microsoft* range of networks
Audience:	advertisers targeting subscribers to *Microsoft* services
Address:	msnadcenter.com

Future view: systematic platform for organized search and advertising

Microsoft's massive global network operation has been used to form an advertising platform for paid traffic on *Microsoft*-run online services. This includes *MSN Search* and *Windows Live* search sites. *Microsoft* have over 10 years of customer data to draw on, and with their huge global usage *Microsoft* have the largest data evidence to track online consumer behaviour. *Microsoft* can therefore offer the equivalent of a mass advertising service that can accurately predict the scale of *click-throughs* for niche advertising across its entire network.

As a funded advertising structure

As an online information portal, *Microsoft* is able to track where mass-media advertising has stimulated *repertoire*-hunting for the best deals on the net. It uses demographic and click-through data to determine the age of consumers, geographic location (from IP addresses), time and date of internet usage, but *Microsoft* are keen to restrict use of personally identifiable information. *Microsoft's* existing data give them a distinct advantage over broadcast advertising in that they accurately predict which spots will perform effectively in prescribed niche areas.

The main distinction between *Microsoft adCenter* and other online advertising services is that *Microsoft's* software tools have a wider tracking reach and can quickly produce market reports that pinpoint effective platforms and target *prospects* for different types of brand. Therefore advertisers can anticipate higher conversion rates as a return on their investment (*ROI*), and can constantly move their positioning in the search listings during the day and during the week.

Search links are priced per click-through, and *MSN* set out to prove that their superior ability to anticipate the volume of relevant web traffic will result in a larger percentage of *conversions* compared to other online advertising service providers.

Exclusive targeting	Incremental targeting
day of the week	age
time of the day	gender
country & city	country & city

(Source: *Microsoft adCenter*)

What it means for advertising

Although *Microsoft* has 7 per cent of the world's current search traffic, it holds the most comprehensive body of online consumer information. *adCenter* lets advertisers draw on *Microsoft's* vast information database on niche market groups. With over 10 million registered users of *MSN Instant Messaging* and nearly 9 million users of *Hotmail*, *Microsoft* has enough personal data to create accurate customer profiles.

In terms of charging for word-search conversion rates, *Microsoft* offer a comparable operation to *Google*. Advertisers bid for key-word and phrase listings, pitched at particular day and time allocations, which makes this particularly effective for brands with clearly defined niche targets.

> With *adCenter*, you can flight your ads on particular days and times of day. This means that your ads get seen by interested people at times when they would be on the net looking for your type of service. And you only pay on *click-throughs*.
>
> (Mel Carson, *adCenter* Community Manager, Europe)

Compared to broadcast commercials, which have greater potential reach but cannot guarantee that viewers will convert to customers, internet advertising is more accurate in its audience projection, but provides less scope to generate an unplanned, unpaid-for buzz through the strength of creative advertising work. Internet advertising is returns based, and has become more of a selling science than a communication art. Service providers *Microsoft* and *Google* can virtually guarantee which online spaces would be effective for advertising and charge higher rates for premium online spots.

For word-search advertising in 2006, the rate paid per click varied widely across sites in different parts of the world. The highest in the United States was $100 per click (for listing alongside 'mesothelioma', an asbestos-related type of lung cancer: source: *Jupiter Research*), while the highest in the UK is £10 per click. The average is 30p.

Viral distributors

Other content enablers have developed viral distribution channels so that the *word-of-mouth* audience base effectively becomes the main channel for sharing advertising. Firms such as *Digital Media Communications* (*DMC*, UK) pushed viral advertising to new levels in generating talked-about digital videos, making them good value for money as digital advertisements. Whether the format can sustain long-term interest is less certain. As well as (official) *virals* and (unofficial) *subvirals*, distributors have also pushed techniques further by *mashing* existing video technologies to create fresh eye-catching formats. For instance, *Vidavee* (United States) developed a tracking system to measure which bits of video users home in on, by tracking their use of fast-forward and rewind controls. This allows them to tag popular scenes within a video.

In 2006 several online video distribution sites were seeking to establish set-ups with large broadcasting firms to allow user-generated *mash-ups* with established and copyrighted material. While the scale of distribution for mash-ups may be contained, if agreements can be reached, the consequences for advertising could be huge in that they would pave the way for co-designed advertising content, where the consumer is also part-creator.

Summary

What online enablers mean for advertising:

- They provide the formats for advertising, by offering a method of getting advertisements seen and by guaranteeing high-volume *traffic*.
- Online video advertising is using a form of permission marketing (*P-marketing*), whereby customers are rewarded with entertainment for watching an advert.
- Web users are being encouraged to open up their websites and home-made videos to advertising. Search links and tags have become a means for people to earn money from popular material.
- Many search and entertainment sites are still developing means of preventing their systems being manipulated. However, they have devised safe and fair payment methods, and tracking systems are proving useful in determining the effectiveness of web content as advertising platforms.
- In 2006 online advertising is at a stage where consumers can be the co-creators of advertising. *Mash-ups* and self-generated content are becoming areas of substantial advertising investment.

RETHINKING MASS MEDIA 3: THRESHOLDS AND GUIDELINES

This section addresses how advertising's regulatory bodies have addressed the rapid growth in digital and direct advertising.

Most national regulatory bodies were set up in the 1960s following the introduction of US and European measures to protect consumers from unscrupulous advertising. In the old-established commercial advertising economies, most governments felt communication industries were best served by self-regulation, so industry-managed bodies were founded. The advantage of being overseen by a self-regulatory body, rather than statutory law, is that organizations have the ability to be flexible and adapt to changing circumstances. In recent years national bodies have developed international regulatory networks in response to an increasingly globalized advertising industry. Most national and international associations publish details of adjudications on their websites, which means that the volume and type of complaints can be readily found for different advertising media.

Broadly, most complaints in all countries concern direct (junk) mail campaigns – usually because of claims made within the advertising. Other *direct advertising* tends to receive similar levels of complaint to commercials, billboards and press. Internet advertising is starting to be brought to the attention of the regulators. While there have been few complaints, most regulators are still defining ways to handle complaints about web advertising within their existing systems.

Better Business Bureau

Region:	United States
Representation:	advertising and broadcast agencies in the United States
Address:	www.bbb.org and www.bbbonline.org

More than advertisers in most countries, US advertisers are subject to strict government regulation and industry self-regulation. Federal courts can respond to cases of misleading advertising under the Lanham Act (passed in 1946 to prevent trademark infringement and false advertising). The main government regulatory body for advertising is the *Federal Trade Commission* (*FTC*). However, rather than one overall body, different laws and regulations cover different product types, for instance the *Food and Drug Administration* (*FDA*) and the *Bureau of Alcohol, Tobacco and Firearms* (*BATF*).

Of several self-regulatory organizations in the United States, the *Council of Better Business Bureaus* is the main body for the US advertising industries. Founded in 1912, the *BBB* is funded by advertising and mass-media agencies and acts as a watchdog to raise public confidence in advertising practices.

The aim of the *BBB* is to promote truth in advertising practices, and its methods are persuasive – it can pressurize unethical advertisers with boycotts and bad publicity and it has even been known to prosecute major offenders. The *Bureau's* remit is confined to reporting bad practices because it is not a governmental agency, although agencies still tend to use the *BBB* as an industry body to resolve disputes.

In terms of extending its remit to new media advertising, the *BBB* actively seeks out new advertising scams and highlights good practices – which have in the past included alternative uses of mass media. Any schemes that are seen to reinvigorate advertising platforms are encouraged – as long as the practices are deemed ethical by the Bureau's review board.

A US egg producer was asked by the *Better Business Bureau* to stop advertising its methods as 'humane' until it refrained from clipping chicken's beaks and depriving birds of food. *BBB* recommended the producers withdrew 'animal care certified' from their ads and packaging or changed it to stop misleading consumers. *BBB's* statement made national headlines in the United States.

JARO (Japan Advertising Review Organization Inc)

Region:	Japan
Representation:	Japanese communications industries
Address:	http://www.jaro.or.jp

JARO was launched as a self-regulatory body on behalf of the *Japanese Advertising Federation* in 1974 to ensure fair advertising and labelling practices. It does not receive state funding but is funded by more than 950 industry members (spanning advertising, newspapers, broadcasters, publishers and production practices). The organization was launched when most countries in the West were also seeking autonomous self-regulation for their advertising industries in the wake of strengthened consumer rights legislation internationally. *JARO* reviews contested claims, handles complaints from individuals and corporations, and offers advice to members. It operates in conjunction with other Japanese self-regulatory bodies and consumer associations and its remit is mostly to comment on the clarity, quality and fairness of communication. *JARO* also represents Japanese advertising industries interests at fair trade councils.

As a response to the growth in new media, JARO has updated its standards governing online communications through close liaison with media industries. It holds regular meetings with related associations and develops its position on new advertising through its consultative panel. The range of services *JARO* currently offers reflect the growth of advertising – its archive of case studies now includes integrated advertising campaigns and the data in its information centre also reflect current best practice in a wide range of media which acknowledges the emergence of new media advertising. *JARO* offers skills courses for advertisers and operates as an information centre with a large collection of advertising data, although most concerns press and television rather than direct advertising.

The consumer and industry correspondence *JARO* receives mostly addresses media advertising. Complaints about internet communications still only account for 41 of 585 annual complaints received by *JARO*, compared to 230 for direct marketing – magazine inserts, handbills, direct mail and free pamphlets.

Ofcom (the independent regulator and competition authority for the United Kingdom communications industries)

Region: UK
Representation: national advertising regulatory bodies throughout Europe
Address: www.ofcom.org.uk or www.asa.org.uk/asa/links

Ofcom is a government-sanctioned regulator and competition authority for the UK broadcast and telecommunications industries. Its remit spans television, radio, telecommunications and wireless communications. Like other national bodies *Ofcom* is independent and aims to serve the best interests of both the communication industries and consumers. The organization's duties reflect this: one aspect of its provision is to ensure that the UK population is connected to the full span of communications services available. Another aspect is that audiences receive adequate protection from offensive material or unfair infringements of privacy.

Ofcom has a technology research and development section to monitor technological developments and the impact that they might have on the sectors they regulate. As *Ofcom's* website notes, 'Technology developments are driving change throughout the communications industry at an unprecedented rate... Understanding the impact of technology developments on the communications industry is vital to *Ofcom's* role as the regulator and competition authority for the sector' (http://www.ofcom.org.uk/research). The scale of broadcast convergence has made it easier to pool the functions of several regulators into one – and *Ofcom* in the UK is best positioned to manage the bigger picture of commercial broadcasting (Leonardi, 2004).

In regulating change, *Ofcom* can respond only to media within its jurisdiction. Its remit has become harder to define since mobile, telecom landline and broadcast operators, formerly regulated by different bodies, have expanded their operations and overlap to the extent that they are at times indistinguishable from one another. In terms of managing issues to do with narrowcasting, *Ofcom* has tended to recommend related issues to associated regulatory bodies such as *WebtraderUK*, a scheme to encourage consumer confidence in online shopping (other countries have similar schemes which correspond with online marketing and advertising practices). *Ofcom's* verdicts tend to have implications for the advertising industries' own self-regulating body in the United States, the *Advertising Standards Association*; both investigate complaints bought by consumers but *Ofcom's* mandate is to represent consumers' interests in communication matters.

Ofcom offers advice to agencies on broadcast advertising, so many of the campaigns featured in this section would have been cleared by *Ofcom* or the equivalent national broadcast body. *Ofcom* is best placed to assess whether unconventional uses of media formats fall within the principles of commercial broadcasting or impinge on any broadcast guidelines.

China Advertising Association

Region:	China
Representation:	advertisers, advertising and broadcast agencies in China
Address:	www.china-aa.org/china_aa/xh_e.asp?id=38
Regulations:	www.ad163.com/salon/bbsshow.php?bbsid=1&number=6714

The regulatory system in China is a complex one that repays careful explanation. The *China Advertising Association (CAA)* offers certificates of approval for advertising work that tests the conventions of advertising. As with bodies in other countries, its main role is to consider accurate representation in advertising, and to ensure that the content of advertising is not misleading. The *CAA* operates as a consultant in the advertising censorship system rather than a gatekeeper. The Advertisement Law of the People's Republic of China (PRC) is the basis ruling Chinese advertising creation and publishing.

The *CAA* is under the administration of the *Ministry of Civil Affairs of PRC* and the *National Industry and Business Administration Bureau*, and has for many years supervised China's advertising practices and regulation. The *Bureau* compiles regulations and is the prime body that oversees advertising legislation. The *Bureau's* prime role is to protect consumers' interests, so much of its work is concerned with the accuracy of advertising content.

A number of other bodies maintain the standards of advertising work distributed throughout China. In terms of self-regulation, people in the media – print and broadcast – sometimes act as the final gatekeepers in the censorship process. They can reject an advertisement even if it has obtained a certificate of approval from the national office of the *CAA* (Chan and McNeal, 2003).

In conjunction with this, the *State Administration for Industry* and the *Commerce and State Planning Committee*, set up in 1993, regulate the content of advertising, while the *Propaganda Department* of the *CPC Central Committee* has influence on advertising content and sometimes has decided on the approval of broadcast advertising. There is also a *State Administration of Radio, Film and Television*, which has a voice in the censorship process.

Multimedia approaches to advertising are beginning to appear in China. Personal communications such as *SMS* messaging are further progressed than in the West, though *new media* advertising has not yet required any review from the *CAA*.

European Advertising Standards Alliance (EASA)

Region:	Europe
Representation:	national advertising regulatory bodies throughout Europe
Address:	www.easa-alliance.org

EASA is based in Brussels and was founded in 1992 to support self-regulatory bodies across Europe. It is a not-for-profit organization funded by its members. Its website states that its mission is to demonstrate how 'issues affecting advertising in the Single Market could be successfully dealt with through co-operation rather than detailed legislation'. Its role and membership expanded in 2001 to include what it described as 'European industry federations supportive of advertising self-regulation and representing advertisers, agencies and media'. *EASA* presently represents advertising organizations and self-regulatory bodies in 28 European countries. Its role is to resolve cross-national advertising issues – what it terms Cross-border complaints – and to operate as a measure of parity across its member countries. The organization's clout can be recognized in that large non-European advertising economies including the United States, Canada, South Africa and New Zealand are also members of *EASA*. They also produce a guide on self-regulation – called the 'Blue Book' – which is a thorough overview of regulations, both statutory and self-regulatory, governing European advertising.

The majority of cases that *EASA* is called on to adjudicate concern product claims made in direct mailers. However, the number of internet advertisements referred to EASA through national associations has increased since 2005. Internet advertisements are treated in the same manner as other forms of advertising, where the central issue hinges on whether advertising copy is misleading. *EASA* have produced recommendations for 'issue papers' on unsolicited commercial communications (spam) in response to complaints they received. However, problems arise where an internet advertisement's country of origin falls outside *EASA's* European members: while non-EU countries are members, their advertising output is outside *EASA's* jurisdiction, so complaints through EU members cannot be pursued. They can, however, transfer the case to the appropriate international regulatory bodies.

A French consumer contacted French regulatory body *Bureau de Vérification de la Publicité* about a mailer from Switzerland referring to clairvoyance. The complaint was that the text played on fear and made sweeping promises that could not be guaranteed. The mailing was in breach of French rules on occult sciences and was referred to the Swiss regulator *Commission Suisse pour la Loyauté*, which agreed with the complainant. The advertiser was asked not to use such methods again.

Summary

1. All nations have advertising regulatory bodies. Most bodies are self-regulated by communications industries and all act as advisory centres. They tend to adjudicate on cases bought to their attention by members of the public.

2. The 'measure' in all cases is whether advertisements are fair in their claims and not misleading.

3. While some bodies have censorship powers, others 'recommend' actions in their judgements. Some act as pressure groups by publishing their verdicts and shaming agencies to act fairly.

4. National regulatory bodies constantly discuss how to handle international campaigns.

5. Most complaints centre on how truthful adverts are. Shocking or aggressive adverts tend to be cited if their tone is deemed to be unnecessary. New or alternatively used advertising formats are rarely sited for being 'misleading'.

2 Widening formats

This section reviews campaigns that have extended beyond conventional advertising formats. What they also have in common is that they *pull* customers into playing along with their method because they offer a fresh approach.

Of the examples featured, some have used digital methods, from *SMS text* messaging (*Cadbury*) to using sales data to involve existing customers in schemes (*Land Rover*). Others challenge accepted ideas about how posters are read (*Médicos sin Fronteras*) and how public spaces are used (*Carling* in London, *Nike* and *Lips Enterprise* in Singapore, *First National Bank* in Johannesburg). One case study even challenged the conventions of launching new goods by introducing a semi-autonomous brand character to partner a product launch (*Levi's*). The example in question went on to become an icon in its own right.

Cases featured...

Médicos sin Fronteras digital images – effective rethinking of how posters are read
Land Rover Adventures – drew on customer databases to create a social network
Cadbury's TXT 'n' WIN – first SMS personal text messaging campaign
Carling Music Live – created a new sponsorship opportunity in *London Underground* subways
Lips Enterprise Zippo taxis – taking product demonstration on the road in Singapore
Nike vending machines – made playing football any time, anywhere feasible in urban areas
First National Bank towers project – developed a social inclusion project into a commercial opportunity
Levi's Sta-Prest Flat Eric – created a brand character to drive a communications mix.

Suggested reading

Lindstrom, Martin (2005) *Brand Sense: How to build powerful brands through touch, taste, smell, sight and sound*, Kogan Page, London

Ries, Al and Ries, Laura (2002) *The Fall of Advertising and the Rise of PR*, HarperCollins, New York

Smith, PR and Taylor, Jonathan (1993) *Marketing Communications: An integrated approach*, Kogan Page, London

Médicos sin Fronteras multifaceted posters

Product:	*Médicos sin Fronteras*
Target market:	youth in Spain
Agency/city:	*McCann Erickson*, Madrid
Reach:	unknown
Length of customer engagement:	15 minutes
Brief:	through new media, spread awareness of the global battle against killer diseases
Budget:	undisclosed
Lifespan:	launched in 2003 and still in circulation throughout 2004
Benchmark:	effective rethinking of how posters are read

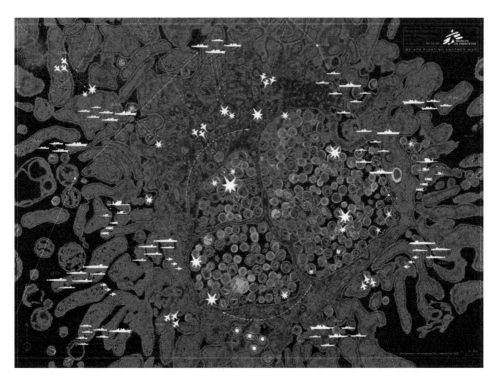

One of six images shared across the internet spanning aids, meningitis, pharyngitis and dysentery. This version is titled *Blue AIDS Virus,* and the line *We Are Fighting Another War* in small type in the top right-hand corner is accompanied by contact details.

Project background

An awareness campaign for international medical volunteer network *Médicos sin Fronteras* ('Doctors without Borders') challenged the notion that *viral* images needed to be immediate and interactive. Six static images created by *McCann Erickson*, Madrid, were highly detailed and repaid careful viewing, but were produced in a relatively low-resolution format which meant that they could be distributed without broadband.

The ease of distribution was half of the solution; it was the imaginative approach to art direction that made web users *want* to circulate the images.

Timeline	02 S	O	N	D	03 J	F	M	A	M	J	J	A	S	O	N
Concept development	■	■	■												
Completed project (constructed)				■	■	■	■								
Launch							☼								
Word-of mouth/blogging							☺	☺	☺						
Additional promotion							◙	◙	◙	◙					
Media exposure							--	--	--	--	--				

The campaign aimed to raise awareness of the battle *Médicos sin Fronteras* was having with a number of diseases, including aids, meningitis, pharyngitis and dysentery. By highlighting the organization as the chief combatant of diseases, the campaign aimed to make *MSF's* work relevant online as a feeder to recruitment and fundraising activities.

The graphic technique employed is simple: small war-type iconography – battleships, bomb blasts and helicopters – overlay a photographic image depicting the problem that *Médicos sin Fronteras* is combating in the developing world – war and disease. The war metaphor was made immediate with the simple juxtaposition of scale, from the 10:1 scale of the 'enemy' – the virus or injury – to the 1:1000 scale plan view of a battleground.

The relatively small size of the overlaid graphics let viewers know there was further horrific detail which they could access. This effectively served as the digital posters' *call to action*, which required the viewer first to be jarred and then to reflect on the message enough to consider responding. Therefore the images work by playing to the strengths of the medium. When the image was reproduced online, it used the ability of digital image packages to blow up the scale of the image and home in on details.

The campaign targeted Spanish youth, who were known to be keen to engage with social issues and were heavy users of the internet. Research before the campaign suggested that much of the target audience used social network sites as their main online tool, so the campaign was seeded for dissemination via e-mail and URL links.

The campaign challenged preconceptions about online viewing habits, notably that online communication motivates 'skim viewing', where viewers glance at, rather than read, information. It also challenged the assumption that online communications need to be immediate: the *MSF* campaign showed that subtlety can be effective on the internet.

Creative direction

The art direction anticipated how the images would be read: their initial hook was provided by their bold use of colour – themes of blue, red, green and purple make them easy on the eye at first glance. As viewers close in on the poster's details, its perspective shifts from the first impression of looking at an abstract to awareness that the image is a photograph of a virus or wound. As the viewer is drawn in further, the graphic representation of a battle becomes apparent. At this closer level the text becomes legible in the top right-hand corner of the frame. By this stage the viewer has engaged with the message enough to be affected by the *call to action*.

Had the awareness strategy been driven as a print campaign it would have cost more to produce and the image would have contained too much information to be read as a poster or press advertisement. To be read it would have had to be circulated by hand or post to named recipients, which would have cost far more to distribute. The internet proved an effective vehicle for this type of promotion, and the method of advertising was appropriate for the intended outcome.

Review

The campaign was seeded through *blogs* and social network sites, but global distribution of the images was mostly achieved through e-mail attachments because they were engaging and there was more to them than first met the eye.

- The digital posters were designed around the ways that posters are glanced at. When they were seen online they played to the strength of digital viewing packages. Viewers could play with the images online by increasing and decreasing the scale of view. Viewers were rewarded by panning in, because it seemed as though they were looking at something different.

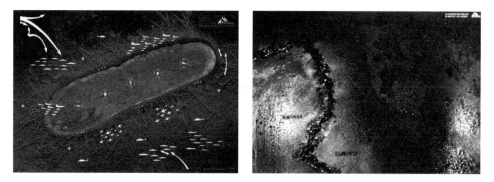

The digital *Médicos sin Fronteras* images – AIDS virus *left*, war wound *right* – were layered to repay careful viewing on a computer screen. At a glance viewers thought they were looking at an ambient image, but closer viewing revealed that it was a virus. A closer look rendered the image as a battleground landscape. At this level the metaphor and *call to action* were effective.

- The campaign resonated on a number of levels: the virus, like the *viral* format, is transmitted socially. The idea of a 'war' against viruses gives the subject topicality. In other words, the image is thought-provoking and makes an impression in a way that other campaigns do not.
- The simplicity of the image lent itself to the web because, as a static image, it was easy to send as a small-kb file.
- This was a rare example that did not need to create a loud buzz. It was relatively understated but engaging.
- The logo borrowed from poster design, but tagged the top left to differentiate it from other advertising formats.

Integrated mix

proportion of campaign

□ Print posters
▪ Online viral

Essentials

1. Using *PC* and *Apple* drawing packages, the images could easily have been produced using basic graphics programs such as *Adobe Illustrator* and *Photoshop*. It was the concept and art direction rather than technique that made the method effective.
2. Consider how the content will be read as a briefly skimmed message. What is its hook?
3. Make sure the styling of the advertisement is tailored to the medium, otherwise it will look as though you have gone online as an afterthought.

For links see www.adstoicons.com.

Land Rover Adventures Scheme

Product:	Land Rover
Target market:	Land Rover owners and 4×4 vehicle owners
Agency/city:	Craik Jones Watson Mitchell Voelkel, London
Planning/production time:	15 months
Reach:	100,000 existing customers and prospects on Land Rover's databases
Length of customer engagement:	day and weekend events, ongoing
Brief:	to bring existing customers closer to the brand and to develop an ongoing engagement with customers and prospects
Budget:	undisclosed
Lifespan:	1993–2002
Benchmark:	fresh use of commercial format, media placement

Project background

Land Rover Adventures was an innovative data-drawn loyalty scheme that, in practical terms, included a magazine and range of activities for existing *Land Rover* owners in the 4×4 car market. Its function, however, was one of *brand saliency* – to develop *Land Rover's* relationship with existing customers in the knowledge that involvement would spread, by word of mouth, to other *prospects* in the 4×4 market.

Timeline	92	93	94	95	96	97	98	99
Concept development	■	■						
Data collection	-------	-------	-------	-------	-------	-------	-------	-------
Launch		☼						
Word-of mouth activity		☺	☺	☺	☺	☺	☺	☺
Mail shots (thousands)		8 10	30	60	100			330

The scheme drew on stored customer data from *Land Rover* dealerships, with details of 33,000 owners, to establish the core *Adventures* membership. It was correctly anticipated that owners meeting up would develop a social interest group and develop a readily identifiable culture around the brand. This would allow the advertisers and brand to use communication channels between members as a

Brochures, videos, mailers were part of the *Land Rover Adventures* project and, later, even a *Little Book of Freedom* was sent to embellish involvement with the brand.

portal for new product information and promotions. So *Adventures* was a platform where *Land Rover* owners could talk about user experiences and test-drive other models at away-days in country parks and at weekend driving events.

The handling of customer data was significant: the agency took great care in the way *Land Rover* owners were approached by ensuring that mailers were not over-personalized and intrusive. The *OneLife* magazine was sent twice-yearly and events were offered only once. At the same time they wanted to demonstrate personal customer care. *Land Rover* owners tended to be loyal to the brand, so customer involvement was highly likely to reinforce connections with the very spirit of the brand that owners had chosen to buy into. *Adventures* was therefore positioned as a passive but enthusiastic mode of communication, flavoured by the brand ethos.

The scheme proved highly effective. Unlike other 4×4 manufacturers during the mid-1990s, *Land Rover* enjoyed a customer retention rate of between 65 and 70 per cent.

Profile: membership schemes

Land Rover's Adventures scheme was one of the first and best examples of how to integrate customer data and marketing techniques with strong creative direction.

The platform effectively became a customer loyalty programme and developed further in other countries around localized *Land Rover* communities. *Adventures* grew from a brand magazine mailshot into a programme that included training days and test-drives at *Land Rover's* specially built testing ground where customers were able to try out a variety of models off-road. The scheme proved particularly effective at encouraging existing *Land Rover* owners to upgrade their vehicles to more expensive – and profitable – models.

Creative direction

All *Land Rover* communications operated to the brand's promise, to work with a sense of adventure. The skill of the creative direction was in ensuring that events, magazine style and content collectively upheld this core brand spirit.

The concentration on existing customers rather than *prospects* was appropriate for *Land Rover* in 2003. Their market was steadily but consistently growing, with over 40,000 new vehicles sold each year in the UK – just under 2 per cent of the total automotive market. Rather than the variable sales rates of other manufacturers, *Land Rover* owners were characteristically repeat buyers, so brand testimonies from happy existing customers with good experiences to tell were an effective way of influencing other potential 4×4 owners in what was a rapidly expanding market.

This was one of the few campaigns that improved with age: during the time *Land Rover Adventures* ran in the UK, the information-communication processes were fine-tuned as digital technology improved. The lengthy relationship and growing trust of *Land Rover* with their direct advertising agency *Craik Jones Watson Mitchell Voelkel* allowed the scope of the scheme to expand, so there was more of a fluid link between above-, thru- and *below-the-line* activity.

The magazine was central to the scheme and created the opportunity to reaffirm the brand's ownership of the sense of adventure. *OneLife* contained spreads of *Land Rover* driving experiences, dealership updates, news of product develop- ments and accessories available. This strategy helped existing customers stay loyal to the brand by actively encouraging them to test and upgrade models on a regular basis, in a way that made it seem that they were graduating through the range.

Review

The scheme was *burst* through an invitation to existing *Land Rover* owners for an owners' away-day in the grounds of a country manor house. Afterwards more frequent one-day rural events were added to the list of activities. Events were preceded by mailshots which included *Adventures* brochures and a *Little Book of Adventures* and even collectors' cards.

> The longer we were involved in DM, the more it's been like rolling a snowball – you can fine-tune the programme, build a more powerful database and develop better direct marketing tools. (Rob Furio, relationship marketing manager, *Land Rover* in the United States, who developed the model further online)

The ideas initially developed in the UK for *Land Rover Adventures* were further developed in the United States, where an online community and active *Land Rover* expedition groups emerged to engage owners with the brand's ethos of outdoor exploration.

- The scheme was estimated to have repaid initial investment a hundred times over within five years. It was a 'slow burn' process compared to most advertising strategies but produced far more longer-term benefits.
- Bringing owners together allowed like-minded people to develop a shared understanding of the *Land Rover* experience and explore the potential of their own vehicles.
- The design of mailers was consistent in tone and styling. This helped to reinforce *Land Rover's* strong corporate identity.
- While the scheme proved effective in keeping owners connected, it was expensive to maintain and was later scaled down because of escalating maintenance costs.

Integrated mix

proportion of campaign

- Online
- Direct
- Events

Essentials

1. Loyalty schemes anchor existing customers to the brand as *brand advocates*.
2. The volume of correspondence needs to be carefully moderated to avoid customer saturation and intrusion.
3. While brands and agencies can make platforms for customers to get closer to their brand, they cannot manufacture a customer-centred brand culture.

For links see www.landroveradventures.com.

Cadbury SMS TXT 'N' WIN

Product:	*Cadbury*
Target market:	young people, 16–24 at point of sale
Agency/city:	*Triangle Communications*, London
Planning/production time:	6 months
Reach:	UK, 10 million (included terrestrial and satellite television commercials)
Length of customer engagement:	1–30 minutes
Brief:	make confectionery relevant to the target audience by involving customers in a promotion
Budget:	undisclosed
Lifespan:	2001
Benchmark:	first *SMS* personal text messaging campaign

Project background

The *Cadbury SMS TXT 'n' WIN* scheme was the first to use mobile phones as an advertising channel and became the model for *Short Messaging Service (SMS)* text-based schemes. As well as engaging customers in a promotion, it also provided data on customers likely to express an active interest in further schemes, and so created the prospect of personal communications at a later stage.

	00				01										
Timeline	S	O	N	D	J	F	M	A	M	J	J	A	S	O	N
Concept development					■	■									
Completed project (constructed)						■	■	■	■	■					
Media exposure							--	--	--	--	--	--			

During 2001 confectionery sales in the UK were flat compared to previous years. The confectionery market was looking to new ways of revitalizing its market presence, at a time when the mobile phone market was taking off and young people were spending more on phone cards. The biggest spenders on confectionery, female adults, who tended to buy for themselves and their family, were also heavy users of top-up mobile phones. *Triangle Communications* created a way of making the consumption of chocolate relevant to mobile phones by devising the SMS scheme, with more than £1 million worth of prizes.

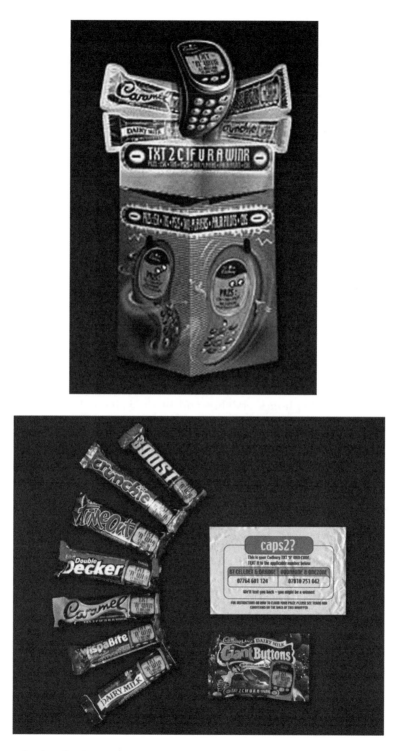

Cadbury packaging for the *SMS TXT 'n' WIN* scheme, which generated a one-to-one dialogue channel and SMS advertising platform for the brand.

Triangle Communications' strategy worked by making a virtue of the individual serial numbers on chocolate bar wrappers, which were printed to identify batch distribution. The campaign invited customers to check individual serial numbers on *Cadbury's Crunchie*, *Time Out* and *Fuse* purchases with *SMS TXT 'n' WIN* graphics, printed on some 65 million *Cadbury* wrappers. All customers had to do was text the serial number from the bar's wrapper to a free-phone *Cadbury* hotline to see if they had won a prize. All calls and *SMS texts* were logged into a database and prizes were randomly allocated. Customers were notified if they had won, and if their code did match a winning number all they had to do was send in their wrapper to claim their award. There were cash prizes of up to £5,000 and a variety of digital audio-visual equipment to be won.

The scheme immediately helped to make *Cadbury* more relevant by realigning its confectionery range with the activities of younger people, which was its primary aim.

Creative direction

Two original ideas were linked through the *SMS TXT 'n' WIN* campaign: the first involved using mobile technology as a means of customer response to a promotion. The second was the idea of finding a second use for product serial numbers which appear on packaging.

The graphic styling bore little difference from other promotions, but the involvement of mobile phones as a direct advertising channel made the offer and the brands seem progressive, up to date and relevant, simply because it was a digital medium. The promotion was aided by the immediacy and convenient ease with which customers could respond.

Review

Television commercials helped burst the promotion, while on-pack graphics, promotion information and point-of-sale paraphernalia reinforced the presence of the campaign.

> It gave sales a big lift at a time when the confectionery market has been pretty flat. (John Sunderland, *Cadbury Schweppes* CEO)

> Looking back at the work now, it looks quite basic and you see everyone using text as a mechanic to enter competitions, whereas in its day *Cadbury TXT 'n' WIN* was very innovative and the mechanic itself was the idea. The barrier we had to get over was the technology to make it work, which is where *Flytxt* came up trumps. Previously no one else had managed to crack this on such a mass scale. (Nick Presley, Group Creative Director, *Triangle Communications*, 1988–2005)

Cadbury's campaign for *SMS TXT 'n' WIN* ran through their brand range for individual and bulk pack purchases.

- The campaign utilized sound observations on how British youth filled their leisure time and ultimately rejuvenated the brand among younger consumers by connecting two key 'social break' activities – texting and eating confectionery.
- Chocolate consumption has long been considered as a break-time ritualistic activity, along with other *FMCG* snack foods, drinks and smoking. More recent work-break activities include internet searching, personal phone conversations and texting. When *SMS* traffic was established in young people's consciousness (the number of text messages hit the 1 billion mark in 2001) and expenditure on mobile phone air time was increasing, *Cadbury's* connection with a break-time rival helped combine the two activities. Texting and eating *Cadbury's* brand of chocolate became synonymous activities in the mind of consumers.
- Over 5 million text responses were received by *Cadbury* data analysts *Flytxt*, which amounted to approximately an 8% response rate (very good by sector standards).
- SMS communications proved effective in reaching the youth audiences – a segment of the market that was notoriously difficult to reach through mainstream channels. The *one-to-one* channel also proved to be good for maintaining continuous dialogue and supporting other multimedia activities.
- The scheme involved people having to key in the numbers and send a text, so they were being required to involve themselves in the campaign through a medium that they would identify with social activities.

Integrated mix

proportion of campaign

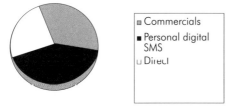

◨ Commercials
▪ Personal digital
  SMS
▫ Direct

Essentials

1. The medium can become as much part of the advertisement as the message. With the *SMS TXT 'n' WIN* campaign the brand realigned to current youth activities through the medium used, by association.
2. Campaigns can double up in function, through the traditional means of raising awareness and through the contemporary means of involvement. Customer data can be recorded and used to create insights for further promotions.
3. Customer involvement can be made fun – as long as it is easy to follow and engage with.

For links see www.flytxt.com/cgi-bin/template.pl?t=cspd&ID=43.

Carling Live Underground Music

Product:	Carling alcoholic beverages
Target market:	18–34 predominantly male, London
Agency/city:	*Vizeum/Kinetic*, London
Planning/production time:	16-week trial
Reach:	*London Underground* station visitors and commuters
Length of customer engagement:	up to 5 minutes daily
Brief:	Extend *Carling's* associations with live music and provide an opportunity for *Carling* to engage with consumers in a different and unexpected way
Budget:	not disclosed
Lifespan:	launched May 2003 (ongoing)
Benchmark:	placement, involvement

Buskers were auditioned to perform on *Carling Live* pitches on the *London Underground*.

Project background

To enhance the experience of travelling on the *London Underground*, *Transport for London* devised an innovative advertising platform: sponsored busking pitches. The measure acknowledged that illegal busking had become part of the *London Underground* experience. Regulating the activity was seen as a way to recognize its value, establish a quality threshold and distinguish busking from unauthorized money soliciting, as part of *Transport for London's* move to improve the underground railway network.

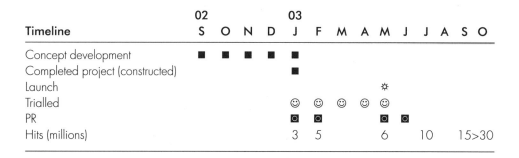

Timeline	02 S	O	N	D	03 J	F	M	A	M	J	J	A	S	O
Concept development	■	■	■	■	■									
Completed project (constructed)					■									
Launch									☼					
Trialled					☺	☺	☺	☺	☺					
PR					◙	◙			◙	◙				
Hits (millions)					3	5			6		10		15>30	

Transport for London approached brewer *Carling*, sponsor of a wide range of music events throughout London, to partner the venture. *Carling* bought its experience and credibility from setting up similar ventures and a recognizable 'live music' profile.

The first phase involved *Carling* and *Transport for London* locating pitches in subways leading to train platforms and setting up auditions for buskers, for which auditioning acts were charged a refundable registration fee. *London Underground* first had to lodge a legal appeal to change laws and bylaws to legalize live music in *Underground* subways. *Vizeum* and *Kinetic* were commissioned to develop a scheme for busking platforms, which were not allowed to obstruct passengers heading for the trains.

Profile: How the system operates

The recruitment, audition and management of buskers and busking zones is sponsored by *Carling*, which, through its continued engagement with the entertainment industries, ensures a high level of both talent and variety. The rota is managed by a professional artiste management company, and buskers rely solely on donations from customers.

Licensing has proved a big hit for both customers and buskers. A survey conducted for *London Underground* showed that 82 per cent of commuters favoured the scheme, while buskers valued the chance to perform to huge daily audiences (3 million passengers daily). The licensed buskers have managed to attract international media interest and are regularly booked for events and recording sessions – more so than when buskers performed illegally.

The project has proved successful. From a starting base of 256 buskers at 12 main central *London Underground* stations, the number of *Carling* licences rose to 400 at 25 stations in 2006, providing over 3,000 hours a week of live music each week. The success of the scheme has been acknowledged in that it has been awarded a permanent role on the network.

Creative direction

The design direction had a practical problem to solve in defining busking zones while maintaining clear passageways. Styled zones with branding helped to bridge *Carling's* live music sponsorship activities and featured ambient graphic images of live performance venues. They also managed the PR launch for the scheme.

The scheme required classic *third party association* tactics so that the project bought mutual benefits to all parties:

- *Carling* benefited by reaffirming its commitment to live music events in London.
- *London Underground* benefited by making subways safer.
- Tourists and London's commuters benefited because the ambient vitality of live music filled the tunnels leading to the trains.
- Buskers benefited by being guaranteed regular pitch sites. The sites themselves created a performance space, and tube travellers felt easier about giving money to a bona fide cause.

Review

Licensed busking trials were announced in early 2003 and news stories were later picked up by a number of news agencies. The full scheme trial was launched in 2003 with 25 busking pitches at the 12 underground stations. Selected buskers were awarded blue busking licences following their auditions and police background checks.

Perspectives

Buskers provide a welcome distraction from the hustle and bustle of the Underground for many London commuters. Even in the age of MP3 players, live music is still an important part of people's lives and (emotionally) it makes us feel happy. Sponsorship of the scheme extends *Carling's* associations with live music and gives an opportunity to engage with consumers in a different and unexpected way. (Andy Cray, *Carling* Brand Manager)

I'd never busked on the Underground before I applied for a licence – I didn't want to come up here and fight people over the pitch. With the licence I know where I can go and play, and there won't be any arguments from anybody – shopkeepers, environmental health or beggars.

(Bass player Justin Manser, 33)

The branding and corporate identity of other *Carling* music sponsorships carried through to the London Underground busking spaces. Defined *Carling Live* pitch spots gave buskers an official space to perform.

- According to Dr Michael Bull, an expert on sound in consumer culture, the buskers have humanized the Underground by transforming routine journeys with live musical performances. The subways have become more of shared experience, claims Bull (Bull, 2002).
- Auditions, licensing and rota systems had to be centrally managed to ensure quality and variety at all stations.
- *Carling* and *London Underground* were keen to highlight that all performers were independent and not in the pay of sponsors. This was flagged up in all publicity for the scheme in order to prevent regulation diluting spontaneous 'good will' by commuters.
- Busker zones were styled as a space somewhere between stage and street performance. The aim was to make spaces look official, but at the same time make musicians seem approachable and receptive to donations. Graphics clearly separate commuter space from the *Carling* music 'platform', which is reinforced by back-lit poster boards normally reserved for advertising.

Integrated mix

proportion of campaign

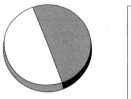

■ Programme
  sponsorship
□ Ambient

Essentials

1. The strength of a strong advertising idea comes during the planning stage: with *Carling Live* the benefits for stakeholders were considered first, which helped shape the development of the project.
2. The project's advertising work was channelled into the design of the licensed busking system and the busking zones. Within the campaign buskers are effectively *brand ambassadors*.
3. For a new promotional platform to become a fixture a careful check of relevant bylaws and a consideration of beneficiaries at many levels are first required.

For links see www.tfl.gov.uk/tube/arts/busking or www.carling.com.

Lips Enterprise Zippo cab roof mounts

Product:	*Zippo Windproof Lighter*, for *Lips Enterprise*
Target market:	smokers in Singapore
Agency/country:	*McCann Erickson*, Singapore
Planning/production time:	3 months
Reach:	island-wide
Length of customer engagement:	fleeting; generated word-of-mouth activity
Brief:	to highlight the unique attribute of *Zippo Windproof Lighter*
Budget:	80,000 Singapore dollars
Lifespan:	January–June 2003
Benchmark:	taking product demonstration on the road

One of a number of cabs in Singapore with roof displays demonstrating *Zippo's* windproof lighters.

Project background

The roofs of taxis are often used as advertisement space, but a stunt for *Zippo* lighters in Singapore captured the imagination of passers-by for a number of reasons: real flames flickered out of what appeared to be a *Zippo Windproof Lighter* mounted on cab roofs, which looked daring, provoked curiosity (*how did they make it work?*) and managed to demonstrate clearly the USP of the *Zippo* lighter.

Timeline	02 S	O	N	D	03 J	F	M	A	M	J	J	A	S	O	N
Concept development	■	■	■	■											
Completed project				■	■										
Launch					☼										
Run					☺	☺	☺	☺	☺						
PR					◙	◙	◙	◙	◙	◙					
Media exposure					--	--	--	--	--	--	--				

The campaign was commissioned by *Lips Enterprise*, a Singapore-based shop specializing in retailing *Zippo* lighters, with the aim of dramatizing the performance of the lighter by reinforcing the *Zippo's* ability to hold a flame in adverse weather conditions.

The project used techniques that are familiar to advertising: exaggeration of the key product quality and 'placement' of the message in environments where the product would have the greatest significance – on the streets of Singapore, where most smokers would see it parading past as they strolled the pavements or stood outside buildings on smoking breaks.

As a three-dimensional demonstration, the project made a bigger impact than static billboards or posters in the same environment. Mounted on top of a taxi, the advertisement was circulated through the main city-centre taxi routes and in the suburbs. The *Zippo* cabs with their flame alight became a topic of conversation and a mark that people looked out for.

Creative direction

The cost of the campaign – estimated to be approximately 80,000 Singapore dollars – would have only just been able to reclaim its outlay from the Singapore market alone: it was understood that the campaign would be a loss-leader in generating images that would circulate though web *blog* sites because it looked different and intriguing. As an image the scenario could been manufactured graphically, but people who saw the cabs became witnesses to the fact that it was real.

The six-strong *Zippo* fleet operated the normal course of cab journeys – although they were often specially requested by callers to Singapore's central taxi offices.

The strength of the campaign is in its choice of context. Travelling around the streets of Singapore was more likely to reach smokers at a time when they would be contemplating smoking. Therefore it appealed at the heart of the circumstances and environment of the product activity (Schmitt, 1999). The theme of re-appropriation is not unique to advertising: other creative areas such as furniture have long since been reusing artefacts in different contexts (see *Marlboro Motel*, chapter 3). However, cab rooftops provided an ideal test for Zippo, and the cab served its purpose as a unique travelling billboard.

Review

The taxis were launched without pre-publicity, so they appeared as a bit of an enigma. The campaign's marketing firm contacted the national press, who put the story and images of the cabs onto the internet. Publicity then developed *word-of-mouth*, online and offline.

> If clients deserve the kind of work they get, *Lips Enterprise* is definitely one of the boldest we've witnessed. From what was originally a brief for a simple print ad, they had the foresight and gumption to go with a brilliant piece of out-of-the-box thinking. (Somjai Satjatham and Juliana Koh, two of project's team at *McCann Erickson*, Singapore.)

- Since its launch, the ambient piece had never ceased to be a show-stopper. Being a living proof of outsmarting and not outspending one's competitors, the *Zippo Windproof Lighter* taxi-top had created more impact and achieved more brand awareness than any print ad or television commercial could.
- This campaign had many billboard-based precedents: perhaps the most notable was a 1982 campaign for *Araldite* glue in the UK, which featured cars glued to billboards. However, this was a moving 'billboard' that demonstrated *Zippo's* USP across the city, on a route determined by the cab drivers' normal course of work.
- The mystique of *Zippo* taxis' sudden appearance on the streets of Singapore city centre did not cloud the concisely demonstrated advertising message, that the strength of *Zippo's* flame can withstand adverse weather conditions.
- The message is dependent on the medium: it takes the cab to move and the usual everyday weather conditions to make the advertisement work.

Zippo Windproof Lighters cabs drove around Singapore city and suburbia so that passing pedestrians, in outdoor spaces where they could smoke, could compare the strength of the *Zippo* flame with their own lighters.

● By re-appropriating taxis the perfect environment is made for the message to work, because it is different, moving and appealing to its target audience in an environment conducive to smoking.

Essentials

1. For an outdoor stunt to communicate well, the medium has to fit the message. The environment also has to be where the right audience will see it.
2. The impact of the stunt should not overwhelm the message.
3. Such approaches need to be managed long before they are launched – in this case, the safety of the light and various local authority and transport safety procedures had to be cleared before the project was allowed to go live.

For links see www.adstoicons.com.

Nike 90 Swift football vending machines

Product:	*Nike 90 Swift* football (sports goods)
Target market:	men, 12–24 years old, Singapore
Agency/country:	*Kinetic*, Singapore
Reach:	urban youth
Length of customer engagement:	lasting experience and association (length of product's lifespan)
Brief:	develop the brand as an any time, anywhere interactive experience
Budget:	not disclosed. *Nike 90 Swift* footballs vended for 26 Singapore dollars (US $16.50)
Lifespan:	from February 2005
Benchmark:	placement, involvement

Nike football dispensers, situated where youths had re-appropriated urban spaces for street football.

Project background

In terms of inspiring international press attention, customer participation and delivering a product to its audience through a simple placement, *Nike*'s football vending machine would take some beating.

Nike aimed to reach urban youths hanging out in Singapore's city centres and parks by installing football vending machines close to areas where they already kicked footballs: by the main MRT railway station, in concreted public squares and in an open paved area next to the shopping centre. The idea was to make playing football accessible at any time and anywhere – not just on grass. For 26 Singapore dollars youths could get hold of a ball where they would normally be kicking it around – without having to go to a sports shop.

Timeline	04				05									
	S	O	N	D	J	F	M	A	M	J	J	A	S	O
Concept development	■	■	■	■										
Completed project				■										
Launch						☀								
Word-of-mouth/blogging				☺	☺	☺	☺	☺	☺					
Additional promotion				◙		◙		◙		◙				
Media exposure						--		--		--	--	--		
Hits (millions)				0.5	1	3	5		6		8			10

The concept was simple. Vending machines were remodelled to vend *Nike*'s new *90 Swift* footballs. The machines had a clear *Perspex* front mount and graphics-covered casing which sported the campaign's motifs and copy. The graphics helped the vending machines to tie in with their surroundings.

The strategy extended *Nike*'s plan to encourage sports and fitness activities in urban areas, and by putting dispensers in unusual locations they faced no competition in the immediate environment.

As an *ambient* campaign the success of the vending machines was measured not solely by the number of balls sold but also in terms of how the campaign raised awareness of the brand's urban positioning. The worldwide press coverage it generated certainly boosted *Nike*'s presence significantly in the sporting press.

The vending machines outperformed expectation by selling more footballs in one week than were sold in two months from stores. People were even willing to queue for the novelty of buying a football from a vending machine. The agency responsible, *Kinetic*, has been able to extend the vending machine idea to other ball games elsewhere in the world. As an advertising platform it was particularly strong because people were familiar with the vending machine concept and because it made products accessible 24/7.

Profile: 'cultural capital'

The vending machines brought *Nike* cultural advantage: by blending in where youths had already made space for group games, *Nike* could claim to belong in that environment. Rather than simply developing their mainstream credibility, this project develops *sub-cultural capital* by acknowledging unauthorized urban locations as sporting environments. The graphic styling of the machines made *Nike* look as though they belonged in the spaces where youths hung out, in urban environments 'reclaimed' as unofficial leisure zones. Although the agency, *Kinetic*, had to seek council approval to install the vending machines, their placement undoubtedly added value to the brand.

The machines' locations encouraged a spirit of innovation and reinforced *Nike* as an advocate of individuals playing by different rules: the project echoed *Nike*'s outlook as an innovative and unprecedented brand.

Creative direction

The vending machine's design reinforced the ready-to-play spirit. The display featured balls stacked in columns. When a ball was purchased it dropped to the bottom and out of the machine ready for play.

The idea was an extension of *Nike's Play to Win* campaign, which ran in Singapore, and the line even ran across the top of the vending machines. Television commercials showed footballers demonstrating tricks with the same design of football in urban spaces. By buying a *Nike 90 Swift* football from a dispenser, others could do the same.

Review

There was no pre-publicity for this campaign. Vending machines appeared in locations overnight.

- The project worked as an extension to an existing *Nike* television commercial. It reminded street footballers of the campaign in a space where they practised football.
- The positioning of vending machines was strategic. High-traffic urban locations close to designated and undesignated street playing areas were targeted to maintain the any time, anywhere theme of the commercial. Football was played day and night in these spaces.

A *Nike Play to Win* football dispenser outside Sungei Wang Plaza, Singapore.

- Existing uses of vending machines – confectionery and fizzy drinks – provided a reference for the *Nike* footballs that was about affordability and convenience. This made the balls and brand appear more accessible than they would be if confined to sports shops.
- The originality of the concept helped the brand claim territory in environments they were targeting.

Integrated mix

proportion of campaign

- PR
- Ambient

Essentials

1. By placing branded artefacts in relevant environments, existing associations can be reinforced.
2. Contexts for stunts need to be appropriate to the brand – in this case street play, high-density urban spaces and the vending machine theme were harnessed.
3. The any time, anywhere theme underpinning the project fitted with other brand promotions.
4. Approval was needed for the stunt – even though it appeared counter-cultural.

For links see www.adstoicons.com.

First National Bank Cooling Towers Mural

Product:	First National Bank, South Africa
Target market:	citizens of Johannesburg
Agency/city:	*FCB 361-degrees*, Johannesburg, SA
Reach:	Johannesburg, SA regeneration
Length of customer engagement:	ambient – varies
Brief:	use commercial channels to rejuvenate the business district of Johannesburg
Budget:	850,000 rand
Lifespan:	2002 – until area redevelopment plan implemented
Benchmark:	community involvement

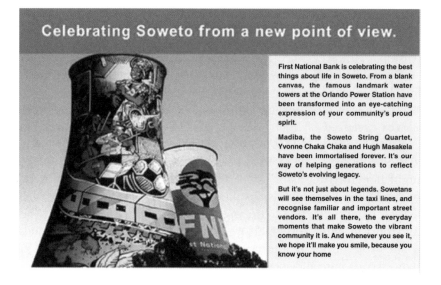

Two cooling towers, one branded with sponsors *First National Bank*, the other with a mural titled *A celebration of life in Soweto*.

Project background

For three decades preceding the new millennium, the business district of Johannesburg lay derelict. Its most prominent landmarks were two crumbling cooling towers which became seen as symbolic of the region's state of decay.

A project funded by the *First National Bank* of South Africa and coordinated by environmental advertising firm *FCB 361-degrees* in Johannesburg sought to make over the towers to symbolize the beginning of reinvestment in Johannesburg and in particular the regeneration of the business district. The aim was to help the area 'from within' by developing a community-centred project to restore pride within the area.

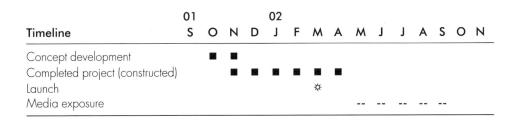

The *Orlando Power Station* cooling towers and huge turbine hall had previously been one of Johannesburg's first coal-fired stations and once pumped smoke over the townships. However, once Johannesburg had switched power supplies, the towering stacks had fallen into a state of disrepair, which was mirrored in the economic decline of the area.

In 1999 the towers were earmarked for regeneration as part of the *Johannesburg Metropolitan Council's* 'iGoli 2000' urban renewal strategy but the project had difficulty attracting funding. *FCB 361-degrees*, with the aid of local government, sought to solve the problem; stakeholders were enlisted with a view to considering how they might benefit from association. It was soon realized that it was not just Johannesburg's residents but also its businesses that had a vested interest – some because their identity was tied to the region, others because they were involved in travel and tourism, while developers were keen on pushing the value of land in the region. The project drew all interested parties together and worked on a strategy that balanced corporate and social considerations. The outcome was a scheme that resulted in one commercial and one locally decorated tower – a striking and symbolic addition to Johannesburg's urban landscape.

Profile: strategic design plan

The murals had to complement each other and the surrounding area, but communicate different values. The left tower depicted the branding of the main sponsor, *First National Bank*, which has its head offices in Johannesburg, and had already invested in the (re)development of the city's main football stadium. The prominent towers were able to provide a visual reminder of the bank's home and served as a reminder of the region's strong history as a financial centre.

The right tower's motif was a tribute to the cultural history of the region. The huge, colourful mural in local hues of blue, yellow and red was called 'A Celebration of Life in Soweto', and depicted scenes and stories from the region. With such detail in the mural, the towers quickly became part of the tourist itinerary of Johannesburg visits, and went some way to moving on from Soweto's tragic history.

As a rejuvenation scheme the project helped pull businesses, residents and the government together and provided a solution that fulfilled its commercial and cultural roles equally effectively.

Creative direction

The clever thinking underpinning this project was developed in the planning stage, which turned a community project into a commercial proposition that would symbolize something positive for all parties involved. For the main backers, *First National Bank*, the project provided a visual presence that also publicized their involvement in regenerating the scheme. For local residents it was a scheme they could be part of and co-create; the community was involved in actually painting the towers in a process that was carefully documented. Recording the process was used to further generate interest and investment in the area, and may prove useful for the marketing of future projects. For the *Johannesburg Metropolitan Council* the project not only tidied up an eyesore but produced a graphic regional marker, which combined the visual language of the region with its aspirations – vibrant, colourful and positive.

As a scheme the project therefore fulfilled a range of functions – all progressive – in creating a revitalized presence, through the intelligent coordination of an advertising process and a socioeconomic constituency.

Review

The re-launch of the towers was a major event in Johannesburg, attracting political dignitaries and local celebrities. It was handled as an opportunity to broadcast the region's renewal as a commercial centre in South Africa.

- The community was involved in designing one tower and painting both, in a process that was carefully documented. The footage will also have cultural and commercial currency because it shows the region pooling sources to complete the project.
- The project also highlighted the local visual language of Johannesburg, and in terms of promoting the region created an icon on the skyline that gave the region distinction.

Views of the redeveloped *First National Bank*-sponsored towers, dominating the skyline over the business region of Johannesburg, South Africa.

● The project was not the first commercially branded urban regeneration scheme, nor was it unique in using murals to reinforce regional identity. However, it was unique in tying together marketing, environmental and cultural schemes through an advertising-oriented approach.

Integrated mix

proportion of campaign

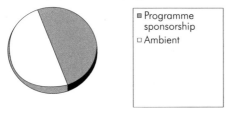

- Programme sponsorship
- Ambient

Essentials

1. Projects on this scale require more time in planning and negotiation than in the design phase. Selling the vision and negotiating agreement is the key behind getting approval.
2. To create a landmark not only requires local authority approval but also has to be recognized as fulfilling all stakeholders' interests.
3. If a large community-based project is planned, it is worth first identifying potential stakeholders that would benefit from the project. It is worth considering parties whose interests could be motivated by location or relevance to their core activities.

For links see www.adstoicons.com.

Levi's Sta-Prest Flat Eric

Product:	Levi Strauss **Europe, Middle East and Africa**
Target market:	16–24-year-olds
Agency/city:	*Bartle Bogle Hegarty*, London
Reach:	Europe, Middle East and Africa
Length of customer engagement:	varied during campaign. Points of online and offline contact were created
Brief:	create opportunities for core market to engage with the brand ethos
Budget:	undisclosed
Lifespan:	from 1999 for 12 months
Benchmark:	brand character, driving a communication mix

Flat Eric, the brand character used to assist the launch of *Levi's Sta-Prest* jeans.

Project background

Flat Eric was a puppet created to launch a new cut of *Levi's* jeans in the UK. The campaign followed a legendary series of commercials for *Levi's 501* that emphasized the brand's heritage. The launch of the *Sta-Prest* sought to distinguish the promotion from its predecessors and to update the brand's positioning, in tune with the new style, tone and wit of youth.

Timeline	98 S	O	N	D	99 J	F	M	A	M	J	J	A	S	O
Concept development			■	■	■									
Completed project/viral circulation								☼	■	■	■			
Launch (commercial burst)											☼			
Word-of-mouth/blogging										☺	☺	☺	☺	☺
Media exposure									--	--	--	--	--	--
Hits (millions)									0.1	0.5	10			30

The character *Flat Eric* initially appeared to have little to do with promoting the brand, but his presence on the site created an opportunity for *early adopters* to claim him first as an icon. This was because the puppet was one of the first caricatures to be seeded on the internet through *viral* activity before having a mainstream presence in commercials. Eventually *Flat Eric* was put out in his own right as a soft toy.

Flat Eric was styled by *Jim Henson's Creature Shop* for a pop music video being made in France. His popularity is enduring – there are websites still devoted to him in the United States, Australia, Spain and Germany, even though the campaign stopped running in 2000.

In his commercial lifespan as *Levi's* 'spokesperson' (sic; ironically, he didn't speak), *Flat Eric* became a youth cult icon – one of the first advertising creations to do so, with a life beyond the frame of the advertisement. Unlike other brand 'icons', *Flat Eric* did not wear the product nor was he featured on the product. His association to the brand was maintained in an enigmatic way.

Profile 1: incrementally managed release

The character was first seen on *Levi's* website, which allowed *early adopters* to discover *Flat Eric* first before he featured in *Levi's* commercials. *Early adopters* spread the word by mailing images, wallpaper and URLs to their friends online. *Flat Eric* therefore became familiar in schools and colleges first because he was developed through an online clique that created initial *subcultural capital* for *Levi's*.

The launch of the television and cinema commercials featuring *Flat Eric* became something of an eagerly anticipated event. The advertisements had an American road movie theme running through them: they featured *Flat Eric* and travelling companion 'Angel' – a modish figure wearing *Sta-Prest* jeans, evading the law as they drove through the open landscapes of California. The commercials developed like a series, ending when they were finally captured. Within a year the campaign achieved mass appeal. The launch of the *Flat Eric* soft toy offered another way into consuming the cultural phenomenon. More websites and an organized fan club were created to support those who felt a bond with the character.

Profile 2: the design of Flat Eric

Levi's Flat Eric was on a puppet that had earlier featured in a pop video with French dance music artist *Mr Ozio* (the soundtrack for which was used in the *Levi's Sta-Prest* television commercials and went on to reach number one in the British music singles charts). In one sense, this gave *Flat Eric* a 'pre-life' history that did much to boost his credibility among youth.

Earlier storylines, later discarded, featured a longer-haired *Eric* being run over – hence the name *'Flat Eric'*. In the narratives that were used, *BBH* cast him as a heroic figure on the run from the law. The plots are short on detail – no explanation is offered as to why he is on the run or why he has a human companion – in the enigmatic style of cult films such as *The Blues Brothers*.

Flat Eric was very much of his moment: at the time in the UK, the *BBC's* children's television character *Gordon the Gofer* and *ITV Digital* brand character *Monkey* created a similar (if smaller) buzz. Neither had a human voice, but both had a human friend in their storylines. In a similar vein to *Flat Eric*, *ITV Digital's Monkey* lived in an assumed world where the situations he found himself in seemed at odds with the personality on view – which did much to define their popularity with youth.

Creative direction

The idea of a lo-tech puppet stemmed from the observation that fashion advertising tended to take itself too seriously, and the makers wanted to have some fun. Because *Levi's* had established great kudos through earlier campaigns, the puppet was a gentle nudge that repositioned *Levi's* existing *brand equity*.

Press release 1999:

The pale creased one (Angle) and the funkin fluff (FE) return with some more anecdotal foolery, sharp both in talent and in Levi's® Sta-Prest® tailoring. YOU get 5 × 30-second cuts for the short of attention span and the busy of mind. A collection of snapshots documenting nothing much more than Flat and Angel's thoughts on taking it as it comes and how to do it well... Sharp enough to cut the unwary, Angel casually shows the way to wear the crease...

Living with style: advanced thinking for the sharper individual.

Review

Much of the campaign's success was down to the way *Flat Eric* was incrementally launched. Images of *Flat Eric* were seeded on the internet and distributed as URL attachments as *virals*. Next, the character was popularized through the *Levi's Sta-Prest* commercials and the video accompanying the re-released soundtrack. Then *Flat Eric* was produced as a toy in *Levi's*-branded packaging. Therefore *Flat Eric* effectively had three launches: as a *sub-brand*, brand character and as a *brand extension*.

Flat Eric, the *Sta-Prest brand ambassador*, as he appeared in the commercials and an image, posted on the web, of a *brand evangelist's* collection of *Flat Erics*.

- *Flat Eric* was by no means the first brand creation to become mainstream. The *Michelin Man*, Tony the *Frosties* tiger, *Trebor's* Bertie Bassett and *Tango's* Gotan doll all pre-dated *Flat Eric*, but the commercial impact of the puppet surpassed earlier versions. As a caricature deliberately designed to be a cult object, Flat Eric was perfectly pitched as a silent, cool rebel.
- Creating opportunities for a character to exist outside advertising allows space for cultural tagging and the accumulation of *(sub)cultural capital*.
- People can get far more involved with a brand and its values if they are given attainable access points. The production of a toy and numerous internet opportunities generated by *Levi's* rewarded people for showing interest and established a level of loyalty beyond that achieved by most brands.

Integrated mix

proportion of campaign

□ Commercial
■ Online

Essentials

1. A strong advertising idea that chimes with the times can grow beyond being an advertisement.
2. Creating opportunities for people to invest time and money in 'hobbying' a brand can be rewarding if the commercial avenues have been designed before launch.
3. People look for ways to identify with themes they enjoy. Providing this through commercial channels can allow ads to be come icons.

For links see www.adstoicons.com.

3 Events-driven

This chapter presents cases that have advertised through staged events. Each example has made advertising three-dimensional by creating or re-appropriating spaces and objects.

The first series of examples are *brand environments* such as television (*Orange Playlist*) and urban sidewalks (*IKEA*). This includes constructed environments which were designed to convey the mood of the brand (*Marlboro* and *COMME des GARÇONS*).

Other examples are *re-branded activities,* and include the subversion of a bar (*Singapore Cancer Society*), street (*Britart.com*) and billboard environment (*adidas*). This section also includes an iconic fashion accessory, which became an event in itself and drew a major social concern to prominence (*LAF LIVESTRONG*).

Cases featured...

Orange Playlist programming – programme content as a branded platform
IKEA Everyday Fabulous – widening awareness through guerrilla tactics
Marlboro Motel after-show 'green room' – creating a (non-)branded environment
COMME des GARÇONS guerrilla store – temporary fashion stores as exclusive social hubs
Nike LIVESTRONG bands – social awareness accessories – a new product type
Britart.com street captions – re-framing the environment as ad space
Singapore Cancer Society ashtrays – challenging consumers by subverting spaces
adidas vertical football billboards – creating a buzz in live advertising space

Suggested reading

Godin, Seth (2006) *Small is the New Big: And 193 other riffs, rants, and remarkable business ideas*, Penguin, New York

Kaden, Robert J (2006) *Guerrilla Marketing Research*, Kogan Page, London

Mikunda, Christian (2006) *Brand Lands, Hot Spots and Cool Places*, Kogan Page, London

Orange Playlist

Product:	Orange telecommunications
Target market:	youth
Production company/city:	*Initial*, London
Planning/production time:	9 months
Reach:	1 million (broadcast on terrestrial TV with satellite channel repeats)
Length of customer engagement:	22 minutes/36 episodes
Brief:	create an environment to promote *Orange* telecommunications download music services
Budget:	undisclosed
Lifespan:	series 1: from October 2004; series 2: October 2005 (26 shows). Series ongoing
Benchmark:	programme content as a branded platform

Part of the opening credit sequence to the first series of *Orange Playlist*, commissioned for *Orange* telecommunications.

Project background

Orange Playlist was a commissioned television programme that demonstrated how a strong brand idea could be developed as entertainment. Rather than producing an advert, the core concept behind *Orange Playlist* was that the branding went beyond programme sponsorship into the set, the styling of programme graphics and merged with the programme content itself, which was honed to highlight a range of music accessible through *Orange* telecom's download services.

Timeline	05										06				
	M	A	M	J	J	A	S	O	N	D	J	F	M	A	M
(series 2)															
Pre-production								■	■						
Launch										☼					
Word-of-mouth/blogging								☺	☺	☺	☺	☺	☺	☺	☺
Broadcast run									◉	◉	◉	◉	◉	◉	◉
Hits (10,000s)									120		100	170			184

The show was first aired in October 2004 on the UK's largest terrestrial commercial channel, *ITV1*. Repeats were broadcast on digital channels *ITV2*, *VH1* and *TMF* later in the year.

In the first series a different guest featured in each episode and the show gave viewers a rundown of the top five MP3 downloads and ringtones of the week (a top 20 of each chart featured on the official website). The charts helped reinforce the presence of *Orange's* download ringtones service. The second series of *Orange Playlist* dropped the charts and made the weekly guests more of a feature. Guests (who have included Christian Slater, Jodie Marsh and Burt Bacharach) picked five tracks – from the past, present, future, an all-time favourite and a dedication.

Viewers had a number of opportunities to actively engage. *Opera Telecom's* technology infrastructure enabled viewers to enter *Playlist* competitions, join discussions, comment on entertainment topics using *SMS* or *IVR* messaging services and send via *MMS* short anecdotes for a feature called 'The song that changed your life'. Selected entries scrolled across the screen during each episode and one would be featured as a 'downloaded' music video. In addition to the show's structure reflecting values of the sponsoring brand, the programme's makers, *Initial* (part of *Endemol*), drew on *Orange* telecom's identity as a significant aspect of the programme's on-screen styling.

The format chimed with viewers – within a year the series even attracted the largest viewing figures for a UK music show in 2006 (1.84 million for an episode featuring musician Ozzy Osbourne).

Creative direction

Orange Playlist was created to champion *Orange's* download music service. Morgan Holt, former Executive Producer of Interactive at *Initial*, noted that 'The ringtone market alone is anticipated to account for 12 per cent of total music sales by 2008 [source: *Ringtonia.com*] and so we developed *The Orange Playlist* to reflect the definite changing patterns in music sales'. By integrating mobile technology into series 1 the broadcast was able to interact with viewers, and strengthen *Orange's* position as the most prominent mobile music download brand.

The programme title alone, *Orange Playlist*, featured in TV listings and served as a reminder of the telecommunication firm's connection with music. Yet it was within the 22-minute show format that a brand environment was created.

Profile: advertiser-funded programming

As a method of promotion, advertiser-funded programming incorporates sponsors within the broadcast content, so that the treatment, topics discussed and tone of the show reflect the target environment of the sponsoring brand. Insurance firms, mortgage brokers and sports equipment manufacturers have championed this format through network home improvement and fitness programming. Unlike commercials, advertising through programme content sponsorship has potential as a promotional vehicle because it is not as compressed by the timeframe of commercial breaks and there is scope within programmes to shape the screen around the sponsors, in terms of a programme's content and aesthetic. As a form of persuasion it is more subtle than television commercials but has more opportunity to give a flavour of the product or service.

The idea of using television in this way has become an increasingly popular strategy in the UK. In 2005 car manufacturers *Audi* even produced their own television channel – *Audi TV* – which scheduled *Audi*-specific programme content under the assumption that channel-surfing viewers would dip into and out of shows. Broadcast radio shows have used this model for some years, but as a television vehicle this approach had to negotiate stringent regulatory codes to avoid editorial imbalance.

Review

Given the complex multi-channel nature of the production, just over nine months' lead-in time was required before the programme was first aired. For instance, separate elements such as mobile messaging, live studio feeds and pre-recorded (and post-production) elements had to work in sync for the pilot episode. Incorporating live interactive elements made the organization of production complex before production.

> By integrating mobile technology into the programming we were able to interact with our viewers – helping them to get more from their mobile and building our own brand awareness. (Martin Holt, Executive Producer, *Initial*)

Orange Playlist episodes: series 1 with host Lauren Laverne and guest, musician Nick Rhodes. The updated logo for series 2, hosted by Jayne Middlemiss with guest, model Jodie Marsh.

- Rather than pushing *Orange's* download service as an obvious pitch, an environment was created through the programme's content and styling, where a feel for the network was channelled.
- The association between the brand's downloading service and its role in overseeing download music charts gave *Orange* an authorial positioning.
- The association with music celebrities illustrates *Orange's* involvement with musicians and performers, and not just the distribution of music.
- The interconnection between regular programme content and interactive elements helped *Orange* incorporate viewer involvement. Web activity extended connections between the show and *Orange's* digital music service.
- The freshness of the format gave the brand a contemporary television presence.

Integrated mix

proportion of campaign

▫ Programme
  sponsorship
■ Online
▫ SMS/promotions

Essentials

1. *Programme content* as a branding platform requires the type of subject and format that is consistent with the brand's target market, to create the right presence. It is a way of showing a context for a brand outside the traditional commercial format.
2. Mapping and exploring the potential of multimedia communications projects requires a long lead-in time. The benefits are that more than one income stream can be generated.
3. Interactive aspects help consumers to 'own' an aspect of their viewing choice – just as they 'own' the content of their personal communication media.

For links see www.adstoicons.com.

IKEA Everyday Fabulous street exhibits

Product:	IKEA furniture and accessory range
Target market:	pedestrians in Aoyama (Japan) during the opening of the *IKEA* Funabashi Store and New York (United States), during New York Design Week
Agency/city:	*Deutsch Inc*, New York
Planning/production time:	3 months
Reach:	Aoyama and Manhattan city dwellers, pedestrians and motorists
Length of customer engagement:	varies
Brief:	take IKEA to the people
Budget:	the cost of the furniture and transport (estimated $1,000 in total)
Lifespan:	2006
Benchmark:	widening awareness through guerrilla tactics

One of many guerrilla installations produced by *IKEA*: these are in a bus shelter on 57th Street, New York (left), and a 'house Cube' in Aoyama, Japan (right).

Project background

The idea of taking products to the people is not new, but *IKEA* made the method literal by strategically placing *IKEA* goods in public places to create an unexpected buzz among passers-by.

In a simple and direct approach, *IKEA* managed to persuade environmental authorities in Aoyama (Japan) to let them create a series of installations with *IKEA* products for promotional launches during 2006. Arrangements of *IKEA* goods appeared in bus shelters, along streets and in 'breast pocket' parks (small park plots between high-rise buildings), set up by an *IKEA* team of rapid assemblers.

While some people tended to treat the arrangements as if they were art installations, others actually used the furniture in situ. The furniture was not guarded so passers-by would not feel inhibited and were able to respond any way they felt. The sudden appearance and disappearance of the goods provoked much blogging activity in New York: Who put them there? Were they being stolen? As one blogger remarked, 'steal away, those side tables are $12 at the store – less than the cab fare it'd take to get that thing home'.

| | 05 | | | | 06 | | | | | | | | | | |
Timeline	S	O	N	D	J	F	M	A	M	J	J	A	S	O	N
Concept development	■	■	■	■											
Completed project (constructed)				■	■	■	■								
Launch							☼								
Word-of-mouth/blogging							☺	☺	☺	☺	☺	☺	☺	☺	
Additional promotion							◙	◙	◙	◙					
Media exposure							--	--	--	--	--	--	--	--	--
Hits (100,000s)							1	5	10		20				30

The idea initially ran in Japan, where outdoor 'showroom' displays were created in glass boxes by *IKEA* along a street in Aoyama. The spaces were called *IKEA 4.5 Museum*, referring to the measurement of four and a half tatami mats to emphasize *IKEA's* suitability for small living spaces. The project attracted widespread attention, so it was decided to extend the concept to New York during the city's annual *Design Week* festivities.

The aim in New York was to make the unannounced displays an enigma: to most that saw it, the furniture had appeared without explanation. Whereas the displays in Japan were in showcases, the version in New York was directly on the street. *IKEA* staff simply turned up in a van, quickly arranged furniture in location and drove off to the next installation.

Placements included:

- *IKEA* furniture – sofas, bookcases and curtains, arranged in bus shelters;
- *IKEA* dog bowls and watering cans adjacent to a fire hydrant;
- fliers attached to lampposts in *IKEA* picture frames;
- an *IKEA* plastic bag dispenser and pooper scooper in a tree pit;
- *IKEA* cushions at the bottom of slides in a playground.

The street presence was supported by other *Everyday Fabulous* activities, including give-aways such as a free down pillow for the first hundred 'suddenly singles' to claim them.

Creative direction

The project was effective because it contained a lively and imaginative approach. While street placement was not new (see britart.com, pages 138–141), the layout of the goods and use of existing street furniture was. The arrangements were organized to inspire city folk living in small flats by offering contained imaginative sets, or were witty juxtapositions such as pooper scoopers in tree-lined streets – in which case they sparked word-of-mouth activity.

As an ambient campaign the project was effective because it showed *IKEA's* contemporary styles and demonstrated neat arrangements. It also caught people's attention by being out of context. The project was an extension of *IKEA's* campaign to brighten the home – this idea effectively demonstrated how furniture can work in tight environments and how good and affordable design can improve the quality of life.

Review

Furniture simply appeared on city streets unannounced, in the same manner that flash stores pop up and disappear with little notice. Word-of-mouth activity helped direct discussion to the opening of a new store and the development of IKEA's product range.

> 'I saw little dog bowls with a water can next to it [sic] on 5th avenue between 16th and 17th as well as numerous "flyers" in colorful picture frames.'

> 'This is an inspired advertising ploy as well as a little gift to the city. I say props to Ikea and welcome to Brooklyn.'

> 'I like this smart, eye-catching guerilla advertising. And yes, nothing was being guarded, and thus it was all up for grabs. Even so, most people were just leaving it be.'
> (Bloggers in New York)

● The campaign was a benchmark in widening access by taking the products to their audience. It gave people access to try goods they might not have done in a showroom. The unusual situation made the experience all the more memorable.
● The placement of goods – cushions at the bottom of slides, bar stools in telephone boxes – made the re-appropriated places seem witty additions, rather than branded environments.

Furniture arrangements around street furniture and parks in Manhattan and *IKEA's* tag explaining the idea that *Good design can make the everyday a little better*.

- The approach to guerrilla advertising
  hit the right button – it got attention from humorous juxtapositions and looked a bit like a series of art installations.
- The project generated much word-of-mouth 'did you see…?' activity.
- Assuming that most of the furniture was eventually taken by passers-by, the loss of stock still amounted to a good return on unpaid-for publicity.

Integrated mix

proportion of campaign

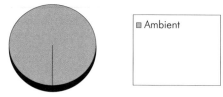

☐ Ambient

Essentials

1. Loss-leaders can generate a big impact for little cost.
2. Campaign tag lines have tended to provide the starting point for successful brand-related stunts.
3. Avoiding traditional media to advertise can be more of a 'come-on' to passers-by because they are confronted with things that they do not expect. This is how experiencing advertising can become an event.

For links see http://info.ikea-usa.com/ IKEAEverydayFabulous/photos.html.

Marlboro Motel

Product:	Marlboro
Target market:	exclusive 'in-crowd', existing smokers, *repertoire buyers*
Agency/city:	*Tequila*, London
Planning/production time:	8 months
Reach:	after-show parties for pop bands, approximately 5,000
Length of customer engagement:	30 minutes – all evening/all night
Brief:	create an American motel lounge ambience, the sort of evocative environment and scenario ideal for a *Marlboro Moment*
Budget:	undisclosed
Lifespan:	Summer 2002, for 6 months
Benchmark:	creating a (non-)branded environment

The *Marlboro Motel* was a backstage VIP area for artists and guests at *Creamfields* music festivals in Britain. It included furniture specially designed to create an American Mid-West motel ambience.

Project background

The *Marlboro Motel* was a VIP backstage space for pop acts, their entourages and friends to relax and smoke during and after the *Creamfields* pop events in Britain during 2002.

The project was unique as a *communication* (rather than advertising) platform and even though it took place before the 2003 ban on tobacco advertising in the UK, the environment did not feature *Marlboro* branding or make any claims about the product. Instead, it was simply a shaped space that was conducive to 'meeting' the brand.

	01				02										
Timeline	S	O	N	D	J	F	M	A	M	J	J	A	S	O	N
Concept development	■	■	■	■											
Completed project (constructed)					■	■	■	■	■						
Launch									☼						
Word-of-mouth/blogging									☺	☺	☺	☺	☺	☺	☺
Additional promotion								◙	◙	◙	◙	◙			
Media exposure									--	--	--	--	--	--	
Hits (hundreds)									1	4	10	20	30		

Marlboro Motel was effectively a brand environment as part of an ongoing campaign to create *Marlboro Moments*. The space contained a themed 1950s-style portable set modelled on hi-style American lounges. It consisted of side units containing televisions, carpets, room dividers, low lighting and flocked upholstered sofas in primary colours to affect a lounge mood. Although the sideboards contained packs of *Marlboro*, no fixed branding was evident in the environment. Throughout the summer of 2002 *Marlboro Motel* was effectively the 'green room' for after-show parties at *Creamfields* and another festival, the *Southport Weekend*.

Profile: defining a branded platform

The observation that led to a design-based solution was that music festivals attract a large number of smokers, from late teens to late forties. The crowd with backstage passes enjoyed the culture associated with being on the road: partying, hanging out and drinking. Like being on the road, lounging in the *Marlboro Motel* was seen as a sexy lifestyle choice with a sense of freedom. Others with access to the backstage green room included journalists and promoters as well as magazine and radio competition winners. Therefore *Marlboro Motel* environments provided a backdrop to after-show press shots as people mingled and met up with pop artists.

Marlboro Motel addressed an elite group of music artists and festival goers – it was the sort of environment that fans would be aiming to get into, and consequently the spaces had an exclusive cachet attached to them.

Creative direction

In effect, this design project was an exercise in producing themed environments conducive to smoking. The Mid-West American motel styling created a 'chill out' ambience in contrast with the high-energy on-stage performances and crowd responses.

The 'motel' reference also served as a reminder of the 'on tour' circumstance of pop acts at festivals. The reference to the Mid-West – *Marlboro Country* – nudges on *Marlboro's* historical heritage: rather than images of the *Marlboro Man* on horseback in the Arizona dessert, the motel environment suggested overnight stop-offs on the long American road trip, the type so frequently featured in Hollywood movies such as *Easy Rider*. *Marlboro Motel's* furniture reinforced this – one of the sofas even converted into a bed: in the *Marlboro Motel*, those chilling out were modern *Marlboro* people.

The project specifically targeted existing smokers. Nudging *Marlboro's* heritage in a fresh way was seen as a means of evoking different buying associations when smokers at the festivals next went to buy cigarettes (this is often referred to as *repertoire buying*).

Review

The *Marlboro Motel* platform was launched without pre-publicity. It simply appeared at festivals as a sponsorship by *Marlboro* for music company *Cream*. The project was exclusive to the UK and completed its run by the end of summer 2003.

The furniture and props in *Marlboro Motel* spaces were conducive to enjoying the brand.

- *Marlboro Motel* followed a similar approach to *Team Marlboro* sports promotions, where *Marlboro*-sponsored racing teams competed in landscapes synonymous with *Marlboro Country*.

- *Marlboro Country* is synonymous with the brand's heritage, but was redeveloped here to tie in with the festival environment. In effect, the brand's US flavour was maintained but updated. The theme of travel was retained but reshaped as a stop-off en route through Mid-West territory.
- *Marlboro Motel* worked on a number of levels. It involved people with the brand by giving them an environment conducive to smoking. It also gave people a brand to associate the festival party with. The ambience was enough to convey the *Marlboro* spirit – sales messages and branding were not required.
- Creating unusual environments is an effective form of engagement. It does not *push* customers to buy a brand, but *pulls* them towards an attitude or ambience that ties in with the brand.
- This platform made a virtue of identifying a core market. By appealing to *repertoire buyers* it did not need to make advertisement-based claims; it just had to make the product available.

Integrated mix

proportion of campaign

◻ Ambient

Essentials

1. An advertising approach is not essential to making goods relevant.
2. It is worth carefully defining who the target market is and how an environment is relevant before considering the mode, tone and style of the communication.
3. Talking with (rather than pitching at) consumers is often a more effective means of connecting.
4. While some soft forms of communication can be effective if the environment is characterized by hard sell, *experiential* approaches tend to be more effective for small niche *prospects*.

For link see www.adstoicons.com.

COMME des GARÇONS Guerrilla Stores

Product:	COMME des GARÇONS fashion chain
Target market:	fashionistas, *early adopters*
Agency/city:	*COMME des GARÇONS* in-house, Paris/Tokyo
Planning/production time:	6 months
Reach:	Glasgow, early adopters and fashion-conscious
Length of customer engagement:	stores have limited time span varying between 3 months and 1 year
Brief:	develop exclusive market for *COMME des GARÇONS*
Budget:	approx £7,500
Lifespan:	from 2004; length of runs varies
Benchmark:	retail as adspace

Aggressive fashion publicity:
COMME des GARÇONS flyer, above, aimed exclusively at exclusive fashionistas. Guerrilla stores were deliberately understated and anti-chic. By the time the venues were more widely known, stores were closed to prevent them becoming mainstream.

Project background

The phenomenon of temporary short-lease shops – *flash*, *concept* or *pop-up stores* as they have become known – emerged in Tokyo, New York and London during 2004, and have since sprung up in fashion hotspots around the world. They can exist for a matter of weeks. *Flash stores* rely on stimulating sales in a short time-frame, motivated in part by shoppers' desire to buy before it is too late. The guerrilla store in Glasgow is a classic example of this carefully honed approach.

	05				06										
Timeline	S	O	N	D	J	F	M	A	M	J	J	A	S	O	N
Concept development				■	■	■									
Launch						☼									
Store's run							■	■	■	■	■	■	■	■	■
Word-of-mouth/blogging							☺	☺	☺	☺	☺	☺	☺	☺	☺
Media exposure							--	--	--	--	--	--	--	--	--

Fashion house *COMME des GARÇONS'* store was 'guerrilla' – based in emerging areas and even more exclusive than the other brands.

More than other exclusive labels, *COMME des GARÇONS* have championed the guerrilla store concept. Their first flash store opened during 2004 in Berlin in an open-plan 70 square metre storage space, rented for €530 ($700) a month. It simply contained racks of clothes and made no concession to 'retail experience'. Yet when it started to attract a following the store disappeared without announcement. You could mention that they have since opened many stores throughout the world's emerging fashion hotspots like Athens, Reykjavik, Hong Kong or Warsaw.

Similarly, a *COMME des GARÇONS Guerrilla Store* in Glasgow was designed to become a moment of fashion. The juxtaposition between the location and the chic fashion brand – the store appears to squat in a former garage in Glasgow – stimulated word-of-mouth activity through fashion's social networks. The shops deliberately blurred boundaries in a number of ways – toying between art and commercial space, cult and mainstream, and independent and chain. Emerging artists were brought in to shape the spaces, and organizers staged supporting events as a backdrop to selling fashion.

Profile: how guerrilla stores operate

The *Guerrilla Store* opened for nine months in 2006 and its sudden disappearance sparked a second wave of publicity for the brand. After closure, the buzz created by the store left a positive impression of the store as a branded experience that brought like-minded people together for a moment in time.

It is important to distinguish between *flash stores* and *guerrilla stores*: flash stores tend to be in more central parts of town while guerrilla stores are in areas undergoing regeneration – new cool areas on the edge of the inner city. The stores have the ambience of small exclusive galleries, and operate in a similar way. They are organized through local freelance fashion operators, usually young and aspiring arts events organizers, who take responsibility for the lease but receive support from the brand. As with *Guerrilla Store*, high-end brands tend to supply a store with exclusive merchandise on a sale or return basis.

Creative direction

The site of the Glasgow *Guerrilla Store,* a studio warehouse in Kelvinhaugh, a high-density urban art district away from Glasgow's central commercial retail zone, made customers work to find out where it was located. Visitors had to go out of their way to reach the store. Even from the outside there was little to suggest that the building was home to an exclusive fashion house. Inside, the building had been transformed into a chic space, with the building's existing use as a garage re-evoked: props include a painted *Rolls-Royce* and a customized elongated moped, in the design of 1950s hi-style space.

The merchandise was a mix of seasons, with old and new ranges of clothes and accessories. Little concession had been made to make the user experience comfortable. It was assumed that the quality of the merchandise was enough to appease the ultra-fashion-conscious customers that the store addressed.

Review

The Glasgow store was launched through *flash mob* messaging (see below). From then on, it relied on non-traditional methods of advertising – mostly via e-mail, club flyers and through editorial articles in prominent hip fashion magazines, including *Purple, Another* magazine and *Self-Service*. Otherwise, news of the store spread by word of mouth. A published self-styled 'propaganda' booklet was distributed through the store. It reminded customers of what guerrilla stood for in this context – 'a small group of independent people fighting for what they believe in'.

> It's about being an enigma. The shop was intimate and unique, and now it remains as an event in the memory – which still has bearing on how *COMME des GARÇONS* are perceived. (Jessica Bush, trends analyst and flash store specialist)

- The edgy guerrilla-styled approach reinforces the identity of the label as edgy, youthful and exclusive. Where closing a flagship store would usually spell the end

The interior of *COMME des GARÇONS'* Glasgow *flash store* was hi-style, chic and temporary, with a curious range of props (photographs by Tomonori Goto).

of the brand, the disappearance of *flash stores* helps the brand to maintain its contemporary relevance by seemingly moving on.

- Late opening hours (2–9 pm) reflect the lifestyle of clubbers rather than city workers, and the stores deliberately cease to trade before they get too popular. Brands operating through *flash stores* include *Nike*, *Vertu* and *Prada*.
- By making the launch private and controlling exposure, the stores had an aura of exclusivity, subversion and avant-garde artiness. They attract *early adopters* who, in tandem with fashion press coverage, tend to circulate news of their whereabouts by word of mouth.
- The *massclusive* approach instilled a sense of elite that *early adopters* would want to be part of. As the stores close before they reach the mainstream, they maintain their sense of exclusivity. They convey qualities of a creative community on the move.
- The spirit of *guerrilla* is driven by the narrowcast method of publicizing the launch, *flash mob*, where members of a social network are given short notice through digital channels – mostly e-mail or SMS text – of an event or must-see stunt. 'Planned spontaneity' (a term coined by *trendwatching.com*) helps to maintain the exclusivity because events tends to break as mainstream news after they have moved elsewhere.

Integrated mix

proportion of campaign

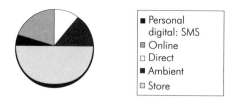

- ■ Personal digital: SMS
- ▨ Online
- ☐ Direct
- ■ Ambient
- ☐ Store

Essentials

1. *Flash mob* is a means of ensuring that only a select niche of people are engaged in the first wave of communication. Normal word-of-mouth channels do not usually have enough time to circulate the message.
2. *Flash stores* are an effective platform to create a buzz around high-end goods. That they disappear before most people discover them serves to fuel the mystique of 'fashion moving on'.
3. Targeting niches need not be expensive, but does require a close understanding of the right communication channels if only the niche audience are to made aware.

For link see www.guerrilla-store.com.

Lance Foundation/Nike LIVE**STRONG**

Product:	**Lance Armstrong Foundation/Nike**
Target market:	cancer survivors, global
Agency/country:	*Lance Armstrong Foundation*, Texas, USA and *Nike*, New York
Reach:	global
Length of customer engagement:	ongoing since 2004
Brief:	raise presence and awareness of cancer charity, and honour Lance Armstrong's attempt at a sixth *Tour de France* win
Budget:	undisclosed
Lifespan:	2004, sales ongoing
Benchmark:	social awareness accessories: a new product type

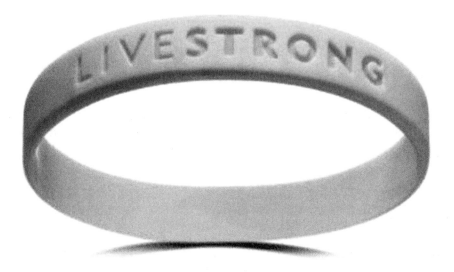

The yellow *LIVESTRONG*® wristbands retailed at $1, but after the first run sold out in the United States a black market developed for the rubber bangles. This created huge demand for further runs.

LIVESTRONG bands were the idea of *Nike*, a supporter of Lance Armstrong and the *Lance Armstrong Foundation (LAF)*, to raise money and support cancer survivors through the Foundation's public health and research initiatives.

Project background

Launched in May 2004, the first 5 million *LIVESTRONG* bands were produced by *Nike*, who distributed them through *Nike* stores and online, giving $1m to the *LAF* from the proceeds. The first batch proved so popular that they sold out within two months. The fact that demand exceeded supply made them even more desirable among teenagers in the United States. By the time the next batch of 6 million were released the demand had become international. Fuelled in part by the huge press coverage following Armstrong's record-breaking sixth *Tour* win, Armstrong wore a *LIVESTRONG* band throughout his record-breaking feat.

The bands' popularity grew through *early adopters* and into the mainstream, then became a fashion code for social awareness. The band carried associations with the cancer concern and the idea of winning – like Armstrong – against the odds. While concern was raised that the cancer awareness message could become lost as the band became fashion, the campaign far exceeded Armstrong's original $5 million target. By 2005, 21 million bands sold had generated funds for the *LAF*.

Profile: products as promotional vehicles

Like the red AIDS ribbon, the global symbol of AIDS awareness in 1991 (which was conceived by an advertising agency), the wristband had the added value of becoming extremely fashionable as the first of a much-copied 'social awareness' medium.

As a campaign, the *LIVESTRONG* phenomenon tapped into people's need to demonstrate their sense of social awareness for issues they identified with. It also managed to bring social conscience and trend consciousness together in a way that set the tone for other social marketing campaigns.

Creating products such as the wristband around specific causes, campaigns or charities is a relatively recent idea, although producing objects as extensions of campaigns is an advertising device that dates back to the late 19th century. What makes cause-related products particularly effective is that they provide an opportunity for people to buy into an issue. The associations that the object embodies and the means of distribution are intrinsic to the way it operates as a revenue-earning platform.

The accessory proved so popular that it spawned a genre of awareness bands – *Nike* introduced black-and-white pairs to symbolize the campaign against racism, while pink came to represent breast cancer awareness; while white bands raised

'Must wear' fashion accessories

		$
2007	mobile phone jewellery	5 approx.
2006	charm bracelets	20 approx.
2005	stop poverty & stop racism bands	5
2004	*LIVE**STRONG*** bands	1
2003	Kabbalah strings	20
2002	moon beads	10
2001	friendship bracelets	5
2000	power beads	10

funds against world poverty, blue bands came to stand for 'anti-Republican' in the United States during 2005. One firm even produced a range of school colour bands in the United States.

Creative direction

Armstrong's *LIVESTRONG* bands were yellow for two reasons: the first personal (Armstrong associates the colour with hope) and the second commercial – it is the colour of the *Tour de France* winner's racing jersey, so readily associated with sportiness and winning. Armstrong's final tour win helped seal this, and the breadth of coverage Armstrong received in his final *Tour* helped the campaign wash through international markets.

In terms of costs, the bands themselves were flexible and cheap to mass-produce, and the embossed *LIVESTRONG* marque made them difficult to reproduce on the black market. They also worked effectively as bright and iconic accessories that were highly visible in photographic reproductions.

Review

Nike announced the launch of the *LIVESTRONG* bands at a press conference with Lance Armstrong. An announcement was also published on the *LAF* website. The first bands could be bought individually from *Nike Stores* and in bulk from the *LAF*. The initial launch prompted the first sales rush for the bands.

> Young people with cancer should be empowered to fight hard, dream big and live strong. (Lance Armstrong at the launch of the bands in May, 2004)

● The bangles were skilfully positioned. They were sported early on by Hollywood actors (including Robin Williams and Gwyneth Paltrow), pop stars

(Bono and Sheryl Crowe), politicians (Nelson Mandela and George Bush) and numerous sportspeople – the original intended market – who were able to wear them while competing because they were made of light silicone rubber.

- The bangles were carefully priced. At $1 they were a twentieth of the cost of authorized Kaballah strings, so they were easily affordable though initially hard to obtain. However, this only fuelled demand from *early adopters* for the exclusive accessory.
- The cause was both moral and hip. It operated through the idea of dress codes as communication. To work, however, it needed a big cause (cancer), a big personality (Lance Armstrong), a big event (breaking the record for *Tour* wins) and a big distributor (*Nike*) for the concept to bite globally. In one sense it was an extremely powerful form of *third party association*.

Integrated mix

proportion of campaign

■ Online
□ Direct

Essentials

1. Marketing a new product type requires a very strong existing market presence.
2. The association between Armstrong, *Nike* and the numerous celebrities seen wearing the band was persuasive. The right associations can appeal beyond the initial target audience.
3. A new product type will be more successful if it can be finessed into a 'family' of other objects.

For link see www.livestrong.org.

Britart.com re-appropriations

Product:	**Britart.com**
Target market:	affluent Londoners with disposable income (30–50-year-olds)
Agency/city:	*Mother*, London
Planning/production time:	4 months
Reach:	Londoners, national press
Length of customer engagement:	placement (varied). Generated word-of-mouth activity
Brief:	create awareness of *Britart.com*'s art-purchasing website
Budget:	£220,000
Lifespan:	from September 2001
Benchmark:	public awareness through placement

One of a series of street re-appropriations, announcing the launch of art-trading website *Britart.com* in 2001.

Project background

For the launch of *Britart.com*, a large online art dealership and gallery, advertising agency *Mother* used the idea of ad-hocism to turn the streets of London into a 'gallery'. They created a series of poster-cum-environmental captions, where the pavements became galleries for the *Britart.com* launch. Pedestrians were challenged with captioned street furniture, which made them look at their everyday journey surroundings in a new way. As an advertising campaign it got noticed, created buzz and generated enough word-of-mouth activity to produce a large volume of web traffic for *Britart.com's* new website.

	01										
Timeline	J	F	M	A	M	J	J	A	S	O	N
Concept development						■	■	■	■		
Launch									☼		
Word-of-mouth/blogging						☺	☺	☺	☺	☺	
Media exposure						--	--	--	--	--	--	--

'Installation captions' were placed on commuter routes where they would be seen on the way to and from work by their target audience, defined as 'adventurous, technologically literate and financially well organized', in the city of London, Hoxton and central London business districts.

The campaign exceeded expectations by generating nearly half a million hits on the *Britart.com* website by the middle of 2001 and provoking a large quantity of unpaid-for media publicity.

Profile: re-appropriating landscapes for advertising

The *Britart.com* campaign aimed to distract and surprise passers-by as a means of creating intrigue and fuelling curiosity around the launch.

The *objets d'art* ('art objects') subjects of the posters were existing pieces of street furniture – banal, ordinary artefacts not unlike artist Marcel Duchamp's notorious *Urinal*, one of the most famous and controversial pieces of 20th-century art. This was the witty reference that the *Britart.com* campaign intended to make. When the campaign was launched, the work of the *Young British Artists* was attracting much controversy in the national media, so the idea latched on to the buzz already being played out in the popular press.

When the campaign was launched, fly-posting was common in London, and such use of the urban landscape as part of the stunt captured the imagination. The

Britart.com campaign appeared like fly-posting, although *Mother* had fact received permission from *London Underground*, to prevent the posters being removed by local borough authorities.

The creative team referred to the posters as 'artalizers' because they transformed anything they were placed on or alongside into art. In fact they made the environment an intrinsic part of the advertising campaign. Whereas advertising usually stays within its frame, the boundaries to these 'commercials' were less clear.

Further generations of the campaign targeted everyday items found in the office and home, and were sent as mailers for people to place themselves.

Creative direction

The overall strategy of *Mother's* campaign was to make buying art seem like an everyday activity. To bring a new audience to buying art, it targeted *prospects* with sizeable disposable incomes who might not normally feel comfortable about buying art in the stuffy surroundings of a gallery environment.

The more openly accessible 'art of the street' approach was light-hearted enough to engage people in a humorous way, at the opposite end of the spectrum to the more elitist, esoteric approaches often associated with modern art networks, which the campaign sends up.

Review

Posters went up overnight and appeared in situ without announcement. This element of surprise was needed to surprise regular passing pedestrians.

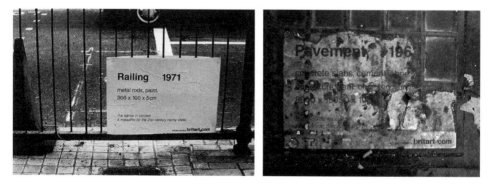

Are these posters advertisements or installation captions? The text on the poster, left, reads, '*Railing, 1971 metal rods, paint 300×100×5 cm. The barrier in context – a metaphor for the 21st century nanny state. Art you can buy. www.britart.com.*'

- The message that modern art could be accessible beyond existing art communities was conveyed by making the advertising just as accessible. It took the tone as far away from art galleries as possible.
- The posters mimicked art gallery caption cards in detail, by describing 'media' used and giving an art-speak description of each banal object, as if to over-determine its artistic credentials. Beyond the web address no other information was given about *Britart.com*. So the posters were cryptic for a target audience that were more inclined than most to 'play the game' and find out more.
- The fly-posters relied on people reading between the lines and deducing the message. This assumed a level of sophistication in the target audience. This is one of the rare examples of advertising where it paid to leave most of the 'message' out of the advert.
- The campaign succeeded in a number of objectives. It announced the arrival of a new website, set the tone and context and operated like a *teaser* advert to stoke interest.

Integrated mix

proportion of campaign

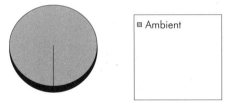

▫ Ambient

Essentials

1. To create a buzz, a campaign has to create a context, set the tone and ensure that the brand and its activity are core to the promotional strategy.
2. To refer to phenomena outside the frame of the advertisement, attention to detail is essential if viewers are to spot the reference.
3. An advertising medium and its placement can communicate as much as the words it contains.

For web link see www.adstoicons.com.

Singapore Cancer Society Ashtray

Product:	Singapore Cancer Society
Target market:	smokers/people in bars, Singapore
Agency/country:	Y&R, Singapore
Planning/production time:	2 months
Reach:	ashtrays: Singapore. Image of ashtrays: global
Length of customer engagement:	intermittent
Brief:	remind smokers of the significance of their actions
Budget:	1,000 Singapore dollars (for 100 trays)
Lifespan:	2004
Benchmark:	subverted spaces

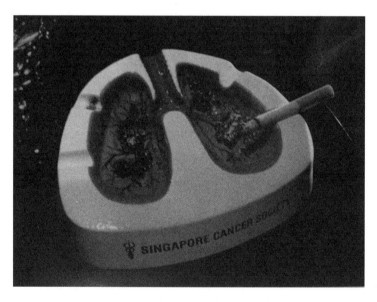

Singapore Cancer Society lung ashtray, placed in bars and given away to remind smokers of the damage smoking causes. Circulated during 2004.

Project background

In 2004 the *Singapore Cancer Society*, a charity with limited funds, placed specially designed ashtrays in bars and public places where smoking was permitted. The ashtrays bore the branding of the society, but, most poignantly, the troughs of the ashtray modelled the shape of lungs, complete with painted arteries. While the ashtrays were witty in their juxtaposition of lungs and smoking, they were effective in communicating a serious message to their target audience.

As with many guerrilla stunts, measuring the approach's effectiveness is not straightforward. The number of people who would have rethought their attitudes to smoking cannot be registered effectively, but the distribution of the ashtray as an image can: it received widespread coverage, with images of the ashtrays reproduced in the national press as well as international magazines on health and communications. At least 200 *blogs* are known to have sported images of the ashtray.

The idea of lung effigies in smoking environments appealed to smokers directly because of the dark humour involved. The wit of the design was often the reason that images of the ashtrays were so widely circulated online. The message worked like an advertisement – it was immediate and needed no translation.

The concept is very much in the frame of *experiential* advertising, in that it appeals to the target audience – smokers – at the very moment that they would be likely to smoke. A timely reminder of the repercussions of smoking would also make the experience less pleasurable and might provoke those using the ashtrays to reconsider their actions in mid-smoke.

The idea of targeting smokers during the act of smoking has become an effective tactic for anti-smoking campaigning because it taints the pleasure of smokers with a sense of guilt. On *London Underground* platforms in 1998, adverts for *Nicotinell*, a chewing gum designed to help smokers cut down on their consumption of cigarettes, offered a 'way out' for smokers. The line *'at times like this, it needn't be hell with Nicotinell'* was printed on enamel plaques and placed directly beneath 'No smoking' signs in subways (see below).

Creative direction: subverted spaces

The *Singapore Cancer Society*'s approach to advertising is symptomatic of a more widespread move to use artefacts as advertising messengers. Compared with print or digital advertisements, artefacts are more likely to have a longer lifespan. For a campaign that was not constrained by time limitations in the way that traditional advertising formats might be, the move to push the campaign message through an ashtray had a number of benefits. It put the message in a context where advertising was not normally seen, so it created an element of surprise. With products there is often a sense of their worth, so the product had a greater value than other communication media. The artefact served a function, so it was less likely to be junked. If anything, it was more likely to be stolen. Even if was stolen the piece would still be a potent talking point. The product took on a uniquely memorable significance for the people confronted with it.

Review

The project required minimal pre-publicity. The ashtrays were simply smuggled into spaces and a photographer took shots on behalf of the *SCS*. These were later circulated through the internet via e-mail.

> I dunno, I think it's a clever way of getting their message across without becoming too preachy. (blog site pundit)

Plaque placed beneath a 'No smoking' sign on *London Underground* station platforms in 1998. It reads: 'At times like this, it needn't be hell with *Nicotinell*'.

- Only 100 of the ashtrays were ever produced (at a cost of $10 each), but the scale of publicity generated by online word-of-mouth viral activity made the campaign extremely cost-effective as an awareness scheme.
- The juxtaposition of the lungs, burning cigarette and *Singapore Cancer Society* branding made the communication work in any language, and in a bar environment it would certainly jar observers.
- The method of communication is similar to that used in government information posters of the mid-1940s, in that cause and action are demonstrated through a single image by compressing information.

- The message shaped in its ashtray format communicates on two levels: the *image* is itself easy to understand and makes use of the smoking ritual itself. It invites smokers to flick ash and stub cigarettes on a miniature replica of lungs – the very part of the body most often affected by smoking. This (metaphoric) gesture is enough to jar smokers into thinking about their actions.

Integrated mix

proportion of campaign

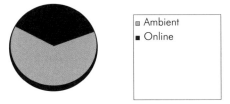

■ Ambient
■ Online

Essentials

1. Advertising through three-dimensional objects rather than two-dimensional media can have the effect of confronting target audiences during the appropriate moment of consumption, if the artefact is placed in the right environment.
2. 3D artefacts as advertisements tend to have a longer lifespan than 2D advertising formats.
3. An advertising object's central message, if effectively juxtaposed against the context that it is placed in, will generate an impact.

For link see www.adstoicons.com.

adidas vertical football

Product:	*adidas*
Target market:	urban youth in Tokyo and Osaka
Agency/city:	*TBWA\Japan*, Tokyo
Planning/production time:	3 months
Reach:	sites overlooked two of the world's most crowded pedestrian intersections
Length of customer engagement:	each 'match' lasted 15 minutes, and began every hour on the hour, 1 to 5 pm daily. People literally stopped in their tracks to watch
Brief:	reinforce *adidas*'s football dominance. Engage and 'wow' the core target audience
Budget:	US $180,000 for both venues
Lifespan:	September 2003, three weeks in Tokyo/four weeks in Osaka, five times a day, 15 minutes a time
Return:	to date, has received over US $160 million in free publicity
Benchmark:	local ambient, global reach

adidas vertical football billboard, mounted on a building above Japan's busiest pedestrian intersection.

Project background

The agency *TBWA\Japan* devised a novel way of reusing an old advertising medium. In September 2003 two soccer players played 'vertical football', fully kitted, suspended on bungee ropes (as was the ball), five matches of 15 minutes each day, on advertising billboards high up on office blocks. The one-on-one sessions took place against the backdrop of printed, *adidas* branded billboards on two existing sites in Tokyo (four weeks in Shibuya) and Osaka (three weeks in Dotonbori). The buzz generated at both venues bought traffic to a standstill.

	02				**03**										
Timeline	S	O	N	D	J	F	M	A	M	J	J	A	S	O	N
Concept development				■	■	■	■	■							
Completed project									■						
Launch									☀						
Word-of-mouth/blogging									☺	☺	☺	☺	☺	☺	☺
Media exposure									--	--	--	--	--	--	--
Hits (100,000s)									1	3	5			10	30

Both billboards were in prime locations – the Tokyo site overlooked the world's busiest pedestrian intersection while the Osaka site was close to the city's town centre.

> People would literally stop in their tracks to watch the aerial footballers. Normally reserved Japanese were cheering and clapping, and generally carrying on much like they would in a stadium. They photographed it. They called their friends to come join them. They came back the next day and the day after that. All for an ad! (John Merrifield, then-Chief Creative Officer, *TBWA\Tokyo*, creative director of vertical football)

The idea underpinning the project was that if you are passionate enough you can bring sport to life anywhere – as text on the billboard-cum-playing surface noted, *own the passion and you own the game*.

Several aspects contributed to making the project work. First, the staging: two players playing soccer at a 90-degree angle, 10 storeys from the ground. The players' efforts to generate a game of football kept passers-by spellbound. Second, the intrigue: Was it authorized? Who were they? What was it about? Third, the association: *adidas* trainers have excellent performance quality, as the footballers demonstrated. Finally, making the project work created a number of practical problems for the advertising team. The billboards required steel scaffolding reinforcements and dry runs were done off-site to test the structure. The footballers also needed practice time to work out how long they could sustain their game.

Profile: local ambient, global reach

This is one of the first staged 'live' stunts to benefit from instant photo-messaging services on a global scale. In Japan, text messaging from bystanders spread news of the stunt, and both sites were *flash-mobbed* as crowds gathered to witness the spectacle. As crowd sizes grew, images were mailed to news offices around the world. Coverage generated by the stunt spanned all media channels globally. Apart from being featured in all formats of the *Wall Street Journal*, it also featured on broadcast channels, including the *BBC, CNN, EPSN, Canal+, ABC, NBC* and all major Japanese networks. The stunt drew an estimated 100 times more in unpaid-for publicity than the project actually cost.

This was the first of two ambient projects developed by *TBWA\Japan* that helped *adidas* build credibility with youth through ambient advertising techniques. The second, titled the *Impossible Sprint*, appeared during the 2004 Athens Olympics and featured a sprint tournament on 100-metre tracks vertically up two skyscrapers, reinforcing the *adidas* brand message that *Impossible is Nothing* (see chapter 10).

Creative direction

The idea that football can be played anywhere – even if it defies gravity – was the core message that related to the brand's tag line.

> All billboards are vertical. All football pitches are horizontal. Our first idea was a horizontal billboard. It would jut out from a building five stories up, a sort of mini 'pitch' complete with goalposts. Our players would get into a bit of two on two in full view of the crowds below. Clients loved it. Then we got the quote. Shit. Um, er... all right, how about this: what if we cheat physics and have a vertical pitch with players and a ball hanging by ropes. And we'll get that big billboard that's 10 storeys up on top of the building overlooking Hachiko. And that's precisely what we did. Isn't it wonderful that Japan's so damn expensive? (John Merrifield and Hirofumi Nakajima)

The project demonstrated how effective 'live' events can be, and proved that billboards were still capable of creating a buzz if used imaginatively.

The media owners had been keen to revitalize one of their best-earning platforms, so the novel use of billboards caught the imagination of the public as well as world's advertising bodies, who awarded the project numerous accolades. As the project's Chief Creative Officer John Merrifield noted, projects are more likely to capture the public's imagination if they 'challenge conventional wisdom and overturn assumptions that get in the way of imagining new possibilities'. The medium might have been old and familiar, but the use of it was fresh and challenging to the audience and to the agency. Although the agency had to go to great lengths in getting safety certificates and local authority approval, the impact made it worthwhile.

Review

Before the stunt burst, the national press were notified that something was going to occur at the sites, but no public press release preceded the stunt. The small-scale seeding did the trick: within 24 hours the vertical footballers had featured on every single television station in Japan. The stunt mostly appeared in variety programmes and magazines, and one Japanese comedian even tried his hand at vertical football on one of the sites.

> It's become an *icon*, in fact, and has been featured in dozens of articles and features in trade publications locally, regionally and globally.

(John Merrifield)

adidas vertical football billboard attracted large crowds of pedestrians, as eager mobile users called their friends to join them in front of the spectacle.

- To make a buzz for the brand; without prior publicity, the event had to be immediate. All aspects reinforced the clarity of the message – the fact that it was on a billboard sponsored by *adidas*, the fact that the copy line across the players' 'pitch' matched the activity and the fact that it fitted with *adidas*'s existing campaign theme helped fix the stunt to the message.
- The action was regulated: 15-minute bursts were the right length for the players to endure, and the 5-sessions-a-day frequency helped viewers work out when they were likely to appear next.
- The sites were selected because they would have space below for people to gather. The billboard was high enough to be seen from a distance. This took careful planning and required various forms of permission from local government authorities (see chapter 10).
- A small-budget idea can generate publicity that has far more impact than big production campaigns. As this project proves, strong and original ideas still capture consumers' imagination.

Integrated mix

proportion of the overall campaign

- ◼ Word-of-mouth
- ☐ Ambient

Essentials

1. If you are going to create an event, keep the message simple and the event manageable.
2. Consider how the message will be captured and conveyed to others not present. In other words, how will the story be recounted?
3. If you are producing a stunt, consider if it is a viewing or a participatory spectacle. How it will create intrigue and how will the environment affect the customer experience?

For web link see www.adstoicons.com.

4 Shaping product experiences

This chapter features advertising projects that have centred on people's involvement within campaigns. Each provided a way in to central values of the product or brand being advertised, and each created a buzz that went beyond the usual boundaries of an advertising campaign.

Some of the cases featured tapped into the spirit of the age by creating cryptic icons (*Polska Telefonia Cyfrowa*), by leading a crusade for personal fitness (*Nike*) and by stoking a public frenzy in the popular press (*FHM*). Others featured used direct address to demonstrate a product (*Siemens*), challenge preconceptions (*Skoda*) to bond with existing customers (*O₂*) and to illustrate the potential of *mashing* digital media (*Sony Ericsson* and *Crystal Romance*).

Cases featured...

Nike 10K runs – brand-centred involvement, managed online
Polska Telefonia Cyfrowa Heyah – teaser leading to brand adoption
FHM projections – tapping the zeitgeist
Siemens cab drivers – person-to-person product demonstration
Skoda Live with it for a while – personal challenge through direct address
Sony Ericsson W750i 5 Seconds of Fame – user-centred launch integrating narrow-cast and broadcast methods
O₂ customer retention – one-to-one relationship platforms
Crystal Romance – television programming and integrated communications mix

Suggested reading

Dru, Jean Marie (2002) *Beyond Disruption*, Wiley & Sons, New York
Julier, Guy (2000) *The Culture of Design*, Sage, London
Schmitt, Berndt H (1999) *Experiential Marketing*, Free Press, New York

Nike Run London

Product:	Nike
Target market:	runners
Agency/city:	AKQA (London) handled all digital aspects of the campaign (web, e-commerce, mobile and e-mail)
Planning/production time:	6 weeks from initial brief, alongside an ongoing activities programme
Reach:	people – fun runners and those looking for a physical challenge – near the London area
Length of customer engagement:	12 months, with opportunities to continue
Brief:	involve customers with the brand, and help *Nike* participate in fitness programmes
Budget:	not disclosed
Lifespan:	2001–ongoing (annual, self-liquidating)
Benchmark:	brand-centred involvement, managed online

The 2005 home page of *Nike's Run London* website, which outlines the ease with which people could join up to the scheme.

Project background

Nike's promotions strategy aims to provide innovation and inspiration to athletes by creating opportunities for customers to engage with the brand. Their approach to advertising has moved over a decade from a mass-media-centred ('*just do it*') approach to targeted interactive platforms and events.

In 2001 *Nike* created *Run London* – 10-kilometre races held in the London area, open to the first 10,000 who wanted to take part. *Nike's* runs have subsequently become part of the London events calendar.

Timeline	00				01									
	S	O	N	D	J	F	M	A	M	J	J	A	S	O
Concept development	■	■	■	■	■	■	■							
First race										☼				
Word-of-mouth/blogging						☺	☺	☺	☺	☺	☺	☺	☺	☺
Additional advertising								◙		◙		◙		
Media exposure			--	--			--	--				--	--	--
Hits (100,000s)											6		8	10

The *Run London* idea created a platform for people to experience *Nike's* ethos by getting fit with them, by training with a year-long *Nike* schedule leading to the runs in London's parks. Participants were given the opportunity to get fit with *Nike*, and those working or living in London could even follow the regime by meeting and running with others at set times from *Nike Town* at London's Oxford Circus.

Run London has proved a success on many levels. As well as motivating return purchases from existing customers, it has boosted *Nike's* relevance in the sport and fitness industry as well as confirming *Nike's* iconic presence online. During online registration periods, the volume of *Nike.com* traffic and *click-through* rates boomed to the extent that it becomes one of Europe's highest trafficked e-commerce sites. Although it cost £25 to enter in 2006, race places were selling out in under 40 hours of being made available.

The scheme has put *Nike* in a position to demonstrate *corporate social responsibility* in the areas in which it operates. For instance, *Nike* has donated equipment to *Sport4London* schools from *Run London* proceeds and fulfilled a moral obligation by creating a platform for customers to improve fitness levels. *Nike* has also extended opportunities for their customers to become *brand advocates* by taking part in *Nike* programmes.

Customer insight

Digital advertising agency *AKQA's* early research explored the psychology of training and addressed the reasons why people choose to run. One insight revealed that people are more likely to do something if they tell someone else about it – especially if they commit to making a pledge. This distilled into a *call to action* – '*I will run a year*'; *Nike* would help them keep to this pledge by providing the tools to fulfil it.

Diets, warm-up routines and programmes were provided online for subscribers. Once customers had selected their lead-in time (one year, six months or two months) they were presented with a training regime prepared by leading coaches and *Nike*-sponsored athletes. Each runner's online *click-through* responses informed the tone of future messages from *Nike*, which rolled out through the period leading to the race date.

Click-throughs were even used to shape training regimes. For the 2003 *Run London* events, three virtual coaches with distinct personality traits were created, allowing runners to choose the coach they felt would be most effective at training them.

Review: creation of a web community

While the project was supported by in-store and point-of-sale activity, the campaign centred on the website. Web activity provided the main portal for *Nike 10 Kilometre* communication. There was ample opportunity for a *Nike*–runner dialogue from the point of registration. Data from the major 'touch points' – registration, group training-run attendance, visits to *Nike Town* – were used to hone customer data for future correspondence through personal e-mail, *SMS* and *MMS* alerts. This helped enhance the individual customer experience. The registration pack even contained a digital chip which runners attached to their race shoes so *Nike* could track race attendance and provide runners with their race times and a finishing line photograph, accessible through their personal 'My *Run London*' account on *Nike's* website.

Online activity developed from being a registration tool in 2000 to being the main tool for a running community. The site could be shaped by personal preferences and, depending on customers' choice of training regime, contained features hidden until the schedule unravelled. It also allowed message distribution, response tracking and personalized dialogue to be managed economically and without a time-lag. By the 2006 events, people could enrol onto a rolling *Run London* schedule, sign up for training runs, set run reminders and monitor their running performance. Over 30 unique pieces of communication were planned through the duration of the campaign in 2006, and *third party* collaborations are stretching *Run London's* potential further. *Mash-ups* with *Google's API* mapping allow runners to plot new training routes, and the hook-up with *Apple,* enables music to train with and online performance competitions.

Creative direction

Each annual *Run London* schedule has a different theme and graphic identity, but design elements run consistently through all online and offline activities, including race packs (shirts and registration numbers) and medal, presented after completing a 10-kilometre run. In other words, the corporate identity was managed consistently through all channels and points of contact with participants.

Annual *Run London* themes and slogans

2001	July is a runner
2002	I'll do it if you'll do it
2003	Choose your coach (Paula the athlete, O'Keefe the sadist, Carter the hippie)
2004	Go nocturnal (night runs)
2005	I will run for a year (events throughout the year, including monthly 5-kilometre runs)
2006	North versus South (North and South London runners competing as teams)

Review

Run London was burst through a mass-media *burst* campaign but details of events were managed in-store and online. Customers could enrol in-store or online and supporting activities were rolled out through *Nike's* flagship *Nike Town* store. Subscribers needed to make at least one *Nike Town* visit in central London to collect their running T-shirt and race pack.

> *Nike* is about bringing sports inspiration to everyone in the world. *Run London* is a great way to make sports more fun and accessible for a large number of people. (Ajax Ahmed, Founder and Chairman, *AKQA*)

- Participants actively engage within *Nike's* ethos and have many opportunities to be inspired by its confident spirit. The tone of the site is light-hearted, fun and enthusiastic. Consistent graphic styling and use of language reinforce the buzz and excitement of running through London.
- The end of the journey – race completion – finishes on a high with participants having achieved their objective and having a *Nike Run London* medal to prove it.

Scenes from *Run London* day and night events, 2002, 2004 and a *Nike* text, 2006: As well as receiving a medal for completing the run, runners receive a text with their finish time. They can also see an image of themselves crossing the finish online.

● *Run London* has enabled *Nike* to move into the territory of self-fulfilment: *Nike* provides the means to achieve it. So the act of getting fit and feeling better about oneself is inextricably linked with *Nike* in the minds of participants.

Integrated mix

proportion of campaign

▣ Commercials

■ Online

□ In-store
   Activities

Essentials

1. Involvement creates a much closer customer bond than traditional advertising platforms.
2. Taking customers on a journey means that they can 'feel' the brand in their own way and at their own pace.
3. Consistency through design and advertising communication helps maintain the overall experience.

For link see www.runlondon.co.uk.

Polska Telefonia Cyfrowa Heyah launch

Product:	*Polska Telefonia Cyfrowa* sub-brand *Heyah Mobile* network
Target market:	Warsaw youth, Poland
Agency/city:	*Polska* and *OMD*, Warsaw, Poland
Planning/production time:	6 months
Reach:	100,000 subscribers
Length of customer engagement:	ongoing, rolled out over 3 months
Brief:	launch campaign; aim to get target market talking by creating suspense and being involved in their environment
Budget:	undisclosed
Lifespan:	launched March 2004
Benchmark:	teaser leading to brand adoption

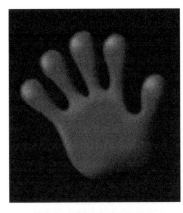

The *Heyah* mark and brand mascot, a bulbous red hand, was put out in a range of media (above: candy; right: in seat form) as a taster preceding the launch of the *Heyah* mobile phone brand in Poland.

Project background

Heyah was a mobile phone sub-brand of *Polska Telefonia Cyfrowa*, devised to target Poland's urban youth in 2004. For its launch, a through-the-line agency were commissioned to create a buzz prior to launch, so that *Heyah* would already have an environment and a rapport with the target market. The agencies came up with a *teaser* project that became a marketing phenomenon and created cultural capital for *Heyah* – even before the brand name was released.

Timeline	03 S	O	N	D	04 J	F	M	A	M	J	J	A	S	O	N
Concept development	■	■	■	■											
Tasters					■	■	■	■	■	■					
Launch									☼						
Word-of-mouth/blogging						☺	☺	☺	☺	☺	☺	☺	☺		
Additional promotion						◙	◙	◙	◙	◙	◙	◙			
Media exposure						--	--	--	--	--	--	--	--	--	
Hits (100,000s)				1				5		10			20		

The campaign started by raising curiosity around the city of Warsaw with the sudden overnight appearance of red hands. Red hands appeared as street objects, sweets, fly leaflets, stencil graffiti and on what appeared to be handmade posters. Many assumed that it was the work was of a *tag* artist, but the press were not so sure. Red-hand images and objects started to appear in more obscure places, and some assumed the iconic hand was being propelled as a youth-generated icon, without a brand attached. The symbol soon became readily adopted by Warsaw youth, because it seemed hip and created intrigue – no one was clear where the red hand had come from.

Eventually the hands were put out in a form that people could buy: chunky cherry-red hands with bulbous fingers were retailed as toys, and started to feature on the *blog* pages of Poland's youth.

Before *Heyah* had even been launched, its red-hand logo had already established itself in the everyday environments of youngsters. On its release the campaign agenda was clear, and the *Heyah* brand name fell into the identity already established for it through the red hand.

The advertising campaign surpassed expectations as a seeding device, boosting *Heyah* sales on its release in March 2004. One million people subscribed to the pre-paid service by July, making it the number one brand among urban youth in Poland. Demand was so great that, for the first half-year, demand surpassed supply. In terms of publicity, over 85 per cent of the press and word-of-mouth exposure was unaided (not paid for). The campaign took off simply because it created intrigue among its target audience.

Creative direction

The aim of the campaign was twofold: to introduce and embody a new mobile brand within young urban youth markets and to give the branding currency as a brand of desire.

The commercial meaning of the red hand was deliberately not released at the outset, and keeping its purpose secret helped boost its popularity: it had become an adopted symbol because of the mystique surrounding its origin.

The red hand set up *Heyah* with a pre-established target market. In other words, the hand had established a place within youth culture on its own terms and served as a dormant portal, waiting for the launch of *Heyah*.

Review

To create intrigue, a range of unbranded red hands appeared overnight in posters and as objects throughout Warsaw city centre. Street furniture and *agitprop* (agitating propaganda) graffiti collectively looked like the work of youth looking to *tag* the environment with its own esoteric mark.

The level of exposure and number of red hands flooding the streets and shops increased before *Heyah's* launch. The hand was marketed separately after launch as a brand extension, while sweets, street projections and other paraphernalia increased in presence throughout Warsaw.

The 'reveal' came over a weekend in March 2004 when television and cinema platforms, along with magazines, finally connected the red hand with *Heyah* in a series of advertisements to launch the brand.

Analysis

- The red-hand symbol first existed without reference to any commercial operation. This allowed it to develop its own identity first. As no information on its origin was available, people were left to make of it what they would. Once the mysterious hand had established an identity from the intrigue, the launch was ideal to give it a commercial meaning.

Heyah's red hand was sold and established cultural capital in its own right as a *brand extension* before the mobile firm it represented, *Heyah*, was even launched. This gave the mobile phone brand a ready-established market position and kudos by its launch, right, through commercials and other above-the-line media.

- The hand had plenty of character – its cartoonesque fingers and primary red colour made it appear like a clown's prop. In its many formats those keen to discover more about the hands were able to connect to other 'hands' found around Warsaw.
- As a campaign it was effective because it developed its reputation mostly through *word-of-mouth*. What started as an ambient campaign developed as intrigue grew through *blog* sites. The launch of the mobile phone rebooted interest in the hand, because it gave youth another way to consume the popular branding.

Integrated mix

proportion of campaign

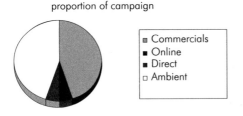

- Commercials
- Online
- Direct
- Ambient

Essentials

1. The launch of teasers to incite interest can be successful if the seeding is in the right environment for the intended target market.
2. Launching a product through established portals runs the risk of appearing to be a scam. The brand, mark and tactics must closely relate to the product being launched.
3. Youth markets are unique in that they are inherently media conditioned and brand savvy. Youth are adept at absorbing high volumes of on- and offline information, so new symbols are more likely to stoke curiosity than they would in older audiences.

For link see http://www.letranger-stellaartois.com/springerlinks.com.

For Him Magazine street projections

Product:	For Him Magazine
Target market:	young men
Agency/country:	*Cunning Stunts*, London
Reach:	over 40 million people worldwide (after TV exposure)
Length of customer engagement:	stunt: 4 minutes press: approx. one week
Brief:	raise awareness for *FHM's* '100 Sexiest Women' issue
Budget:	£3,000
Lifespan:	1999
Benchmark:	tapping the zeitgeist

Image of model Gail Porter projected 24 metres high onto London's Parliament buildings in 1999 on behalf of the magazine *FHM*. Press releases connected the stunt to the brand before it featured in *FHM* as an editorial.

Project background

A famous one-off stunt to promote youth magazine *FHM* proved that a wide-reaching, well-reported promotion need not be expensive.

Timeline	99 J	F	M	A	M	J	J	A	S	O	N
Concept development				■							
Pre-publicity				■							
Launch					☼						
Word-of-mouth/blogging					☺	☺					
Media exposure					--	--	--	--	--	--	
Hits (100,000s)					5		10			20	40

In May 1999 a promotions agency called *Cunning* projected a 24-metre-high image of model-cum-actress Gail Porter onto the side of London's Parliament buildings at midnight on a Sunday in May. A tagline – *vote Porter* – was added, but it need not have been, because all subsequent reports mentioned the magazine in their dispatch. The actual live projection was not seen by many people: only late-night commuters and tourists in central London reportedly stumbled across it.

However, it was photographed and written about by invited press reporters, who made it a topical front-page news story. The unauthorized stunt, the model and the use of Parliament struck a chord with the British press to the extent that it generated the equivalent of several millions of pounds' worth of free publicity for *FHM*.

Cunning's brief was to generate an event to raise awareness for *FHM*'s '100 Sexiest Women' issue. This is an annual issue in which readers are encouraged to vote for their favourite 'sexiest woman'. Furthermore, the stunt was to drive sales of the magazine at a quiet time of the year and develop *FHM*'s reputation as a sexy, cheeky, irreverent, youth-oriented magazine. Projecting Gail Porter against the Houses of Parliament, the country's oldest voting institution, neatly linked the concept of 'sexy women' and voting.

Profile: exploiting the issues of the day

When the campaign was being planned, there was widespread concern over the dwindling turnout in British elections. The broadsheet and 'serious' tabloid press apportioned blame in a number of directions. Editorials condemned what was termed the 'dumbing down' of news and popular entertainment. Concerns were also being raised that youth were disenfranchised and disconnected from politics, while celebrity culture and bland 'high ratings/low content' programming were being held responsible for stoking the demand for junk culture. Magazines such as *FHM* were being cited as part of the symptom. The combination of these ingredients made the story take off.

The choice of Parliament for the *FHM* stunt was interpreted by many as a riposte. It cast *FHM* as the 'spokesbrand' for a genre of entertainment at which criticism was being levelled. *FHM* were well positioned to step into the debate: Gail Porter was one of several celebrities that frequently featured in magazine and tabloid press articles. Pictures of a naked Porter would have been a prime example of what the 'serious' press termed the 'cult of celebrity' displacing 'real' news.

The stunt immediately made news headlines in the UK. By Tuesday every tabloid contained the story – most as a front-page leader. By Wednesday the stunt had attracted broadsheet coverage and became a global news story within the week. The *FHM* projection is still widely regarded as the most successful *guerrilla* advertising campaign ever.

Creative direction

As an advertisement, the skill was in distilling the idea into a simple broadcastable event. It had a simple graphic and immediately apparent message. It relied on a lo-tech construction and was easy to photograph and distribute.

The idea of young men voting for Porter in *FHM's* Sexiest Women poll – rather than voting in a political election – was graphically apparent in the *Vote Porter* tagline. Parliament was simply used as a symbol of voting. The juxtaposition was iconic and the fact that the projection was unlicensed enriched the story as an act of youthful subversion. The cost of production was low because the stunt did not use paid-for ad space. The production just required two mobile laser projectors, two slides, a press release, a photographer and reporters on hand to record events. Yet the output was big: one 24-metre 'billboard' in a prime stand-alone site without any other advertising in frame.

Review

Prior to launch, the spaces around Parliament were checked out as projection bases. Cunning also had to consider how Parliament would work as a projector screen.

Just one photographer responded to the photocall notice. We really wondered if the image would ever be seen by anyone but us.

(Anna Carloss, the *FHM* stunt's creator, *Cunning*)

Several reporters and photographers were notified ahead of the event, although only one photographer responded to the press call. Fortunately his images ensured that the stunt was recorded. The pre-launch press release enabled newspapers to shape the story, and ensured that the connection between stunt and brand was not lost in the coverage.

The cost of a good idea can be just your own time.

(Anna Carloss, the *FHM* stunt's creator, *Cunning*)

● Projecting onto the Parliament buildings was not original: watch brand *Swatch* was projected onto Big Ben, and music promoters *The Ministry of Sound* had projected their logo onto the walls of the Parliament buildings two years earlier. However, the significance and timing of the message made it resonate as a news story.
● The simple juxtaposition of model against Parliament made the image provocative. Most reproductions omitted the 'vote Porter' caption: it was left to viewers and the press to re-caption the image and debate its significance.
● The stunt's success was tied to its topicality. It filled a space created by public debate by providing a simple graphic image.

Integrated mix

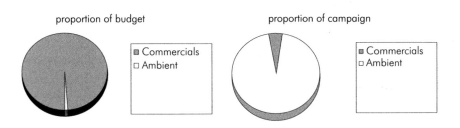

proportion of budget   proportion of campaign

■ Commercials
□ Ambient

■ Commercials
□ Ambient

Essentials

1. A large amount of press coverage can be achieved without great expense.
2. A strong, topical idea has the potential to make a big impact.
3. Ideas that are distilled to their simplest essence have far greater potential to catch on.

For link see www.ideasfactory.com/business/marketing/know_it/feature2.html.

Siemens cab drivers

Product:	*Siemens S10* executive mobile phones
Target market:	businesspeople in London taxis
Agency/city:	*Impact FCA*, London
Planning/production time:	2 months
Reach:	London, within the M25 motorway
Length of customer engagement:	potentially the length of a cab journey (typically between 10 and 60 minutes)
Brief:	business market brief for in-cab advertising – reach London businesspeople with the message that the *Siemens S10* business phone offers *Better talknology from Germany*
Budget:	Approx. £15,000
Lifespan:	over a four-week period in 1997
Benchmark:	person-to-person product demonstration

London cab drivers as *brand advocates*: if you were lucky enough to get a *Siemens*-sponsored cab driver you could use the *Siemens S10* business phone and hear about product benefits during your journey.

Project background

In 1997 the advertising agency *Impact FCA* involved 100 of London's black cab drivers in a project to talk about the benefits of *Siemens* mobile phones during the course of their daily journey. As *brand advocates*, they could let customers phone ahead on the phone, explain product benefits and use the journey to demonstrate how *Siemens S10* business phones could meet their needs.

Timeline	97 J	F	M	A	M	J	J	A	S	O	N
Concept development	■	■	■								
Launch			☼								
Word-of-mouth/blogging			☺	☺	☺	☺	☺	☺	☺	☺	
Additional promotion			◙								
Media exposure			--	--	--	--	--				

The cab drivers received a flat fee rather than commission, plus free use of the mobile phone for the duration in return for their participation. The ethics of 'chat-up advertising' was considered at length before the project went ahead. In the end it was decided that cabbies should not initiate conversations, but if a passenger engaged in a conversation the chat could be swung round to the *Siemens* mobile phones. If customers objected, cabbies were briefed to back off.

So that the cabbies explained the products properly, they were given pre-launch direction. They were coached by *Siemens* staff on the mobile phones so that they had a working knowledge of how the phones worked, the system set-up, and contract schemes. They were also given a prepared script and sales advice by the advertising agency *Impact FCA* on how to highlight particular features. Tips included how to drop important details about the product into conversation.

Cab drivers' prompt points:

1. Where are you going?
2. Would you like to call ahead? Use this phone…
3. Did you know that you can get as much as 10 hours' talk-time from one battery?…

Three key selling points:

1. German technology
2. Small but powerful battery
3. You can upgrade the telephone for more services

As part of pre-planning, the agency were also required to strike a deal with London's *Public Carriage Office*, which controls London's licensed black cab drivers, in order to get clearance for the campaign.

While the cab-based project reached a far smaller section of the public than a media campaign, it reached the appropriate target market at a time when they could experience the product benefits, and one-to-one salesmanship enabled a dialogue to develop around the phones. The project led to a far higher response rate than conventional advertising would have generated.

Insight

Preliminary campaign research indicated that traditional media would make little impact on the niche of business mobile phone users, who in 1997 would have been considered *early adopters*. Research also revealed that businesspeople in London spent a lot of 'dead time' on journeys: cabs shook too much on London roads for them to do work and their portable communication technology tended to fail. Most business travel by cab was therefore filled by having ad hoc conversations with drivers.

Creative direction

The campaign strategy acknowledged that German technology was well regarded for its reliability and capability, but was often seen by Britons as being too technical. Business users were known to want technology made easy for them. The campaign line *Better talknology from Germany* honed the *call to action* around the fact that the phone was more reliable than rivals in the sector and was designed around the needs of business users.

To create the right tone and environment for the promotion, cab drivers were carefully whittled down before and after training.

Review

One press release preceded the launch, which was focused on the product benefits rather than the ensuing stunt. It was the news media that turned the project into a news story that spread around the world. *NBC* were the first to broadcast the campaign, followed by London's *Evening Standard* newspaper. Within 24 hours news of the launch was dispatched worldwide by *Reuters*.

> Messages passed on from people closer to the issue, from customer to customer, are far more powerful messages than mass media.

(Shaun McIlrath, Creative Director, *Siemens S10* London Cab campaign)

- London's black cabs and their drivers are iconic, so using them in a commercial way was bound to generate press attention because the 'story' was easy to recount. As a recognized symbol of London, cabbies were regarded as talking authorities on a number of subjects, so word-of-mouth plugging fitted in with their usual banter.
- The circumstances for the promotion were right. Potential customers had an opportunity to use the product with a demonstrator, in a way that would not be as comfortable in-store. It made effective use of consumers' 'dead' travel time.
- The 'platform' – cab drivers – were seen as a trustworthy 'voice'. Using the *Siemens S10* phone during journeys gave businesspeople the opportunity to test the cabbies' claims, in an environment where the phones could be fully tested.

Integrated mix

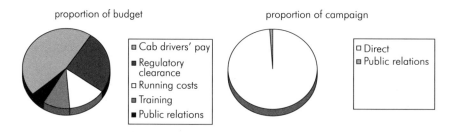

proportion of budget

- Cab drivers' pay
- Regulatory clearance
- Running costs
- Training
- Public relations

proportion of campaign

- Direct
- Public relations

Essentials

1. *Ambient* strategies can involve customers personally. If they include the product advertised, customers' first experiences of the product can be shaped.
2. While direct approaches target smaller niches, they generate a far higher response rate.
3. A novel approach is more likely to make an impression, but it must have relevance to the product advertised.

For link see www.adstoicons.com.

Skoda business-to-customer mailer

Product:	Skoda automotive
Target market:	drivers in the UK
Agency/city:	Media campaign ('*It's a Skoda. Honest*'), *Fallon*, London; direct mailer, *Archibald Ingall Stretton*, London
Planning/production time:	6 months
Reach:	100,000 prospects
Length of customer engagement:	direct mail gift
Brief:	reposition perceptions of the *Skoda* brand following the campaign line '*It's a Skoda. Honest.*'
Budget:	£20,000
Lifespan:	from 2001 for 18 months
Benchmark:	personal challenge through direct address

Skoda car badge, sent as a mailer to challenge *prospects'* preconceptions of the brand.

Project background

A mailer on behalf of *Skoda* used a direct way of combating the preconceptions of people that mattered.

As part of a measure to change *Skoda*'s brand image after its acquisition by *Volkswagen* in 2001, media-neutral agency *Archibald Ingall Stretton* challenged the drab image the brand had by sending 100,000 registered *prospects* from *VW* and *Skoda* databases a small 10×10 centimetre black gift box. In it was a *Skoda* car badge. A message printed in the box read, '*Live with it for a while and see how you feel*'.

Timeline	00				01									
	S	O	N	D	J	F	M	A	M	J	J	A	S	O
Concept development			■	■	■									
Completed project						■	■	■						
Launch									☼					
Word-of-mouth/press									☺	☺	☺	☺	☺	
Media exposure									--	--	--	--	--	--
Hits (thousands)									5					10

Until its re-launch in March 2000, *Skoda's* advertising strategy concentrated on their cars' performance rather than the real problem, the brand's reputation. *Skoda* had developed a stigma for being an old person's car, safe but cheap and bland.

A mass-media campaign in 2000 (created by *Fallon*) re-booted the brand by challenging its unfashionable reputation. It was launched through television and press advertisements that showed *Skoda* cars were far better than their reputation suggested. Each finished with the line *It's a Skoda. Honest.*

While the commercials sought to change public opinion, *AIS* were commissioned to change the opinions of *Skoda prospects* through direct address. Their strategy was to challenge customers' opinions by making them reconsider the significance of a brand badge over its performance. The *call to action* was to follow up the challenge laid down and take a test drive.

One hundred thousand mailers were sent to cold *prospects* nationwide and achieved a better than 2 per cent response rate – more than double the expected pre-launch response.

Within a year of the relaunch there was a clear change in attitude, reflected in national press coverage. More importantly, consumers also responded positively to the mass-media campaign and the direct response mailer that followed. The number of people who would not consider buying a *Skoda* fell, while sales significantly increased in the UK.

Creative direction

How do you double the value of a Skoda? Fill the tank!

In the UK *Skoda* had become the butt of jokes. Fortunately this was limited to the UK, so the tone of *AIS's* 'rebuttal' could be nationally specific.

Insights confirmed that *Skoda* cars functioned better than most of their sector competitors, but their identity was a stigma for target *prospects*. However, research also highlighted that *Skoda* drivers were characteristically independent and thought for themselves.

AIS's response in the mailers, *Live with it for a while and see how you feel*, was direct, challenging and bullish. It demonstrated confidence in the brand and a somewhat ironic wit. The stereotypical view of *Skoda* was being thrown back at customers. Like the classic *Volkswagen Beetle* ads of the 1960s, the direct mail challenged the consumer to question their own prejudices about the brand. It challenged recipients to confront a second-hand perception with first-hand re-evaluation. *AIS*'s strategy therefore exercised the insight that *Skoda* drivers were independent-minded by positioning *Skoda* as the independent thinker's choice.

The quality of the mailer was important in challenging people's personal experience of the brand. At a cost of £2 per item, the badge's weight and shiny finish made it a respectable gift, not cheap, so it was less likely to be binned.

Review

Commercials re-launching *Skoda* were broadcast four months before the mailers went out, so recipients would already be aware of the campaign message. The mailers required no prior announcement. Their impact relied on a cold-call drop.

Clean, unfussy art direction delivers this quirky brand message quickly and effectively. (Matt Morley-Brown, Creative Director for the *Skoda* mailer)

- The *Skoda* badge was, for a free mailer, a quality gift and quite expensive for a mail shot, but proved effective, with more than 1 in 50 taking up the offer.
- Defining the audience profile and deciding on the tone of address proved essential, as the message and *call to action* were daring. Sound research made the strategy less of a risk.
- The bullish irreverence of the treatment demonstrated confidence in the brand. This is a tactic commonly used by brands with a *brand salient* reputation. *Skoda* were repositioned with the best in their market by simply changing attitude.
- The timing of the mailer helped to take the widespread re-launch message to individuals who were more likely to act on their change of opinion.

Integrated mix

proportion of campaign

▣ Commercial
■ Online
□ Direct

Essentials

1. Tackling consumer preconceptions directly is often more effective than ignoring them.
2. If direct mail used, it is better to spend more on fewer realistic *prospects* than cheapening the quality of the mailer.
3. Consider the necessary lifespan of mailers. The better the quality of artefact, the less likely it is to be binned.

For link see www.adstoicons.com.

Sony Ericsson 5 seconds of fame

Product:	*Sony Ericsson D750i* mobile phone
Target market:	18–80 year-old high-volume digital users: mobile and online *snackers*, gamers and bloggers, Germany
Agency/country:	*b+d new media* GmbH, Germany
Planning/production time:	2 months
Reach:	TV trailer campaign on *VIVA Plus*: 4.78 m contacts Microsite: over 0.65 m page impressions
Length of customer engagement:	between 5 and 60 minutes, intermittent
Brief:	highlight the *D750i's* unique product features through engagement with *Sony Ericsson* platforms. *Give Sony Ericsson users the chance to be famous.*
Budget:	undisclosed
Lifespan:	competition November 2005–February 2006. Gallery still online
Benchmark:	user-centred launch, integrating narrowcast and broadcast methods

A frame from the *D750i* website, where *Sony Ericsson* users can shoot and send 5-second clips which would be broadcast on television shortly afterwards.

Project background

For *Sony Ericsson's* launch of the mobile phone model *D750i*, a series of digital platforms – mobile phone, website and broadcast television – were brought together in
a unique move to involve customers in the advertising output.

The scheme invited *prospects* and subscribers to create and upload 5-second
video clips with their own uploaded picture, via a 'clip creator' on the phone's
website. The best clips were featured in programme slots on German television
channel *VIVA Plus*. The idea was that, as in a talent competition, viewers had the
opportunity to get '*5 seconds of fame*' on the prominent German pop channel.

Timeline	05				06										
	S	O	N	D	J	F	M	A	M	J	J	A	S	O	N
Concept development	■	■	■												
Launch			☼												
Word-of-mouth/blogging			☺	☺	☺	☺	☺	☺	☺	☺	☺	☺	☺	☺	☺
Additional promotion			◉	◉	◉	◉									

The scheme was one of the first fully digital cross-platform campaigns and
required a tie-up between *Sony Ericsson* and the *MTV* network channel. Both
brands benefited: cheap and original content was given to the channel while the
consumers had an opportunity to create material for broadcast. Their footage on
television bore the branding of the telecommunications brand, so the clips were
effectively framed for *VIVA Plus* viewers as *Sony Ericsson* moments. The coup for
Sony Ericsson was in facilitating a unique short-term 'extra feature' through their
phones for customers. This made the promotion a unique *Sony Ericsson* experience. It was also the sort of novel experience that consumers would talk about to
their friends, so more young people would be attracted to the phone while existing
users would become *brand evangelists*.

How the strategy worked

By going to the *D750i* website, viewers were given the chance to create online their
individual 5-second video clips with the 'clip creator' and post them to the site.
Most clips went out on *VIVA Plus* and were published on the website in a 'best of'
gallery. Every week a *Sony Ericsson* and *MTV* jury elected the clip of the week,
which was rewarded with a *Sony Ericsson D750i* cellphone.

The format proved highly effective. *Sony Ericsson* was guaranteed a unique presence on television that was distinct from commercial breaks, while customers got to
experience the capability of *Sony Ericsson* technology.

Creative direction

The project put mobile phone users centre stage by involving them at the front end of the campaign. The hook was that they could be stars for a moment with the equipment at their disposal. Brief fame could be achieved through *Sony Ericsson* with little effort. This involved getting customers to read through and play with a range of narrowcast and broadcast platforms *Sony Ericsson* are involved with, including mobile phones and press advertising.

By opting for an integrated approach, the project served as both a public awareness campaign and a one-to-one advertising opportunity. It gave the impression that through *Sony Ericsson*, technology could compress personal and mass communication to a matter of minutes: no sooner had customers recorded material than it appeared on television.

Review

The website was launched along with a burst campaign announcing the show on *VIVA Plus* television.

> Given that customer-to-customer conversations are now the most powerful way of selling, let marketing and advertising people create the process and platform and let consumers create the advertising content. (Shaun McIlrath)

- The campaign creates a fluid link between digital (personal) narrowcast and (mass) broadcast platforms.
- The 'advertising' was built into the infrastructure for users to create their own broadcastable content. Using customers' videos as the 'face' of the campaign demonstrated the technological reach of *Sony Ericsson*.
- *5 seconds of fame* was billed as a 'cross-media videoclip contest': the format borrows from the 'reality show' genre of popular entertainment. Within this campaign, anyone had the opportunity for a moment of fame if they used the channels provided imaginatively.
- Co-created adverts, where platforms are made by advertisers for *user-generated content*, are a method often favoured by digital brands for giving customers branded experiences through involvement. It is also a strategy that advertisers can control *for* a brand – unlike *mash-ups* (see *Diet Coke and Mentos experiment*, chapter 9).

After being broadcast on *MTV Germany* channel *VIVA Plus*, clips were put on a website gallery where they could be voted as 'clip of the week'. The scheme gave young people the opportunity to explore the graphic techniques available with their material on the site.

Integrated mix

proportion of campaign

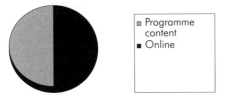

■ Programme
content
■ Online

Essentials

1. Digital formats have created new possibilities for cross-platform advertising that link narrowcast and broadcast methods.
2. Co-creation allows participating customers to share experiences with friends, colleagues and family. *Word-of-mouth* is one of the most powerful forms of promotion.
3. *Sony Ericsson's* campaign demonstrated the shoot-and-share potential of their *D750i* mobile phone: campaigns that involve activities should involve the advertised product.

For link see www.adstoicons.com.

O_2 *customer retention scheme*

Product:	O_2 '10% rewards' scheme
Target market:	current pre-paid O_2 customers – to develop *brand salient* positioning
Agency/country:	*Archibald Ingall Stretton*, London, and O_2 UK-wide
Planning/production time:	one year
Reach:	5 million existing O_2 customers
Length of customer engagement:	over one year (ongoing)
Brief:	remove the perception of O_2 that, like other mobile phone brands, *'they give with one hand and take with the other'*: develop O_2's relationship with existing customers, increase retention and identity as a *brand salient* company
Budget:	undisclosed
Lifespan:	since 2005
Benchmark:	one-to-one relationship platforms

Some of the activities involved in the O_2 customer retention scheme. Note the spread of media that converges through a user-centred approach.

Project background

In 2005 a campaign targeting customers of telecom firm O_2 used personal communication channels to shape new information around the activities of each customer. It became the first of its kind to avoid information time-lags and succeeded in redirecting other media platforms for the attention individual customers.

Timeline	04				05										
	S	O	N	D	J	F	M	A	M	J	J	A	S	O	N
Concept development			■	■	■	■	■								
Completed project (construction)						■	■	■	■						
Launch									☀						
Word-of-mouth/blogging									☺	☺	☺	☺	☺	☺	>
Additional promotion									◙	◙	◙	◙	◙	◙	>
Media exposure									--	--	--	--	--	--	>
Hits (million)									5		5		5		

How the strategy worked

The aim of the strategy was customer retention. Where other telecommunications brands focused on customer acquisition, targeting new or dissatisfied customers from other brands, O_2 realized that the mobile phone market had matured. Consolidation was the key and existing customers needed greater recognition in the promotions strategy. Most of O_2's *Pay & Go* customers felt they deserved recognition for their loyalty. They were wary of the small print in promotions and thought all mobile brands' promotions looked the same. O_2's strategy was to put customers at the centre of the promotion by orchestrating events and communication around individual users.

Pay & Go customers were called to discuss how and where they could receive free benefits. The campaign was accompanied by impromptu street 'giveaways' to O_2 customers. Outdoor 'O_2 Angels' in high-pedestrian traffic spots offered 'random acts of kindness' including free massages, soft drinks and flowers to O_2 users. In-store spaces were reworked to reward returning top-up customers. O_2 even sent *SMS* texts so that viewers could tune in to offers broadcast in television commercials. As a reward for being loyal, customers were given back 10 per cent of the top-ups they had used. The aim was to ensure that the O_2 promotion revolved around individual customers' lifestyles so they could tell that the *10% back* promotion was specifically about them. Therefore the timing of correspondence was important.

The timing of texts was informed by customer data, from which patterns of when the target audience were likely to be working and watching on television were deduced. If customer profiles indicated that they used O_2's picture messaging service, a picture message was sent to them with the offer. O_2 WAP users were directed to interactive pages on their mobile handset for offers.

The campaign succeeded in reducing O_2's drop-off rate by 8 per cent, while 78 per cent of O_2 *Pay & Go* users stated they would be more likely to stay with the brand as a consequence of the campaign.

Creative direction

The texts were designed to be unobtrusive. The language used to describe the 'no strings' offer was succinct in text messages and phone calls. All O_2 staff involved in the promotion's interface – at the call centre, as O_2 Angels and in-store salespeople – received briefing packs outlining the aims and objectives of the scheme. Above all else, they were encouraged to emphasize that there was no hidden catch involved.

> From O_2: get 10% of your top-ups back every 3 months. No conditions, no catches, no closing dates – text reward to 50202 and it's yours. To stop SMS call 2220.
>
> (*SMS* text sent to O_2 *Pay & Go* customers)

Review

The customer reward scheme was *burst* through a media campaign, while the programme of direct events was unrolled incrementally during the promotion. This enabled further impromptu events to be staged during the scheme's run.

> Today 85 per cent of the population in the UK and similar numbers across Europe own a mobile phone. The 'land grab' for early subscribers is almost over. The focus now is on loyalty rather than just customer numbers. (Peter Erskine, CEO, O_2 *Plc*)

- The shift to a retention strategy came at a time when mobile phone penetration reached saturation point. Eight in ten people had phones, yet the annual 'churn' rate (of brand swapping) was high – nearly 35% – which meant that customers did not see the value in staying with one brand.
- Communicating with existing customers meant that aggressive marketing or snappy advertising was inappropriate. The brand had to demonstrate customer care through the organization of its services, incentives and customer care. In effect, behind-the-scenes operations became the main aspect of advertising. This campaign illustrates that advertising practices can play a valuable role in all aspects of the customer interface.

SMS messaging reinforced the print and broadcast campaign by making the strategy personal.

- The campaign acknowledged that customers' experiences of a brand define their sense of its worth. If customers have had good experiences with the brands they use, they are more likely to share it with friends, colleagues and family. In effect, good experiences encourage customers to do the advertising on behalf of brands, by *word-of-mouth*.
- For the project to operate fluidly across advertising platforms, the different agencies working on the account had to collaborate as partners. A meeting of minds between the agencies' planners ensured that one big idea connected different platforms in the project in a similar vein.

Integrated mix

proportion of campaign

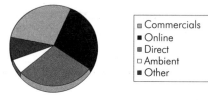

- ▣ Commercials
- ▪ Online
- ▪ Direct
- ▫ Ambient
- ▪ Other

Essentials

1. If brands give customers a stream of good experiences, customers will happily tell others. In other words, if agencies can 'programme' brands well, customers will do the advertising on their behalf.
2. Advertising works best when it goes beyond sowing messages, to where it can link brand practices with good customer experiences.
3. Personal communication channels prevent a time-lag in receiving messages, as long as advertisers avoid intrusion (see chapter 9).

For link see www.adstoicons.com.

Crystal Romance communications mix

Product:	水晶之恋, 果冻	Crystal Romance, jelly products 水晶之恋, 果冻

Target market: | 18–25-year-old young couples and students
Agency/city: | *Ping Cheng Advertising Co Ltd*, Guangzhou
Planning/production time: | 4 months before launch
Reach: | national: 432,000,000 saw the work, 291,700 actively participated by voting
Length of customer engagement: | ran on CCTV for 1 month
Brief: | new media positioning for *Crystal Romance* (jelly brand) range, around the idea of the campaign's slogan, '*Permanent Love, Crystal Romance*'
Budget: | 2.24 million yuan (television accounted for 1.5m yuan)
Lifespan: | December 2004–February 2005
Benchmark: | television programming and integrated communications mix

水晶之恋, 果冻

A communications mix of television, radio programme and web space with consistent branding, above, made *Crystal Romance* an effective multimedia approach. It kept the presence of the jelly brand in the public eye.

Project background

In China, agencies tend to use the traditional media extensively and are very advanced in using new media, but very rarely are different media used in combination. The project for *Crystal Romance* used a communications mix of online and offline media to create a wall of publicity in revitalizing the marketing presence of the well-known jelly brand.

The central activity took place on a specially launched television programme and featured a range of integrated digital media to make the viewing experience interactive.

Timeline	04 A	M	J	J	A	S	O	N	D	05 J	F	M	A	M
Concept development						■	■	■	■	■				
Launch									☼					
Length of run (broadcast)									☺	☺	☺	☺		
Media exposure							--	--	--	--	--	--	--	--
Hits (1,000,000s)							0	300		350	432			

The driver for the awareness campaign was broadcast media, with commercials and a commissioned television programme called *Crystal Romance*, on which the campaign centred. The show featured couples competing for votes to become China's 'Perfect TV Couple'. The programme was also supported by a live-on-air radio show, which discussed the week's issues arising from the television series.

The project also occupied space on *Sohu*, the well-known website and search engine in China. The space was called *Permanent Love* and created a dedicated area for *Crystal Romance* which included downloads, voting platforms, e-cards and a gift-ordering service 'for lovers', as well as music requests for the television and radio broadcasts. The *Sohu* space also connected to the wireless broadcast channel, from which the personal messaging services operated.

A series of live events as well as the online offering helped to keep the television and radio shows topical. For instance, a series of activities were planned around Valentine's Day – with included the conclusion of *Perfect TV Couple* and a fanfare of online offerings including e-cards and special gift offers.

The campaign ran for 47 days and the impact was very high in terms of raising brand awareness and driving product turnover. The campaign was credited with increasing sales by 50 per cent within half a year, for a project that, overall, was calculated to have cost 1.7 yuan (less than 12p) per thousand viewers. This is one of the biggest marketing successes for any product in China, and certainly the biggest that has used a combination of advertising media.

Profile: media mix plan

At the core of the project was a concept called *Permanent Love*. From this all media activities were channelled out to participants and viewers who had registered an interest through any of the campaign's touch-points. These included:

Media used:

- Broadcast:
  - 30-second commercials;
  - television programme *Perfect TV Couple*;
  - radio show *Crystal Romance – Special Area*;
- Narrowcast:
  - webspace *Crystal Romance – Special Area* on *Sohu*;
  - *SMS* images sent to participants, with colour flash animation;
  - text-based *SMS* messaging sent to participants;
  - direct-dial phone music request line;
  - gift service;
  - online voting for the *Perfect TV Couple*.

Creative direction

The brand's existing tone of voice was perceived by the advertiser as being soft, warm, sweet, pure and sexy – more feminine than masculine – so the idea of a promotion project designed around relationships capitalized on the sensual side of the brand's identity.

The website also used *click-throughs* as a means of judging popularity. The most popularly clicked pages clicked by young people featured as prominent buttons in the *Special Area*. Age profiles were defined by using an online questionnaire while the site was running, which helped the web planners and programmers define the listing order.

In common with international reality television shows, the programme's competition was organized in regional and national heats, so that the anticipation grew throughout the series.

Review

Trailers for the television show preceded the online site, but the *Special Area* webspace on *Sohu* was up and running two weeks preceding the first broadcast episode of *Perfect TV Couple*.

Images of some of the message tags, available on the *Special Space* offering on *Sohu*, as part of *Permanent Love, Crystal Romance*.

- This multifaceted approach is widely regarded in China as being among the first to fluidly combine online and offline media activity. The campaign's theme – love – helped project the prime-time programme to mass appeal and help boost ratings for the radio broadcast and web hits, while the radio shows helped to maintain a buzz for the television broadcasts.
- The strategy defined the most relevant ways of getting target customers to respond. For young adults the SMS text service was deemed the best way of stimulating a response, especially colour SMS, which enabled the agency to produce adoptable flash animations for viewers to customize and share.
- The campaign encouraged young Chinese adults to vote, which is a recent experience for the new adults across China. This capitalized on their enthusiasm to exercise choice over the programme they were watching.
- *Crystal Romance* was positioned as contemporary and relevant by appearing to be international, in terms of the way media were mixed and the way consumers had opportunities to interact with and affect the outcome of the campaign. It also introduced the Western concept of Valentine's Day to suggest the brand's international credentials to young Chinese people.

Integrated mix

proportion of campaign

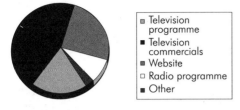

□ Television
  programme
■ Television
  commercials
■ Website
□ Radio programme
■ Other

Essentials

1. A communications mix can be effective if the media used interconnect seam-lessly and the platforms feed one another.
2. An overarching theme needs to be appropriate to, and easily communicated through, each platform.
3. Technological trends can be adopted in order to make products relevant.

For links see www.adstoicons.com.

5 Digital persuasion

This chapter gives prime examples of the potential for advertising online. Some are designed for passive viewing while others require participation, but each case has used entertainment to stimulate people's attention. The cases featured fit into three discrete categories:

1. *Advergaming* – where participants discover the advertisement through play. This spans examples where playing a game helps people learn more about the product (*Jeep*) and where advertising is incorporated in the landscape of the game (*Deutsche Tourenwagen Masters DTM Race Driver*).
2. *Advertainment* – where the commercial message is wrapped with interactive entertainment. This can involve playing with the brand message (for *Burger King*), and discovering the potential of available service (*Verizon*).
3. *Virals* – where (paid for) messages are presented as free to view online entertainment. These can be shocking messages (*Ecko Unlimited*), borrowed messages (borrowed from *Mastercard*), fully involved confrontations (*Sega*) or real-time unravelling stories (*Audi*).

Cases featured...

Deutsche Tourenwagen Masters Race Driver – in-game advertising
Jeep Wrangler Rubicon Trial of Life – product information through play
Burger King Subservient Chicken – most widely accessed interactive ad site
Verizon Beatbox Mixer – brand awareness through play
Mastercard Priceless – most copied web viral
Sega ESPN NFL Football 2K4 Beta-7 – web-centred intrigue
Audi A3 Art of the H3ist – communications-mix burst campaign
Ecko Still Free Air Force One tag – viral stunt as branded entertainment

Suggested reading

Gladwell, Malcolm (2005) *Blink: The power of thinking without thinking*, Little, Brown, New York

Kirby, Justin and Marsden, Paul (eds 2006) *Connected Marketing*, Butterworth-Heinemann, Oxford

Lucas, Gavin and Dorrian, Michael (2006) *Guerrilla Marketing: Unconventional brand communication*, Laurence King, London

DTM TVC in-game advertising

Product:	*Deutsche Tourenwagen Masters*
Target market:	gamers, 12–25-year-olds
Agency/country:	*Energy Source Communications (China) Ltd*
Planning/production time:	6 months
Reach:	over 1 million worldwide
Length of customer engagement:	between 5 minutes and 2 hours, depending on the length of involvement
Brief:	to develop advertising opportunities within a computer game
Budget:	undisclosed
Lifespan:	from 2001
Benchmark:	in-game advertising

A scene from the digital racing game *DTM Race Driver*, which features advertisements prominently within the frame of the game.

Project background

In 2001 the motor racing organization *Deutche Tourenwagen Masters* (DTM) author-ized the use of their branding in computer games, which enabled young enthusi-asts to experience the high-speed thrills of racing sports cars and trucks. As part of making the experience real, virtual environments within the game were handled as advertising space. This gave the brand an advertising opportunity and made the on-screen environment seem every bit as real as an actual racing track.

The communications agency *Energy Source Communications (China)* developed the game's screens as advertising space, and organized a system where advertising would seem natural but feature prominently within the games action.

Timeline	05				06										
	S	O	N	D	J	F	M	A	M	J	J	A	S	O	N
Game development			■	■	■	■	■								
Launch							☼								
Additional promotion							◙	◙	◙	◙					
Media exposure							--	--	--	--	--	--	--	--	--
Hits (100,000s)							1	5	7		10				12

The game's scenes look to be photo-real, and the use of the virtual landscape as commercial space reinforces the credibility of the reconstruction as a 'real' race situation.

As far as advertising is concerned, one of the advantages that virtual billboards and posters have within the frame of a digital game is that the 'camera angle' (the viewer's perspective of the action) can include advertising more frequently in shot than a real-life race. The view can appear to be up close and low down to racing cars, so that more of the environment around the racing track can be prominently shown. In most cases this brings the branded advertising hoardings positioned around the track and on the cars into view.

The placement of sponsors' logos on particular models created a placement hierarchy, in that some cars had properties within the game that made them more attractive to the in-game sponsors.

Profile – in-game advertising

Several advertising agencies in China have championed the use of digital technology for advertising purposes. *Advergaming* is one such platform.

Advertising in games produces additional revenue that publishers can offset against the costs of developing the game. By advertising within a game, the placement makes the brand relevant to gamers because it shows the brand has identified places where core fans of motor racing would go for entertainment outside of actual race times.

It is crucial for the flow of the game that in-game advertisements complement the highly immersive gaming experience. Otherwise they can be seen as disruptive. Disruptive advertising has been commonly used as a pre-game and post-game device and some methods have even blocked the skipping of advertisements. However, within the landscape of a game, advertising seems more authentic and in keeping with a typical race environment, which makes gamers less resistant to ads' placement.

Creative direction

While the advertisements appear to be neutral within the game environment, their prominence during games is dependent on how they are placed: on fast cars with striking branding they may graphically punch out from other imagery. On trackside hoardings they may not often be in view. In other words, the prominence of advertising is similar to that on real racetracks. The difference is that advertisers can select their level of 'sponsorship' based on what are programmed to be the best-performing cars at different levels of the game, and through placement on drivers' clothing, which features prominently during the 'in car' gamer's view and after races.

Therefore most of the creativity in this project was in devising a funding system that incrementally allowed for different levels of advertising placement. The art direction effectively followed the rules of real trackside advertising.

Review

The development of *DTM Race Driver* as an in-game advertising platform attracted some online news coverage during its release in 2001. For most, the advertising content operated as ambient advertising within the game without prior publicity and enhanced the game's credibility as a racing simulation.

- Fewer people will see an advertisement within a game, therefore advertising space is much cheaper than its real-world counterpart. Furthermore, advertisements are more likely to be subject to repeat viewing as games are re-run.
- The advertising content amounts to the placement of brand logotypes. The speed of the game prevents longer messages being read. However, the atmosphere of the game and level of involvement from participants tend to mean that gamers' resistance to advertising is lower than usual because they are concentrating on the action. The branding works by association with the ambience of the game.
- Within *DTM Race Driver*, products associated with motor racing tend to be part of the trackside environment, while brands that are more familiar to the target audience than motor racing tend to feature on the vehicles.

Scenes from the digital game *DTM Race Driver*, which includes in-game advertising space. Most of the brands featured also sponsor motor racing, while for other brands this is an opportunity to claim associations with motor racing.

Integrated mix

proportion of campaign

■ Digital
□ Ambient

Essentials

1. Planners of new digital advertising opportunities need to consider how the platform differs from offline advertising environments. The frequency of advertising placement and prominence of positioning will affect the pricing structure.
2. While fewer people will see the advertisement, those that do will be in an immersed frame of mind. Advertising is more likely to work well as an *ambient* part of a game and, given the niche gaming market, brands know they are addressing a more targeted gaming community.
3. With in-gaming advertising, the advertising content needs to be carefully managed. If it is too prominent it will compromise the quality of the gaming experience, yet if advertisements hardly feature they will not be an attractive proposition to advertisers. A realistic balance needs to be developed.

For web link see http://www.energysource-cn.com.

Wrangler Jeep Rubicon Trial of Life

Product:	limited edition *Jeep Wrangler Rubicon*
Target market:	online gamers (usually aged 16–24; this game assumes up to 35)
Game developer/country:	*Terminalreality.com*, Texas, United States
Reach:	estimated 250,000 unique users (over 500,000 games played)
Length of customer engagement:	games last up to 15 minutes
Brief:	off-brief project (idea developed from a TV commercial spot)
Budget:	undisclosed
Lifespan:	circulated 2003, still accessible on jeep.com website
Benchmark:	product information through play

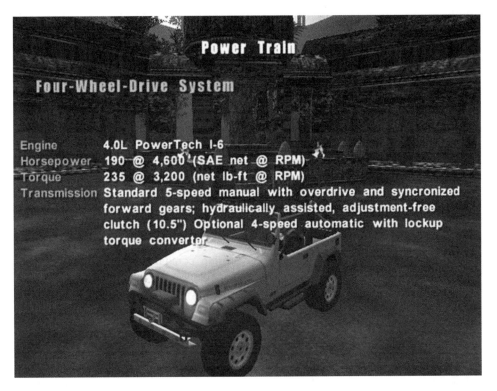

Choosing *Jeep* specifications: an early frame in the *Jeep Trial of Life* game, giving options for the players to drive the *Chrysler Jeep* vehicle of their choice.

Project background

Advergames get consumers to participate in a competition that brings them closer to a brand or product. While this type of advertising has taken many forms, few interactive games have been specifically designed around a product's distinguishing features: the *Trial of Life* was such a game, designed in 2003 as part of a promotion for a special edition of *Chrysler Jeep* called *Wrangler Rubicon Tomb Raider.*

Jeeps featured prominently in the movie *Lara Croft Tomb Raider: The cradle of life*, so *Chrysler* launched a special edition of their *Jeep* to consolidate the product placement. The *advergame* was introduced to develop the connection between the *Jeep* and the film.

As an advertising platform, the digital game format was appropriate because *Tomb Raider* originated from a computer game. The format was also appropriate for more commercial reasons. On *Jeep*'s website it gave internet explorers an opportunity to interact with the brand. Within the frame of a game, participants could explore the performance of the vehicle in ideal *Jeep* environments. Even the modes of progression and incentives, such as points for finding exclusive *Jeep* features, could be controlled to highlight features of the *Jeep*. While players learnt how to win by repeat playing, the messages and experiences they picked up served to advertise the *Jeep*. Therefore gamers' interactive experiences were a pitch for the brand. The format led to a ratio of one in three *clicking through* to discover more about the *Wrangler Rubicon Tomb Raider Jeep*. The *advergame* itself appeared on a number of search engines, including *Yahoo!*

Game description:

It's you and your Jeep® Wrangler Rubicon, engaged in a desperate bid to save the world. You'll need every one of your Trail Rated Wrangler's capabilities as you race through Asian jungles and navigate around primitive villages. Can you meet your checkpoints in time to prevent disaster?

Profile: advergames

The rapid rise in the number of *advergames* (also called in-game advertising) as an advertising method has prompted a great deal of hype around its market potential. Some predict that it will be the next advertising phenomenon, while others describe it as a novelty that, given the rate at which it has grown, won't last long. *Advergaming* has become a more viable option as the number of online gamers has trebled year-on-year since 2002 (source: *PRNews.com*). While some *advergames* appear as pop-ups, *in-game* (advertising frames within the game landscape) and *pre-game* (adverts hanging as a game uploads), others such as *Trial of Life* operate as a form of product demonstration.

Given the emerging capabilities of portable digital communication technology – mobile phone and *BlackBerry* hardware in particular – there is increasing scope for roaming digital users to *snack* on online games.

The market for *advergames*:

- 23% of those who play PC games are between 35 and 44 years old;
- 25% of those who play free online games are between 25 and 34 years old;
- 37% of those who play retail games are between 18 and 24 years old;
- 33% of those who play premium games are between 25 and 34 years old.

Creative direction

In the game, the *Jeep* gets to ride over a selection of terrains that a real *Jeep* would negotiate with ease. Gamers get to drive the *Jeep* through a selection of exotic landscapes that bring out the characteristics and strengths of the vehicle. If they choose, they can act out the type of scenes depicted in *Tomb Raider*.

The styling of the screen shows the *Jeep* in the best possible light – gamers get to see key features such as the dashboard and the shape of the 4×4 as it races through various obstacles in the screen sets.

Playing *Trial of Life* was easy to grasp. Like most *advergames* it borrowed from other game formats, and the standard against the clock provided a challenging objective.

Review

The *advergame* was launched to coincide with the launch of the movie *Lara Croft Tomb Raider: The cradle of life* in 2003. It initially featured on the *Jeep* website to accompany additional online material to support the launch of the limited-edition *Jeep*. Ambient and direct mailers promoting the Jeep around the film launch also profiled the online game. As the game could be easily downloaded, it was soon circulated across the internet via *word-of-mouth*.

> Everything the Rubicon can do in the game, it can do in reality.
>
> (Jeff Bell, vice president, Jeep, Chrysler)

- The game has been designed as a *Jeep* experience, from the sound to the tone of the game, which rewards gamers for exploring as well as racing. As a form of advertisement it is successful in communicating product qualities and user experience through play.

'Your Jeep® Wrangler Rubicon helps you save the world from impending doom!': Viewers get to race the *Jeep* over a variety of terrains, with the distinctive *Jeep* dash in frame.

- The game's screen and sound effects were styled to profile key features. The sound of the car, the unique graphics of the *Jeep's* dash and a dramatic camera angle show how the vehicle negotiates rough terrain. As an advert for the vehicle it highlights many of the *Jeep's* distinguishing features through a series of ideal scenarios.
- For most gamers, playing the game will be the nearest they will get to driving a real *Wrangler Rubicon Jeep*. The game reinforces the idea that *Jeep* is the type of vehicle they should aspire to, because it embodies the spirit of adventure.
- Within the game's design, the rules are designed to highlight exploration and good driving abilities – further reaffirming that the *Jeep* is the vehicle for good drivers with a will to explore.

Integrated mix

proportion of campaign

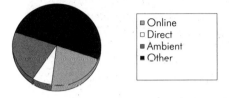

- ▨ Online
- ▢ Direct
- ▪ Ambient
- ▪ Other

Essentials

1. To catch on, *advergames* need to be immediate and easy to access – if not easy to download through mobile technology.
2. The narrative, game format and screen styling need to create the right environment to function commercially as an advertisement.
3. The type of game and its treatment need to be tailored to the target audience: while *advergamers* tend to be younger, older participants will engage if the game's tone and objective strike the right note.

For link see http://www.jeep.com/games/trail_of_life.html.

Burger King Subservient Chicken

Product:	**Burger King, United States**
Target market:	*BK consumers: adults 18–34, with a male skew*
Agency/city:	*Crispin Porter + Bogusky,* Miami
Planning/production time:	less than 2 months
Reach:	over 19 million unique visitors/over 459 million hits in total
Length of customer engagement:	started at 7 minutes, now on average over 6 minutes
Brief:	offshoot of a TV idea
Budget:	undisclosed – (small)
Lifespan:	April 2004 – ongoing
Benchmark:	most widely accessed interactive ad site

Subservient Chicken home page: the chicken's response to inappropriate requests.

Project background

Subservientchicken.com developed as an offshoot of a commercial that agency *Crispin Porter + Bogusky* were shooting for *Burger King*. BK were launching a new product, the *Tender Crisp Chicken Sandwich*, and the campaign finished with the line '*Just the way you like it*'. Rather than *showing* consumers that they could have chicken how they liked it at BK, why not illustrate the point through the *Burger King* site?

The concept of *Subservient Chicken* is simple: visitors type in commands telling the 'chicken' – an actor in a chicken suit – what to do next, and he duly performs in response. There are over 300 pre-programmed responses and various props in the room to give viewers some ideas. The site looks cheap and easily produced – which is part of its enduring charm. The interactive game-cum-joke went on to become one of the world's most distributed internet advertising URL links, and is an internet icon in its own right.

Timeline	03 O	N	D	04 J	F	M	A	M	J	J	A	S	O	N
Planning/production time					■	■	■							
Launch							☼							
Word-of-mouth/blogging							☺	☺	☺	☺	☺	☺	☺	☺
Media exposure								--	--	--	--	--	--	--
Hits (millions)						1	10			100			385>	

The arrival of quicker and visual online communication methods, notably the rich-text format (see chapter 9), enabled ideas like *Subservient Chicken* to be interactive.

Participants would type and send short messages and get a response seemingly in real time, which gave the impression of a live dialogue. Within the scene, the chicken stands facing the camera in a small flat. The impression is that he waits in front of the webcam all day for instruction, and appears to be happy to accommodate most requests that users type in – apart from lewd suggestions or requests to take off his mask, which elicit a chastising wave of his finger.

The light-natured content makes it suitable for all audiences, but those old enough may associate the format with online pornography – the chicken even wears a suspender belt: the design of the screen certainly made efforts to chime with older viewers. *Subservient Chicken* was very much an online *viral* phenomenon when it launched. It relied totally on *word-of-mouth* activity, through the simple addition of a '*send to a friend*' button on the site. Within nine months it had scored over 385 million hits, had been seen in over 190 countries and still attracted over 250,000 per day two years after its release – quite a feat, given that there is no new content or later additions to reward repeat visitors. Furthermore, its commands are only in English – although the commands can be so simple that only a small grasp of English is needed to engage.

Twelve instructions (from over 300) the chicken responds to...

- Watch TV
- Sleep
- Lay egg
- Dances: *Mookwalk, Riverdance,* the *Elephant, Walk Like an Egyptian*
- Eat *Burger King, McDonald's, Taco Bell* or *KFC*
- Fight
- Exercise
- Fly
- Jump
- Yoga
- Read book
- Smoke

(source: *CP+B*)

Creative direction

The tone of voice for *Subservient Chicken* is appropriate to *Burger King* in that it's immediate, witty and encourages play. Warming to the character is effectively like warming to the brand.

The interactive film is on a loop whereby all 300 recorded responses are linked to a spine of footage that features the chicken standing and settling in the centre of the frame. All reactions start and finish in the same neutral position and were filmed in the same Los Angeles apartment.

The responses took time to plan because the creative team had to anticipate a large range of requests. Anything out of the ordinary defaulted to a link where the chicken came close and glared into the camera.

Review

The website was an overnight sensation – literally. When the version was near completion the creative director at *CP+B* e-mailed the URL to several colleagues as a test and requested responses from them and their friends. They sent it to their friends, and from one single 'tester' e-mail the *Subservient Chicken* site ended the day with nearly 1 million hits.

> *Subservient Chicken* was first time an advertiser really went out into the web and created their own web space – aside from corporate sites – to be deliberately entertaining and engaging for consumers. It certainly shifted the paradigm within the advertising industry. (Gillian Smith, Senior Director, Media and Interactive, *Burger King Corp*.)

Some of the moves from the *Subservient Chicken's* repertoire:
above left: spine footage, from which other actions start; above right: response to a request for rival brands; left: request for *Burger King*.

- While the site appears crudely produced its appearance is well measured. The cheap film quality – it looks like a frame-lapse webcam picture, but was in fact recorded on digital video – fits with a product in the *fast-moving consumer goods* range. The speed and reaction of the chicken aimed to re-create the appearance of typical webcam footage. The man in a chicken costume is not unlike a sporting mascot – even though he is wearing suspenders! The association extends the idea of going to *BK* as a leisure activity.
- The chicken suit was made by one of Hollywood's most renowned costume producers. The room was in a flat belonging to a friend of the creative director, and was ideal because the room fits neatly in webcam frame.
- As an extension of advertising, the site offers consumers something from *Burger King* to interact with. It does not offer practical benefits – no promotions or competitions – but emotional ones – a feel for the spirit of the brand. *Subservient Chicken* is an online experience of *BK*, giving it a presence and relevance in a space where *BK* customers are likely to be found.

Integrated mix

proportion of campaign

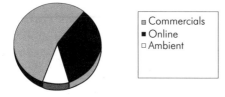

- ▣ Commercials
- ■ Online
- ▢ Ambient

Essentials

1. Interactive elements need to work simply for people to get the idea and play along. They also need to offer variety in order to sustain interest.
2. It is worth considering what the styling of the screen and quality of the film will convey about the product.
3. Even though the product is fast food, the campaign was a means of giving the brand a presence online because that's where their customers spent their leisure time browsing. The site provided light entertainment for online *snackers*.

For link see subservientchicken.com.

Verizon The Beatbox Mixer

Product:	Verizon broadband
Target market:	online web *snackers*, music lovers, people considering broadband purchase
Agency/city:	*R/GA interactive*, New York
Planning/production time:	approximately 6 months
Reach:	over 26 million people worldwide (after TV exposure)
Length of customer engagement:	between 5 and 60 minutes on average
Brief:	show the power of broadband and create a reason for online gamers to explore the *richer, deeper, broader* potential of *Venizon*
Budget:	undisclosed
Lifespan:	circulated 2006
Benchmark:	brand awareness through play

Leading beat boxers are the instruments for online participants to mix and send their own *Verizon Beatbox* samples to friends.

Project background

In 2006 *Verizon*, a telecommunications company, launched an online interactive sampler, *Beatbox Mixer*, to illustrate the potential of broadband. The framework enabled web users to pick riffs from human 'beat boxers' and lay their own mix by combining beats and effects provided. The platform operated as a portal for players to co-create compositions.

It was branded entertainment with an advertising method, in that the site allowed people to interact, engage and discover the platform's message – that *Verizon's* perspective of broadband is fun, relevant and absorbing. As a benchmark of online advertising, therefore, *The Verizon Beatbox Mixer* is a model of online *advertainment*.

		06										
Timeline		J	F	M	A	M	J	J	A	S	O	N
Planning/production time			■	■	■	■	■	■				
Launch								☼				
Word-of-mouth/blogging								☺	☺	☺	☺	☺
Media exposure								--	--	--	--	--
Hits (100,000s)								1	5	10		20

The strategy behind *The Beatbox Mixer* relates to *Verizon's* other online activities, which include a *social network site* shaped around the possibilities of broadband. With an existing *Verizon* 'blue sky' digital community, *The Beatbox Mixer* project encouraged new prospects to play, and in doing so, learn who *Verizon* is. From playing they would also identify *Verizon* as a hip service, in tune with urban culture, and fulfil the campaign's objective, to discover the 'real-time interactive' potential of broadband – and the value in choosing bigger bandwidths. This is also where players would realize the meaning of *Verizon's* 'Richer, Deeper, Broader' tagline. Playing inspired people to spread the word to other newcomers by sending their versions, and motivated them enough to check out other *Verizon* material online.

The Beatbox Mixer was therefore an illustration of *Verizon's* potential and was intended to show *prospects* what they could have access to if they subscribed to its broadband services.

How it works

1. Select your favourite beatboxer and two back-up performers.
2. Lay a base track.
3. Add back-up performers' beats and riffs to produce an original mix.
4. Play back and adjust the mix.
5. When finished, save it to Verizon's online gallery (where anyone can play your mix) or e-mail it to your friends.

Creative direction

By flexing the potential of 'Web 2.0' (see chapter 9), *snackers* were encouraged to discover *The Beatbox Mixer's* potential through play. There were many features to keep people rooted to the site, including the ability to loop track segments and select from a choice of backdrops. In the end, participants were rewarded with a *prêt-à-jouer* ('ready to play') saved version of the game that they could share with others. If they distributed the final version to friends and colleagues, others would be drawn to interact on the site and could even create their own beatbox music.

The design of the site created an ideal dynamic urban environment for *Verizon*. The sharp graphic styling of the mixer, choice of hip cityscape or studio backdrops and the characters involved (all established US Beatbox artists) reinforced *Verizon's* 'street' credentials.

Review

A press release was circulated to prominent new media sites including *Adverblog*, *Webwire* and *YPulse*. From there on, URL links widened the international spread of information via *blogs* and e-mail.

> a cutting-edge cross between a music video, a video game, and a drum machine.'
>
> (*Verizon's* press release)

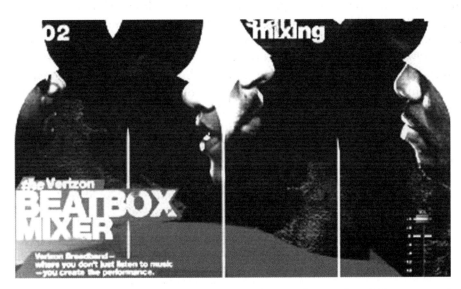

The Beatbox Mixer branding reinforced *Verizon's* dance-culture style, which permeated through the website's graphic layout.

- *The Beatbox Mixer* allowed users to adopt, make and send their own versions. *User-generated content* distributed by participants has the potential to find new prospects in a way that is beyond any one company database of contact addresses.
- Involving people – not simply showing them content – meant that participants were likely to have an experience that they could relate to others. There was even an option after mixing a beat that allowed users to post their mixes to their own websites (the mixer generated a code to make this possible). This approach to play, create and share is at the heart of the best *advertainments*.
- While the rich-text format was still a person-to-data system rather than one-to-one, the experience was created of being in a *Verizon*-shaped recording studio that worked in real time.
- By keeping the game on-site rather than putting it out as a circulated *viral*, links to other content could be updated.

Integrated mix

proportion of campaign

▣ Online
▢ Public relations

Essentials

1. By making platforms for people to create, outputs are more likely to be circulated.
2. Online communication can be used to generate brand experiences.
3. If the platform is engaging, people will play and 'advertise' the platform as brand advocates.

For web links see www.beatboxmixer.com, www.verizon.com, www.richerdeeperbroader.com/beatbox, www.rga.com.

Mastercard Priceless

Product:	Mastercard financial services
Target market:	internet users
Agency/city:	*McCann Erickson*, New York
Planning/production time:	versions vary
Reach:	global
Length of customer engagement:	varies: viewers, seeders and participants
Brief:	allow *Mastercard's* 'Priceless' tag to be circulated and adopted globally
Budget:	undisclosed
Lifespan:	1997 – ongoing
Benchmark:	most copied web viral

Divorce lawyer: $10,000

Loss of house, car, etc.: $250,000

Small marine motor: $275

Disposable camera: $8

Sending your ex-wife a picture of you boating in her family heirloom dining room table:

PRICELESS!

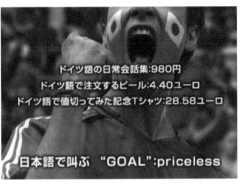

Left: an early corruption of the *Mastercard* campaign, circulated in 2001. Above: a version by *Mastercard* in Japan for the football World Cup in 2006.

Project background

The most copied internet viral ever was originally by *McCann Erickson* for *Mastercard*, from 1997. On *Google images* alone there are well over 500 versions of the campaign – mostly reworked and unauthorized – using the advertisement's format and endline as the frame for a socially networked joke.

Most versions feature the *Mastercard* logo and the word *Priceless*, which – whether intended or not – reinforces the connection between the financial service and its 'ownership' of the word *priceless*. Online communication channels are effective advertising slogan distributors because web users tend to circulate messages they find interesting – whether found, forwarded or customized. Allowing *Mastercard's* format to be adopted proved a masterstroke, because the campaign stemmed far beyond paid-for advertising space around the globe.

Mastercard had previously taken steps to regulate use of their *priceless* mark. The mark is the subject of multiple copyright registrations in the United States where most *priceless* online corruptions originate. It was originally registered as a trademark in most countries because it featured in a media campaign for *Mastercard's* financial products.

Mastercard's policy has been to clamp down on websites that extensively overuse the mark or if it has been used to produce 'infringing material' (offensive or obscene content). This has, however, been handled in a liberal way. Most versions in circulation tend to reference *priceless* as a means to caption a comic image, draw attention to detail in an image that's not immediately apparent, to make a point about the context of the image or, as was originally intended, to adopt the idea that some situations are more valuable than money can buy.

Creative direction

The enduring strength of the *Mastercard* campaign is its copy. Four one-line statements, graduating in price and finishing with the word *priceless*, were originally pushed through above- and below-the-line formats and became used in all six contents. The three-line build-up and punchline is a standard comedy formula, but featuring the cost at the end of each line made the format unique to *Mastercard*, while the line structure was generic enough to be applied in virtually any situation.

As a copy-based advertising solution, allowing internet users to adopt the format has allowed *Mastercard = Priceless* to become an enduring and iconic mark in modern advertising.

Review

Priceless was originally launched through press and commercials early in 1997. It is not clear exactly when the first online version appeared, although versions were adapted online by October 1997.

- The *Mastercard* campaign's copy formula was open-ended enough for a wide variety of subjects to be shoehorned into its format, so it could be made relevant to many situations.

1 × Bull: $142
1 × Hot Pink Bull Fighting
Costume: $299
Copping it up the ass from an
angry Bull:

PRICELESS!!!!!!!!!!!!

One roll of shipping tape: $4.00
Massive amounts of packing material: Free (stolen)
Friends with too much free time on April Fools

PRICELESS

BloodDonor

Donating Used Car ....Helpful

Giving to Charity.........................Worthwhile

Mentoring Young People ....Rewarding

Donating Blood ....**Priceless**

Bastardized versions of *Mastercard's* campaign have been used to make points (left), caption visual jokes (above right) and to promote causes (right).

- The global spread of *Mastercard's* format crystallized the campaign through online communities.
- The format has proved adaptable in local situations with local audiences. Unauthorized versions of the advertisement are often reworked using local parlance, which gets to the heart of moments where the content was topical. As the internet does not contain one online community but many, easy re-appropriation has helped keep *Mastercard* relevant to 'priceless' moments around the world.

Essentials

1. When campaigns are adopted, they need not remain in the full control of the brand.
2. Advertising formats should be easy to 'adopt'. With the example above, this has helped reinforce the *endline's* connection to the brand worldwide.
3. The internet has made *user-generated content* more achievable. Not all brands have been as successful as *Mastercard* in negotiating this online challenge (see chapter 9).

For link see www.priceless.com.

Sega ESPN NFL Football 2K4 game launch 'Beta-7'

Product:	Sega ESPN NFL Football 2K4
Target market:	gamers and online bloggers, *early adopters*
Agency/city:	*Wieden + Kennedy*, New York
Planning/production time:	7 months
Reach:	mostly US, estimated 2,000,000
Length of customer engagement:	intermittent over 2 weeks
Brief:	launch the new product via early-adopter *word-of-mouth*, and maintain a mystique for the launch
Budget:	undisclosed
Lifespan:	June–September 2003
Benchmark:	web-centred intrigue

The website and pirating activities of '*Beta-7*', a fictitious character invented to create intrigue before the launch of *Sega's ESPN NFL Football 2K4*.

Project background

Beta-7 was an online blogger and lobbyist who appeared to be actively campaigning against the launch of *Sega's* digital game *NFL Football 2K4*. He claimed to be involved in trials for *Sega's* new digital game – 'Beta-7' was his trial number. On his website he raised safety concerns, which (in effect) helped to spread awareness of the pending launch. A series of internet *virals* were strategically distributed by *Beta-7* to challenge *Sega*, and *Sega's* responses rebutting his concerns developed the conflict into a newsworthy story.

However, '*Beta-7*' was a fictitious character created by *Sega's* advertisers to create intrigue before the launch.

Timeline	02 S	O	N	03 D J	F	M	A	M	J	J	A	S	O	N
Concept development	■	■	■											
Completed project (constructed)				■ ■	■	■								
Teaser campaign leading to launch							☼	☼	☼	☼				
Word-of-mouth/blogging								☺	☺	☺	☺	☺	☺	
Additional promotion					◉	◉	◉	◉						
Media exposure					--	--	--	--	--					

The specific issue raised by *Beta-7* concerned side effects from playing *NFL Football 2K4*. He claimed that a new camera angle in the game, trialled as 'crash-cam' but re-branded 'first person football', induced strange side effects in gamers. News of the concern spread through *blog* sites and many net surfers tried to discover more – and in particular, why *Sega* were trying to suppress concerns. The story was picked up by chat rooms, and stoked interest around the forthcoming release. People wanted to know if *crash-cam* was safe, what its side effects had been and why *Sega* appeared awkward about *Beta-7's* claims. The air of mystery was maintained right up to *Sega's* release and prompted the most cynical gamers to question whether the confrontation was genuine. It even prompted two genuine websites supporting *Beta-7*.

The unravelling story of *Beta-7's* attack on *Sega* ignited interest over four months, as the saga was rolled out from *Beta-7* and *Sega's* website, through a series of *virals* and *blog* sites and then *Sega* adverts and call lines. Officially authorized, secretly authorized, bogus and unofficial material became *mashed up* and indistinguishable on- and offline, as conspiracy theorists felt *Sega* had something to hide. By September 2003, at the launch campaign's expiry, the story had reached the mainstream through excessive word-of-mouth activity, and as the *Sega NFL* game was *rolled out*, *Beta-7* was exposed as a stunt.

As a teaser, the campaign created a demand for information and even those duped would have enjoyed the drama created.

Action and reaction

'Beta-7'	Sega
ACTION	REACTION
Set up site, posted concerns	Refuted allegations
Generated blog activity	
Sent out pirate versions of the game	Sent legal letters demanding return of pirate
Put out virals showing side effects	copies
	Set up 'unofficial' site rubbishing *Beta-7* and a
	phone line refuting his claims
Exposé documentary posted, showing	
Sega consultants approached and	
challenged on the fly	
Hacked and posted warning on *Sega* site	Put out commercial, tagged with a safety
	message
Claimed *Sega* had personally threatened him	Had *Beta-7* website closed and posted warning
	on his site
	Set up *Sega ESPN NFL Football 2K4* website
	GAME LAUNCH
	Media used: three websites, viral videos, viral
	voicemails, e-mail, blogs, traditional TV and
	print, internet TV, live stunting and collateral,
	packaging design, small-space newspaper

Creative direction

Several types of media were used in sync to make the unfolding story roll out in a realistic way.

The main elements were as follows: first, *Beta-7's* website was launched with a web log documenting *crash-cam's* side effects. It featured symptoms including an uncontrollable urge to tackle people. This led to a range of unauthorized and secretly authorized blog activity. Nine of the most vociferous supporters of *Beta-7's* web log were sent pirate copies of the game, and amateurish *QuickTime* movies were circulated, showing the consequences of *crash-cam*: *Beta-7* was shown physically tackling people in an elevator, in an office and on the beach.

> an intricately layered, deliberately complicated piece of 'live interactive theater' that played out in real time. (*Adweek*)

Sega's reaction took the form of a 'rival' site, denying that tests had taken place. An official-looking legal letter was sent on behalf of *Sega* to recipients of *Beta-7's* pirate copies demanding their return. *Beta-7* was allegedly threatened and barred from distributing further information. A fan website, *GamerChuck.com*, was launched to combat *Beta-7's* claims, but the content looked suspiciously as though it was authorized by *Sega*. *Sega's* own official site was launched and then subsequently hacked by *Beta-7*, while posted threats he received from *Sega* were posted on his own site before Sega had it closed. The actions and reactions developed a keen following and fuelled a wide range of user-generated material, which all served to make the story relevant. A *Sega* television commercial for the game further fuelled the sense of conspiracy by finishing with the message 'excessive playing of the game would not lead to violent or erratic behaviour': This acknowledged that *crash-cam* had become an issue and gave credence to those suspicious of a cover-up.

By the launch date, web activity on both 'sides' had homed in on the game's central feature – crash-cam/first-person football. *Wieden+Kennedy's* plan was so detailed, cross-media and interconnected that it seemed real. It helped *Sega* achieve an estimated 20 per cent rise on the game's sales projections. It also tapped into the sense of *experiential* and intrigue that both agency and manufacturer knew would inspire their target audience, the gaming community.

Profile: strategic thinking

The multimedia strategy was held together by a core idea – conspiracy. At the centre of contention was a unique feature of the game, so its market distinction and dubious safety became an issue. This gave the pending release an edgy reputation before anyone had seen it.

The campaign benefited from well-managed but complex planning. The timing of each response was crucial, as was the sense of whether it was official or unofficial, pro- or anti-*Sega*. Each media had to be a step ahead of consumers by reading their response to each situation.

The planning became tighter as both sides converged close to the launch date: the *Beta-7* and *Sega* sites infiltrated each other so much that the message – launch date and key feature – was consistent through both perspectives.

Wieden+Kennedy had therefore played on a frisson of conflicting ideas – official/unofficial communications, mainstream/counter-cultural, authored and unauthorized. It helped to give the product an agitprop edge.

Review

Initially launched through *Beta-7's* website, awareness was seeded through gamers' *blogs* to establish *word-of-mouth* activity.

I have unpredictable, uncontrollable, violent outbursts that I have no memory of, which have made me a stranger to my friends and family. ('Beta-7', on his website)

What's real and what's fiction is sometimes hard to figure out, but it's fun to go along with it for the ride! (18-year-old gamer, New York)

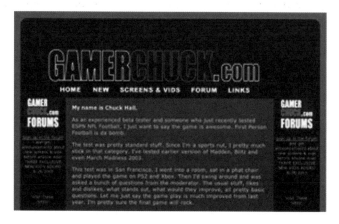

Rival websites, *Beta-7.com* and *Gamerchuck.com*, contested the safety of *Sega NFL Football 2K*.

- The project required active involvement from *Sega*, and those 'in' on the stunt were signed to secrecy.
- Each communication was consistent with the overall strategy and stayed true to the overall project.
- The conflict centred on the product's unique selling point (USP).

Integrated mix

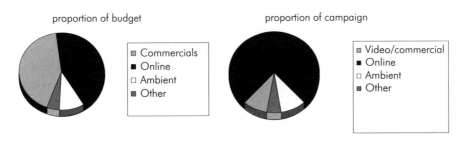

proportion of budget

■ Commercials
■ Online
□ Ambient
■ Other

proportion of campaign

■ Video/commercial
■ Online
□ Ambient
■ Other

Essentials

1. Complex launch strategies tend to engage a core audience, but have to create enough intrigue if they are attract wider audiences.
2. Complex roll-outs require a close working relationship between advertising agency and client.
3. 'Negative messaging' (conspiracy theories) can be used to advantage, but advertisers have little control over how they are interpreted by the wider public.

For link see http://www.beta-7.com.

Audi Art of the H3ist

Product:	Audi of America, for the Audi A3
Target market:	business users 25–50, internet *snackers*
Agency/city:	*McKinney + Silver*, New York
Planning/production time:	6 months
Reach:	throughout the United States
Length of customer engagement:	campaign unravelled over 2 months – takes approximately 15 minutes to get up to date with the story
Brief:	launch the new *Audi A3* car in a way that produces drama and intrigue
Budget:	undisclosed
Lifespan:	3 months in 2005
Benchmark:	communications-mix *burst* campaign

A grainy view from a security camera of the break-in at the Park Avenue showroom, Manhattan – scene of the *Audi* heist. Footage was posted on a website, from which the '*H3ist*' storyline rolled out.

Project background

For the launch of the *Audi A3* in the United States, advertising firm *McKinney + Silver* devised a *burst* plan that was described by some as an alternative reality game.

Using a range of staged events, with on- and offline activities, interested parties could participate in the story and, unusually, help shape events as the next stages were being written as the project unfolded in real time. Many were kept guessing as to whether the initial theft of a new *Audi* was real, while *blog* discussion debated what would happen next as the saga took several unexpected turns. The tactic succeeded in creating a buzz above all other campaigns in the United States at the time and generated a vast amount of free publicity.

Timeline	04 S	O	N	D	05 J	F	M	A	M	J	J	A	S	O	N
Concept development		■	■	■	■	■	■	■							
Launch								☼							
Campaign run								☼	☼	☼					
Word-of-mouth/blogging								☺	☺	☺	☺	☺	☺		
Media exposure								--	--	--	--		--	-	
Hits (10,000s)								5	10		100			150	

The campaign used shock tactics at the beginning with the staged heist of a new 2006 *A3* from an *Audi* dealership in Park Avenue, Manhattan. The *Audi A3* had been on display with five others, but the particular model stolen contained a new form of memory card in its navigation system that happened to carry encryption details for the other five. Security camera footage of the raid was posted on *Audi's A3* website and posters appeared in Manhattan asking for information.

They attracted wide media attention, and many internet *snackers* during work breaks clicked through to find out more at *Audi's* website. The information on *Audi's* site became more detailed in the following days and many internet users became hooked, as speculation grew on the reasons behind the crime. It became apparent that the story was part of the launch and users could follow clues and track the criminals online. People could add to the blog and offer suggestions for the investigation, which were acted upon. A core web-based community joined in and discussed *Audi's* heist as the thrill of an unravelling mystery took hold.

McKinney + Silver and *Audi* chose this *filter advertising* approach because it matched the personality of the *Audi A3* – dynamic, desirable, adventurous, hi-tech and smart.

The main caricatures of the storyline reflected modern lifestyles that the brand would be happy to associate with: an up-market art retriever, Nisha Roberts, and her digital expert boyfriend, Ian Yarbrough, were investigating the theft, while top video game designer Virgil Tatum, who was meant to be modelling a game on

Roberts, became involved in the plot, which involved love and betrayal. The characters in the plot were so well detailed that one has appeared in other games and digital entertainments. The end came at a live filmed event where the characters and plot all converged, three months after the original heist.

As a benchmark of integrated advertising, the campaign is one of the most immersive communication strategies ever attempted, attracting up to 200,000 people to the site in a day and 70 per cent more visitors than the regular *Audi* website. *Audi* estimated that about 125,000 people were regular followers of the *H3ist's* development online.

Creative direction

Media used:

Environment – showroom, posters, print advertisements, billboard
Live events – heist, phone line, end ceremony, live street action (recorded/posted on the website)
Broadcast – television commercials, billboards, radio spots
Digital – website, e-mails, videos, voice transcripts
Extensions – photos, puzzles, documents (clues) posted online.

Although the plot was complex, the approach enabled a high level of customer involvement. People were able to watch, participate and influence events online in live 'retrieval missions', web-cast in real time. The layers of information allowed those following events to choose their level of involvement.

According to *McKinney + Silver*, it was scripted by a team of experienced Hollywood writers who organized material so that people not closely following the story would not lose the plot. The storyline allowed *Audi A3* features to be looped in. For instance, the initial heist information noted the new SD card navigation system in top of the range *Audi A3s*.

A great deal of planning and organization were required to orchestrate events as the ad was *rolled out*, and much of the pre-planning involved developing a working collaboration with *Apple, Sony Computer Entertainment America, Palm, E3, Coachella, URB magazine, VH1, AFI* and *Bose* for the project. The collaborations required consistent briefing and designing into the process.

Review

As the story unfolded...

1. Website created
2. *Heist staged* during the early morning hours of 1 April
3. Posters put out asking for information on the heist

4. More websites and *blogs* set up
5. Security camera footage posted on website
6. Information released about likely suspects
7. Website introduced the central characters – story of them and their relationships unfolds
8. Other interactive elements released on website
9. Hunt gets closer to heist gang
10 *Final* event (held at The Viceroy, Santa Monica, 29 June): launch evening held up as all characters end up in final plot resolution on stage
11. Events posted on website.

The goal was to go beyond what is being done on the internet today and create an alternative world where everything seems real.

(*Art of the H3ist* Art Director Jason Musante, *McKinney*)

The Art of the H3ist represents a true innovation in the way Audi connects with its target consumer. (Stephen Berkov, *Audi of America*'s director of marketing)

Website title page and heist member profile, part of the unravelling campaign for *Audi A3 Art of the H3ist*.

- Both *The Art of the H3ist* and the *Sega Beta-7* campaign (also featured in this chapter) blur the distinction between reality and fiction by unravelling in real time. Both encouraged participation as narratives unfolded.
- The *Audi* drama positions the *A3* as the desirable subject of the story. The spirit of mystery and adventure, of a blue-collar heist and up-market locations – such as the Park Lane showroom – served to create an environment appropriate to the brand.
- The campaign initially blurred fact and fiction, and the live plot development maintained intrigue as the story unfolded. The endpoint and key parts of the story were predetermined, which gave the campaign a clear structure to work around.

Integrated mix

proportion of campaign

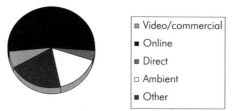

- ▣ Video/commercial
- ■ Online
- ■ Direct
- ☐ Ambient
- ■ Other

Essentials

1. Never underestimate the power of interactive narrative. Engaging customers in the plot also involves them with the brand.
2. Campaigns that involve stunts, online or offline, must ensure that the campaign message features at the heart of the campaign. Otherwise the purpose can be lost on consumers.
3. Events that involve participation require a clearly defined start and end point.

For link see http://www.mckinney-silver.com/A3_H3ist/.

Marc Ecko Enterprises Still Free

Product:	Ecko Unltd/Marc Ecko Enterprises
Target market:	urban youth market (13–18-year-old category) in the United States
Agency/city:	*Droga5*, New York
Planning/production time:	4 months between concepting and development, through post-production to launch
Reach:	over 115 million people worldwide/17,000 separate news outlets
Length of customer engagement:	3 minutes watching the film: length of discussion time immeasurable. Acquired multi-network coverage
Brief:	reinforce *Ecko Unltd's* graffiti heritage. Reinforce Marc Ecko's position as an urban icon
Budget:	$0 media spend (hire of plane estimated $150,000)
Lifespan:	circulated 2006
Benchmark:	viral as branded entertainment

Intended to look low-budget, this is a frame from a digital movie of graffiti artist and fashion designer Ecko 'tagging' Air Force One. It was posted and distributed through video sharing sites around the world, before later, at the height of its infamy, revealing itself as an elaborate advertising ploy.

Project background

A short film was anonymously posted on the internet in 2006 which appeared to show the US president's jet being tagged by a well-known graffiti artist. It caused a furore for a number of reasons: Was it real or a hoax? Should it be censured as a recorded act of vandalism? And later, was it home-made or was it advertising?

The *viral* was in fact a film to promote New York-based clothing designer, video game maker and graffiti-rights activist Marc Ecko and his brand *Marc Ecko Enterprises*, and the issue of whether it was authentic tagging turned the advertising stunt into an international news story – generating much free publicity.

Timeline	05				06										
	S	O	N	D	J	F	M	A	M	J	J	A	S	O	N
Concept development				■	■	■									
Pre-production						■	■								
Post-production							■	■							
Launch									☼						
Word-of-mouth/blogging									☺	☺	☺	☺	☺	☼	
Media exposure									--	--	--	--	--	--	--
Hits (10,000s)									23						115+

The *Ecko viral* featured several men breaking into what looked like *Andrews Air Force Base* in Maryland, United States, at night and spraying graffiti onto the president's personal plane, *Air Force One*, as it sat near a runway. One of the men is shown spraying his tagline and logo, *Still Free*, across one of the plane's jet engines. In fact the set and styling of the video had been elaborately constructed to create the appearance of a risky stunt (see below). The video was seeded on underground websites and quickly spread to major sites, including *YouTube* and *MySpace*, as it became more accessible. Many received it as an e-mail *viral* because its content looked subversive, which then prompted national media interest.

The *viral's* pull revolved around whether it was real or a hoax. The question fuelled mass-media interest because of the context – the president's plane, and security issues involved: had it been an act of graffiti elsewhere the video would have reached a much smaller online niche. As a proposition to get noticed it was therefore bound to provoke widespread interest.

The stunt came to light when the Pentagon was asked to deny the vandalism took place – which they duly did. The film managed to dupe the mainstream press, although there were in-references for followers of Ecko's work to spot the joke. The tagline 'Still free' runs through all of Ecko's output, from fashion to games. Ecko himself eventually broke the news of the hoax and its purpose, to promote *Marc Ecko Enterprises*' new fashion range.

Creative direction

The approach capitalized on the boom in online video sharing, because there was a huge demand for interesting online content: tagging the president's jet was certainly big enough to arouse curiosity. The video's quality did not look polished but more like internet *user-generated content* – another online phenomenon of 2006. Part of the skill was in making the film appear cheap, like typical uploaded digital video – shaky hand-held camerawork, no narration, with some of the dialogue inaudible. The amateurish look made the act of subversion appear all the more real because it seemed authentic.

Yet the cheap production quality belied elaborate preparation. Finding and commissioning a jet to use in secrecy posed a problem early on. A decommissioned Boeing 747 was hired and one side was renovated and repainted at an estimated cost of $150,000. A section of airstrip had to be sourced that looked like the airbase in Maryland, to fool military experts: a spot at *San Bernadino* airport in California was used, and careful lighting helped create the illusion.

Although the film was a hoax and no real act of vandalism took place, disclaimers were still attached to the film. According to creative director David Droga, 'We literally did have seven lawyers sitting in pre-production meetings telling us what we could and couldn't do' (www.theaustralian.post.com.au).

Review

The video was seeded on 20 websites: the 'is it real or not?' debate fuelled online discussion and the clip was in hot demand. It was seen by an estimated 115 million people online before being picked up by US news channels. It went on to feature in over 100 news reports and an estimated 17,000 individual online and offline outlets as a point of interest (www.boardsmag.com).

The film has become a pop culture moment.

(David Droga, of *Droga5*, creator of the campaign)

Still from the film, showing Marc Ecko scaling the airport fence next to *Air Force One*.

- The *Ecko viral* is one the first advertising-funded digital films to break through from *YouTube* online, as homemade entertainment, to the offline mainstream as broadcast news.
- Unlike online *advertainment*, the film maintained an aura of intrigue because its identity was suppressed. It appeared to be non-commercial and subversive agitprop, when it was neither.
- The format follows commercial conventions: the graffiti tag is effectively the *endline* of *Marc Ecko Enterprises*.
- The project sparked debate as to whether it was a legitimate advertising approach – although it was much awarded for its creative approach by advertising industry bodies.

Integrated mix

proportion of campaign

- Digital video
- Online seeding

Essentials

1. Documentary film will arrest people's attention if the content is gripping: while intrigue is important, the end message has to connect with the brand.
2. Disguising an advertisement within another format can dilute the message rather than make an impact. The method only works if it is compatible with the mood required for the brand.
3. To construct a simple illusion takes a great deal of background planning. Detailed preparation produces more convincing results.

For link see www.droga5.com.

6 Online spaces

The examples featured in this chapter have flexed the possibilities of the world wide web and show potential to shape entire virtual environments around advertising. All run from their own branded web or microsite.

Some cases use tailor-made devices to pull viewers to their site (*Amex*, *Volvo* and *Singapore Airlines*), while others have produced a format that invites participants to challenge and explore its format (*Axe Lynx*, *Loctite* and *Monopoly*).

Two of the cases featured are sites that were set up to become social networks (*Sony Ericsson* and *Dove*). They have developed a specialist following for championing subjects that are relevant to the products being advertised.

Cases featured...

Amex Adventures of Seinfeld and Superman – *webisode* campaigning
Volvo Life on Board – creating through-flow, offline to online
Axe Lynx Axefeather – ease of involvement
Loctite Super Bonder– website product demonstration
Monopoly Live! – blending real and virtual, on- and offline activity
Singapore Airlines Boarding Pass Privileges – regional equity, through an exclusive 'brand extension' reward scheme
Sony Ericsson K700 Take Your Best Shot – product-inspired social network site
Dove Campaign for Real Beauty – cause adoption – social network sites.

Suggested reading

Leadbeater, Charles (1999) *Living on Thin Air: The new economy with a blueprint for the 21st century*, Viking, London

Lindstrom, Martin (2005) *Brand Child*, Kogan Page, London

Gladwell, Malcolm (2000) *The Tipping Point: How little things can make a difference*, Little, Brown, New York

Amex Webisodes

Product:	**American Express online**
Target market:	web users, United States – current and prospective *Amex* customers
Agency/city:	cross-functional agency team
Planning/production time:	undisclosed
Reach:	cross-state internet users; estimated 2 million visitors in the first 2 weeks
Length of customer engagement:	up to 5 minutes per visit, over 12+ weeks use the allure of
Brief:	brand endorsement to woo current and prospective customers to *Amex*'s website, via a specially commissioned online programme
Budget:	undisclosed
Lifespan:	March–May 2004
Benchmark:	webisode campaigning

The Adventures of
Seinfeld
&Superman

Amex collaborated with US comedian Jerry Seinfeld, well-known director Barry Levinson and animated cartoon hero Superman as brand guardians, to feature in a series of storylines broadcast exclusively on *Amex*'s website (Superman copyright © *Time Warner DC Comics*).

Project background

American Express devised a unique way of attracting *traffic* to their website. They commissioned two short films featuring American comedian Jerry Seinfeld in storylines written around the potential of *Amex* cards. His co-star was a rendition of superhero *Superman*, which gave the narrative an original twist in a series exclusively available through the *Amex* website.

Both five-minute episodes were made available first only on the *Amex* site. The strategy of combining new and old American icons was such a *pull* that it drew those who use the internet for entertainment to visit the site.

	03				04									
Timeline	S	O	N	D	J	F	M	A	M	J	J	A	S	O
Concept development	■	■	■	■	■	■								
Launch							☼		☼					
Word-of-mouth/press					☺	☺	☺	☺	☺	☺				
Media exposure			--	--			--			--	--	--		
Hits (millions)				0.5	1	3	5	6			8			10

Jerry Seinfeld and *Superman* were previously featured together in an *American Express* commercial during *Superbowl 1998*. The casting had international appeal – Seinfeld was one of the most successfully exported US comedies during the 1990s, while comic book hero *Superman* was a globally recognized character. Episodes were co-written by Seinfeld and directed by film director Barry Levinson (Superman was voiced by Patrick Warbuton, who featured in Seinfeld TV shows). The films blended live action with animation, and *DC Comics* recreated the animated superhero in his original drawn style (as created by artist Curt Swan).

Two episodes were made, titled *A uniform used to mean something* (online from 29 March) and *Hindsight is 20/20* (20 May), and both featured a benefit of *Amex's* customer service woven into the storyline. For instance, in the second encounter, *Superman* and Seinfeld are on a long road journey when they encounter trouble in the middle of a desert. Seinfeld – rather than *Superman* – saves the day by calling for *American Express Roadside Assistance*, a service provided for *Amex* card holders. The episodes were more than just television-styled commercials put online: the website they featured on contained the instalments plus additional point and click content where viewers could find downloadable images, 'behind the scenes' footage and further details of *Amex* card membership and benefits. As a package, all the elements worked together to make the entertainment and advertising content connect. The *webisodes* pulled in a significant audience for web-only viewing and attracted a large number of new visitors to the site.

Creative direction: webisode campaigning

This was an original advertising proposition, and the strength of the strategy was in making the shows exclusive. This meant that people would have to make the effort to find *Amex's* own channel. Additional content to support each episode was on the site, as one might find on a DVD. The more web users *clicked through* the site, the more they were likely to hit on *Amex* customer benefits, so the brand benefited from customers browsing the site in detail.

The films were produced under licence from *DC Comics, Warner Brothers Consumer Products* and Seinfeld, and all parties mutually benefited from the association. The theme that united them was their all-American identity. Even the settings – a New York apartment and desert – were clearly in the United States. The brands and environments involved made this an ideal platform for a *third party association*.

Review

Press and television ran features leading up to the launch – the most prestigious exclusively online narrowcast of its time made the episodes a newsworthy event.

> It's about opting in and opting out; we're trying to create media content where people actually opt in to watch. (John Hayes, chief marketing officer at *American Express*)
>
> (cited in *New York Times* by Stuart Elliott)

Scenes from *The Adventures of Seinfeld and Superman* webisodes.

- Exclusive *narrowcasting* rewarded *Amex's* existing clients and drew new prospects to the site.
- Additional content ensured that visitors had more reason to remain on the site after viewing the *webisodes*.
- Storylines highlighted particular benefits of *Amex* card membership, by demonstrating situations where their unique services would be useful.

- Each short story was layered to maintain intrigue and reward repeated viewing. For instance, the film quality flitted between live footage and animation so that both characters existed in each other's 'worlds'. Also, if one watched the action closely, references were made to their friendship with carefully placed photos in the film frame (these were highlighted in additional material featured on the website). It was anticipated that each episode would be eagerly scrutinized, so scenes were detailed to feed close interest.

Integrated mix

proportion of campaign

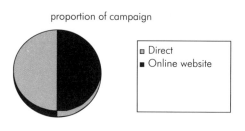

- ◻ Direct
- ◼ Online website

Essentials

1. The *webisode* is a powerful online device in that it creates intrigue for the next instalment and gives web users an incentive to return back to the site.
2. *Third party associations* are appropriate when there is a mutual benefit in brands of similar equity pooling sources.
3. Film viewed online has a different requirement from broadcast – it can be seen at the viewer's discretion and replayed many times.

For link see www.americanexpress.com/jerry.

Volvo Life on Board

Product:	*Volvo*
Target market:	AB1 males, 30–55 (time-poor, prefer information media)
Agency/city:	*Fuel*, Amsterdam, Holland/*EHS Brann*, London; *Euro RSCG 4D*, London
Reach:	1.17 million
Length of customer engagement:	adverts 30 seconds: online approx 4–6 minutes each visit
Brief:	create an experience-based environment that does justice to the innovative nature of this campaign: develop engagement through commercials to online activity
Budget:	undisclosed
Lifespan:	2004–06 (24 months)
Benchmark:	creating through-flow, offline to online

A scene from *Life on Board*, one of the short films designed to *pull* viewers from television commercials to *Volvo's Life On Board* site.

Project background

In 2005 a website was developed as an extension to a pan-European television advertising campaign for *Volvo*. On the site, a series of driver–passenger 'conversations', shown as snippets in the television commercials, were shown in full online. The conversations were unscripted, which allowed the dialogues to develop in a way rarely seen in a commercial. The short travelling conversations were so engaging that they *pulled* over a million viewers to *Volvo's* website, where the brand had more opportunity to convert interested viewers into *prospects*.

	04				05										
Timeline	S	O	N	D	J	F	M	A	M	J	J	A	S	O	N
Launch	☼														
Run		◎	◎	◎	◎	◎	◎	◎	◎	◎	◎	◎	◎	◎	◎>
Word-of-mouth/blogging						☺	☺	☺	☺	☺	☺	☺	☺	☺	☺
TV exposure		◎	◎	◎	◎		◎			◎		◎		◎	
Media exposure		--	--	--	--	--	--		--	--	--				
Hits (millions)							5		7		10			11	

Life on Board was a series of seven filmed conversations 'on board' a Volvo during a long car journey. Extracts were broadcast to draw viewers into watching the conversations in full as streamed narrowcast videos on the *Life On Board* site.

The films each featured two people who had never met before – people with extraordinary backgrounds and different ways of life. They meet and drive off in a *Volvo*, sharing car journeys in different parts of Europe. The hook is rooted in what then follows: more than just 'getting to know you' conversations, they talk about themselves, their lives, their achievements, and share experiences and touching, moving or funny moments. Conversations were varied and at times surprising, ranging from recollections of life experiences – in one case fighting sharks – to philosophical discussions on urban living and more banal themes such as snack foods. The people chosen were based on their affinity to the car – for example, in the *Volvo XC70*, a cross-country all-wheel-drive car built for adventure, two female athletes with interesting and dramatic backgrounds journeyed together.

The strategy of pulling television viewers across to the campaign website stemmed from research that showed that a third of UK car buyers did most of their research on the internet, rather than visiting dealerships. The target audience – Europeans aged 30–55 – were known to lead hectic lives, selectively watch television and want information 'on demand', so they were high users of the internet for information and entertainment. They were also known to do their own research rather than accept information pitched at them.

Therefore the campaign objective was to get people online, because once viewers were already on the site they were likely to view the rest of the site's content. Hence the *Life on Board* website was central to the campaign. It received traffic from the web link given at the end of the commercial, and aimed to divert it through the *Life on Board* films to information about the *Volvo* range.

The channelling process, from mass media to the website, used press, poster and Sunday supplement *sample mounts* to draw a wider target market through a communications mix of online, radio, in-flight entertainment, Bluetooth and 3D screens in *BA* lounges. This proved highly successful – the through-flow from broadcast media to the website was estimated to be nearly 60 per cent across Europe.

Creative direction

The short films operated as *teasers* to coax viewers onto the website. Once they were online, the full films were the reward for following up the link. Therefore the narratives, with their 'slice of life' philosophical discussions, needed to be captivating. The casting ensured this by pairing couples who have conversations 'in their own worlds', discussing issues, outlooks and their personal histories in a way that is unique to long-distance car journeys. Because the conversations are personal, others never usually get to hear them. So watching the films, viewers become voyeurs to private conversations, which make them intriguing to watch.

The website had to be constructed around the fact that people came to the site specifically to watch the short films. The layout was designed to make viewing the films very easy. *Volvo* product information was not pushed onto viewers, but featured as URL links to other pages on *Volvo's* site. Catalogues, product information and dealerships were all obtainable within one click from the *Life on Board* site.

The campaign used:

7 cars
14 passengers (of 10 different nationalities)
50 special guests
6 nations
2 continents
4 directors
141 crew members
3,662 kilometres
73 video cameras
18 shooting days
47 editing days
1,052 hours of videotape
1 photographer
7,680 photographs
11 mechanics
15 production vans

(source: prize-entry.com/volvo/epica)

Review

The campaign launched through a series of *teaser* commercials featuring vignettes of the *Life On Board* conversations, and a web address appeared in the *end frame*. This was followed by separate commercials for *Volvo* models. From then on, popularity snowballed through peer recommendation via word-of-mouth activity.

Two travellers chatting about the profound and incidental during *Life on Board* their *Volvo*: once on the website, viewers have options to scan the scenes in a more interactive way – and peruse other information on *Volvo's* website.

- The overall campaign message was that *Volvo* provides the security and comfort to relax and enjoy reflecting on life in cars. *Volvo* wanted to celebrate life in their vehicles through this documentary-style approach.
- The web was at the centre of the campaign, and all other media *pulled* people in to further engage them by creating intrigue.
- Once online, viewers could view the films interactively – they could flick through bookmarked content and read the background to the journeys through a variety of rich-text links. The site made watching the films more of a user-controlled experience, so viewers felt empowered to explore the site on their terms.

Integrated mix

proportion of campaign

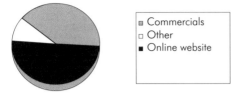

▣ Commercials
▢ Other
■ Online website

Essentials

1. The logic of the filtering process must be carefully devised before creative content. Once a through-flow from mass media to website is constructed, advertising agents can devise content that will *pull* viewers through.
2. Getting viewers online is a useful *call to action*, because once online there is more opportunity to engage with participatory consumers.
3. The 'slice of life' reality approach can be intriguing because it seems less contrived and conditioned to selling things. However, to work for a brand the context and casting have to connect clearly with the selling proposition.

For link see www.volvocars.it/_campaigns/LifeOnBoard.

Axe Lynx interactive fun

Product:	Unilever Axe Lynx deodorant for men
Target market:	men, 18–24 years old, global
Agency/city:	*Dare*, London
Planning/production time:	2 months
Reach:	global, over 10 million viewers
Length of customer engagement:	an average of 8 minutes 54 seconds
Brief:	be relevant to young style-conscious men, without being too precious
Budget:	£25,000
Lifespan:	from 2005, indefinite (non-self-liquidating)
Benchmark:	ease of involvement

A frame from the *axefeather.com* website, where the curser becomes a feather to tickle the model.

Project background

Dare, a London-based digital agency, were briefed to produce an online *viral* campaign, targeting 16–20-year-olds, for the internationally marketed deodorant *Axe Lynx* (*Unilever*).

The aim was to enhance *Axe's* existing market position, developed through several television and poster campaigns. Given that the target market was young men, the proposition was that *Axe* would make them attractive to women. The allure was that it would appeal to women in the right tone – sexy, but not sexual. Buzz words featured in the brief included *cheeky*, *light-hearted* and *playful*.

	04				05									
Timeline	S	O	N	D	J	F	M	A	M	J	J	A	S	O
Concept development	■	■	■	■										
Completed project				☼										
Launch					☼									
Word-of-mouth/blogging					☺	☺	☺	☺	☺					
Additional promotion					◉		◉		◉	◉				
Media exposure				--			--		--	--	--			
Hits (millions)				0.5	1	3	5	6			8			10

Television campaigns preceded the website by 18 months in the UK and had attracted wide press coverage. This was largely motivated by a witty narrative, distinct soundtrack (which went to the top of the UK singles chart) and much internet chatroom conversation.

The observation that led to the web-oriented approach was that the global target audience were the heaviest users of the internet, 18 per cent more than any other age segment. People in this age range were likely to use blog sites, text messaging and e-mail as an integral part of their social activity. This age range tended to surf the net on a daily basis, and edgy material – sexual, striking, interactive – tended to attract the most hits from 16–24-year-olds.

Axe Lynx was positioned similarly elsewhere in Europe and Asia, so a global web-based campaign was appropriate. However, it was distributed under the name *Axe*. So removing the pack shot prevented the site being specific to one country, and the use of both names together helped to reinforce that they were the same brand.

Being online provided several opportunities for customer engagement. *Prospects* could sign up and receive further *Axe* material, and a URL link could redirect viewers to another site featuring the entire *Axe* campaign – television commercials, screensavers and *virals*. The purpose of *axefeather* was to drive traffic to the main site, and web traffic was pushed from the site to the URL links.

Creative direction

The popularity of the website – over 10 million hits worldwide – hung on its simplicity. It was easy to grasp how the interactivity worked without instructions: the way the screens appeared made the operation self-evident. As the page downloaded, viewers saw a model lying prostrate on a bed, viewed from above, looking directly up at the user. The image occupied no more than one-fifth of the screen – easily fitting onto computer screens or Palm Pilots.

The curser turned into a feather and moved with the mouse. The feather/cursor became an extension of the user and the whole experience became very personal. Clicking on the model drew a titillating response, which encouraged consumers to play and test the programme. Of the 25 recorded reactions, some were repeated, some were rare. Hidden responses in the repertoire helped to maintain intrigue.

What made this site effective was that it fully utilized its medium. Rather than simply putting the ad online as a *QuickTime* movie, *Axefeather* pushes the medium by becoming a truly interactive experience. The curser is the user's route to interacting, and by turning it into a feather the user is dressed for role-play. The context is crucial. The figure lying prostrate on the bed is the only thing that emerges as the site downloads. The frame deliberately avoids making overt reference to *Axe* – no product branding appears on the screen; just a simple and discreet return link. This stops it operating like a disruptive commercial.

In terms of the tone of voice used, the agency assumed viewers were active brand-savvy consumers, smart enough to spot the connection between the game and the product's identity. *Axefeather* is offered as 'something cool' that viewers might like to share with friends. The message is that 'coolness' is brought to you by *Axe*.

The advertising works at this level, by imbuing the sense of play and sexiness. The brand is inextricably linked by virtue of the holding page's logo mast. When viewers exit the site, other downloads and campaign previews are offered, via website registration.

Review

The interactive film's art director spent one day registering on as many youth blog sites as possible, then introduced the *axefeather.com* link into conversations. By picking sites used by *early adopters*, awareness of the site spread by word-of-mouth, person to person. The message was circulated by others in the age group, so it was welcomed as shared entertainment and not an intrusive sales pitch.

First we had the idea: feather + tickling + girl = *Axe*. Then we examined the medium = internet and considered how the ad can use the medium to its full potential.

(Oliver Rabenschlag, the film's director)

One of the 25 reactions to discover when model Silvia Valcikova is tickled with the curser/'*axefeather*'.

- The interactive project subtly drew on the source of most online innovation, porn websites, to give the subject a voyeuristic edginess.
- A simple concept enabled the site to be constructed without complex programming, and the simple construction meant the site could be accessed through low-grade equipment.
- The soundtrack was not integral, so the site could be seen without need of a soundcard.
- The site did not pressurize the user to sign up for other *Axe* activities such as messaging services. As a non-committal site it made playing a pleasure and forwarding hassle-free.
- The juxtaposition of feather and model suggested how the site worked. The responses encouraged consumers to play and test the limits of the site.
- The site was gender-specific, but did not put women off. They engaged with the saucy tone of the humour, which stops short of being sexually explicit.

Integrated mix

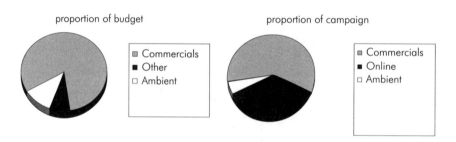

proportion of budget

□ Commercials
■ Other
□ Ambient

proportion of campaign

□ Commercials
■ Online
□ Ambient

Essentials

1. Examine the potential of the medium, rather than using other advertising formats as the basis.
2. Simplicity is the key to success. Try to limit the need for instructions. *Advertainment* should be easy to pick up through interaction.
3. As a general rule, designing for lower-grade equipment enables wider access. If possible, avoid requiring a soundcard.
4. Don't feel obliged to flag up the brand at every opportunity – let the content do the talking.

For link see www.axefeather.com.

Super Bonder live website

Product:	*Loctite Super Bonder* superglue
Target market:	men, 18–24 years old, global
Agency/city:	*DDB*/São Paulo, Brazil
Planning/production time:	2 months
Reach:	global, over 10 million viewers
Length of customer engagement:	an average of 8 minutes 54 seconds
Brief:	reinforce the message that *Super Bonder* 'sticks for real'
Budget:	undisclosed (estimated less than $5,000)
Lifespan:	31 May–1 October 2005
Benchmark:	website product demonstration

The website view of *Super Bonder* glue in action, on *superbonder.com*.

Project background

A website created for superglue *Super Bonder* in Brazil featured a live and continuous webcast for 24 hours a day, 365 days a year. The site showed the strength of *Super Bonder* by showing a computer monitor fixed to an office wall with the glue. The monitor was permanently on and, with a webcam fixed on the screen, beamed live images of the screen. Viewers could type and mail messages to feature on the monitor's screen, while additional links showed the monitor being installed and a counter displayed the length of time since the monitor was mounted to the wall.

When an office worker eventually bumped into the monitor, dislodging it from the wall, the agency publicized the break and rebooted interest in the stunt.

Timeline	05 J	F	M	A	M	J	J	A	S	O	N	06 D J
Concept development			■	■	■							
Completed project					✵							
Launch						✵	✵	✵	✵	✵		
Word-of-mouth/blogging						☺	☺	☺	☺	☺	☺	☺
Additional promotion						◙	◙					
Media exposure						--	--	--	--	--	--	-- --
Hits (millions)						0.5	1	3	6		10	

The interactive element, where viewers could post live messages to the screen, served to prove that the site ran in real time. The website's managers referred to the content as a 'reality show' because it was broadcast in real time, and generated the buzz of a live event. This gave viewers the opportunity to mess with the format. Personal messages and public jokes were posted on the screen, so the screen's content developed a following. Some used it as interactive entertainment while others used it as a chatroom, communicating through messages posted to the screen.

The simple idea underpinning *Super Bonder's* website made it worth revisiting once in a while. However, static content meant that unless viewers enjoyed playing with the format, they tended to spend little time on the site. The concept worked as a short-term proposition, and was not intended to establish a long-term customer base.

It was designed to last indefinitely. However, an office accident saw the monitor dislodged after 123 days, 11 hours and 31 minutes. As 1 million viewers had already visited the site, the broken monitor was itself newsworthy. *Super Bonder's* site celebrated the end by re-enacting the moment the monitor was dislodged. Photos of office staff reactions were also posted immediately after the incident.

Creative direction

The campaign used a conventional *product demonstration* strategy. At the forefront of the site was the project's purpose – to demonstrate the glue's strength. The concept's creative edge came from its ability to beam 'live' images. As the breakage demonstrated, with a live event anything could happen at any time. The site was therefore an ongoing real-time experience, which viewers could passively view or actively participate in.

Even the incident that dislodged the monitor was turned to promotional advantage. Text explained in detail why the bond failed to withstand the sudden impact, while diagrams showed the scale of force required to dislodge the monitor.

Review

Footage was filmed of preparations and installation of the monitor. Pre-publicity was word-of-mouth and when the site went live a link was added to explain the purpose of the site.

● Even though the timing of the monitor breaking was not pre-planned, by recording the event the advertisers were still able to manage the outcome. Pre-planning had therefore helped to capture appropriate film and photographic footage which was later used as an end point to the campaign.
● Live real-time content – *reality advertising* – maintained intrigue in the site.
● Creating interactive opportunities allowed viewers to exercise their own creative ideas on the site.
● Capturing much of the creative process on film gave the advertisers more material to work with during the project's lifespan.

How the website homepage appeared before and after the accident, which dislodged the computer.

Integrated mix

proportion of campaign

■ Online website
□ Blogging activity

Essentials

1. Established advertising methods still have a place in digital communications, as long as they are tailored to the new media.
2. Allowing for viewers to play with content encourages them to discover more.
3. Immediate, simple and visually led campaigns work internationally.

For link see http://infectous.plugin.com.br/reality.

Hasbro Monopoly Live

Product:	Monopoly Live
Target market:	internet users
Agency/city:	OMK London/Tribal DDB, DDB London
Reach:	190,000 people from 218 countries
Length of customer engagement:	varied – minutes or hours during the game's run
Brief:	after 70 years, to make Monopoly relevant for a younger audience
Budget:	£400,000
Lifespan:	28 days (between June and July) 2006
Benchmark:	blending real and virtual, on- and offline activity

Homepage to the *Monopoly Live* website and interactive game, which mixed online and offline activities in a real-time game of *Monopoly*.

Project background

The *Monopoly Live* campaign brought the launch of an updated version of the game to life by involving participants in real games, on- and offline. It created a buzz in the press and gave an absorbing flavour of what the game had to offer.

Billed as *The biggest Monopoly of all time*, the plan involved gamers online playing a 'real' version of *Monopoly* in real time on London roads, featuring real landmarks and using London black cabs moving around a *Here and Now Monopoly* board online. The game was free to play on a specially constructed *Monopoly* website, and the overall competition lasted 28 days. The promotion was designed for the 70th anniversary re-launch of *Hasbro Monopoly* and the final game provided a high point for *self-liquidation*.

	05				**06**										
Timeline	S	O	N	D	J	F	M	A	M	J	J	A	S	O	N
Concept development			■	■	■										
Completed project						■	■	■	■						
Launch										☼	☼				
Word-of-mouth/blogging										☺	☺	☺	☺		
Additional promotion										◉	◉				
Media exposure										--	--	--	--		

The concept attracted wide press coverage and participants globally. With the *Hasbro* central caricature and London cabbies involved, it opened up opportunities for *character migration* and revitalized the demand for the board game.

Prizes included weekend city breaks, and the overall winner received a year's worth of rent/mortgage payments. Cabbies involved were incentivized with a trip to Paris for the one that covered the most miles during the project.

How to play

Eighteen real black taxicabs working London routes doubled up as *Monopoly* playing-pieces as they went about their normal course of work. Cabs were kitted out with global positioning systems so that their exact location could be pinpointed as they conducted commuter rides around London. When a player's nominated cab passed a property on the board, it created the option to buy or make as much (virtual) money from rent as possible from five other players in the game. In other words, five cabs at one time performed the board moves while the online players conducted the business.

Objective

To start you on your way to becoming a property tycoon, we'll hand over £15m – there are three simple steps you must follow to set up your game.

1. Look over the options, then select which sets of properties, utilities or airports to invest your £15m in.
2. Distribute your seven apartments and two hotels across your properties.
3. Select your playing piece, and the cabbie you want to ride around town for you.

Once you're happy with your set-up, the game can begin! Each game lasts for 24 hours; use your £15 million wisely, as once the game starts it's all in the hands of the cabbies.

Profile: interactive strategy

The online game was launched to mark *Hasbro's* 70th anniversary edition of *Monopoly* during summer 2006, whereas most board games are launched for the peak Christmas games market. Consequently, there was no games market buzz elsewhere, to create the right environment for the re-launch. The campaign therefore needed to be self-sufficient and create its own buzz.

The aim of the website was to reintroduce consumers to the game through modern channels, which was appropriate because the game had been updated in many ways. The internet provided a contemporary platform and an opportunity to extend the game's central theme and characteristics, and for old and new players to get a flavour of *Monopoly*.

Preliminary research showed that people have great latent fondness for board games. Playing the games again unlocked their interest and excitement. The interactive online concept would familiarize players with new locations, and would give them a feel for the game. Being online would also produce a virtual community of *Monopoly* players as evangelists for the game.

By bringing the game to life with real cabs, real locations and webcams, the game had a 'real-life, real-time' edge to it. People could participate internationally, which broke new ground for a game's re-launch.

In the 28 days that the *Monopoly Live* competition ran, 190,000 people joined in and some 100,000 people opted to receive further contact from *Hasbro*. It was estimated that the project generated the equivalent of five times more publicity than the promotional budget. Sales of the board game rose dramatically. *Monopoly* became the third best selling game of 2005 during the four weeks that the competition ran.

Creative direction

The *advergame* captured the public imagination because of the *mash-up* between *Monopoly's* strong traditional identity and new digital technology formats. The branding of the online game reflected the strength of the game's branding by carrying the styling through to all web pages linked with the game.

The styling of the screens gave participants a reminiscent feel for the game even though it was on a modern medium. '*Monopoly* community' pages even poked gentle fun at the game's iconic characters by getting participants to *MMS*-message images of their own self-made versions. Weekly tasks were set for keen participants to produce images of new London *Monopoly* landmarks, *Monopoly* cab sightings and Hasbro's *Mr Monopoly*. Some of the web content was therefore created by participants, which made the social network community more interactive.

Review

The site was announced through television, national radio and a widespread online campaign, and was seeded on search engines. It was also presented as a news story, with the angle that the famous old game was rejuvenating its image.

> I think for things to be truly contagious they have to shock you in some way. The very idea of 18 taxis driving around London being pieces in a massive Monopoly game is definitely something that will get people to sit up and take notice.

(Matt Law, Account Director on the project, *Tribal DDB*)

Participants were asked to re-create and send in their versions of '*Mr Monopoly*'.

- The strategy made the promotion a real-time competition, and by using a competition format the campaign finished on a high note with a grand finale.
- The game was concise enough to be a classic 10-minute break-time activity, when people are most likely to surf the net and communicate with friends online.
- Taxis carried the branding of the game, so that participants had proof that the online game was real. The branded taxis also served as advertisements as they travelled around London.
- The site allowed a virtual community to develop. Aspects were created to allow active involvement.

Integrated mix

proportion of campaign

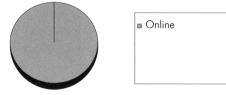

☐ Online

Essentials

1. *Advergames* are a useful device for encouraging *prospects* to participate. Their design must embrace the thing they've been created to represent. Ask what the content says about the brand.
2. Consider how online promotions are destined to 'self-liquidate'. The end point should finish on a high.
3. If the brand advertised has a strong identity, it is worth tapping into existing reputations as a starting point.

For link see www.monopolylive.com.

Singapore Airlines Boarding Pass Privileges

Product:	**Singapore Airlines**
Target market:	passengers across all travel classes
Agency/city:	*Squareroot Singapore*
Planning/production time:	yearly
Reach:	travellers and booking agents using the internet for travel
Length of customer engagement:	annually, started October 2005
Brief:	increase share by differentiating *Singapore Airlines'* offering from rivals and promoting *Boarding Pass Privileges*
Budget:	undisclosed
Lifespan:	2005–ongoing
Benchmark:	regional equity, through an exclusive 'brand extension' reward scheme

Boarding Pass Privileges scheme, styled as a unique extension of *Singapore Airlines* services.

Project background

Singapore Airlines' Boarding Pass Privileges (*SIA BPP*) is a campaign designed to enhance the overall travel experience for *SIA* passengers. However, in achieving this it has expanded the brand's identity as a gateway to South Asia, and developed its identity from business to leisure travel.

By simply presenting their boarding passes within seven days of their flight (at *BPP* partners' outlets), *SIA* passengers are able to access discounts and privileges across five categories – hotel, dining, shopping, tourist attractions and transport – in regions serviced by *SIA*. In 2006 over 400 local and international partners participated in the programme, which incorporated Singapore, Bali, Manila and Australia (among others). The scheme's success enabled it to expand in subsequent years and cater for a larger travellers' market, incorporating Malaysia and Bangkok. Furthermore, the strategy acknowledged that regional identity could distinguish the airline in a highly competitive market.

Timeline	05 J	J	A	S	O	N	D	06 J	F	M	A	M	J	J	A
Concept development	■	■	■												
Website development				■	■										
Launch of promotion				☼											
Launch of website				☼											
Press promotion					☺	☺	☺	☺	☺	☺	☺				
Hits (10,000s)					0.5	1	3	5			7			10	

The project identified areas in proximity to Singapore that have been regarded as attractive business destinations and potential tourist spots and sought facilities that would make the South Asia experience luxurious.

The promotion is run through the airline's overseas offices in conjunction with regional tourist boards and is used as a value-added additional service and a sales aid to attract new passengers. In essence, it differentiates *SIA* from its competitors via a series of exclusive offers. Passengers can review offers available through an online catalogue microsite, which resides on the official *SIA* website. On the microsite passengers can learn about the full range of offers provided by *SIA BPP* and access information on all participating merchants (with links to their websites). Designed with navigation ease and clarity, the microsite also allows passengers to zoom into privileges that they are most interested in. The offers and discounts of *SIA BPP* are categorized by genres – hotel, dining, shopping, tourist attractions and transport.

Creative direction

The creative direction on the *SIA* website centred on establishing the high-class quality of service and the added value the scheme afforded its passengers. The microsite was the central information point, giving *prospects* a chance to test the discount privileges by self-assembling travel packages through the scheme. The microsite's creative function was to develop the sense of exclusivity and the service's strong South Asian identity. Option bars and easy-to-read URL links kept the site's styling understated and made it easy to navigate.

Review

The website's launch was low-key. However, the microsite is now promoted through targeted public media and *SIA* proprietary media from in-flight video and magazine to the *SIA* e-ticket confirmation page.

The presentation of the website, the selection of mini-breaks and design of leisure packages all worked to position *Singapore Airlines Boarding Pass Privileges* as a high-end travel and leisure service.

- The *SIA BBP* scheme makes a virtue of the South-East Asian region's growing prosperity, although the scheme's future development is not programmed or planned for containment within South Asia only.
- The scheme reinforces in the minds of passengers the destinations covered by *SIA* services.
- The organization of the site underplayed its significance as an advertising proposition; instead the layout and functions offered made it appear as an online holiday brochure. This helped to foreground its expansion from travel into tourism and leisure.

Integrated mix

proportion of campaign

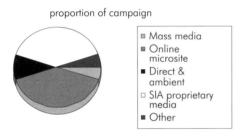

- Mass media
- Online microsite
- Direct & ambient
- SIA proprietary media
- Other

Essentials

1. When looking for *third party associations*, reflect on what the connection is aiming to achieve; will it reinforce regionality or demonstrate investment in your area of operation?
2. It is worth considering how the core business could be developed into related sectors through promotional activities.
3. When shaping an existing brand for a new segment of the market, consider what original contribution the service will make and what makes it distinct. Remember the old adage, 'if you can't be market leader in an existing market, devise a new one'.

For web link see www.singaporeair.com/boardingpass.

Sony Ericsson K750 photographic site

Product:	**Sony Ericsson K750 camera phone**
Target market:	25–55-years-old, looking for image-conscious experiences. They respond to peer endorsement and inspiration
Agency/city:	*Dare*, London
Planning/production time:	4 months
Reach:	over 3 million
Length of customer engagement:	average time on site over 6 minutes; 20,000 registered users and 300,000 votes cast on the uploaded images
Brief:	create an imaging experience that inspires the target audience to take their best shot with the *K750* – and share their images
Budget:	£120,000
Lifespan:	May 2005–May 2006
Benchmark:	product-inspired social network site

Project background

For the launch of the *Sony Ericsson K750*, digital advertising agency *Dare* was briefed to create an imaging experience that inspired the target audience. The strategy was to get customers to take their best shot with the phone/camera and share their images online. This would highlight the *K750's* fast auto-focus and a camera light, which produced good-quality spontaneous images compared to those given by other phone/cameras on the market. A website was created for *K750* users to upload their own best spontaneous 'snapshots of the moment', and top documentary photographer Martin Parr was commissioned to document his travels and upload 10 of his images to the site every week.

Parr's own weekly travelogue uploads became a spectacle in their own right. His journey with the *K750* took him round the world, and many viewers clicked onto the site to see the latest episode of his travelogue. While on the site, many went on to view the efforts of other *Sony Ericsson K750* users.

In the first two months over 2,000 images had been uploaded from around the world, so the range of settings, subjects and style of the shots varied enormously. However, the way uploaded images were framed on the website made them seem well composed: the design of the web pages made the shots look as though they were part of everyday life, with ordinary objects placed around each image, including the *K750* phone, serving as navigation buttons.

Renowned documentary photographer Martin Parr was commissioned to produce an image travelogue using the *Sony Ericsson K750* phone/camera. Shots were posted on a specially constructed site, and other users were invited to post their own shots.

The site was featured in numerous press articles, mostly because of the hook-up with Parr, which drew in excess of 694,000 visitors to the site within the first four weeks. Photographic competitions were held onsite, judged by Parr, which encouraged users to submit their own travelogue series of images (prizes were signed Martin Parr prints).

Timeline	04 S	O	N	D	05 J	F	M	A	M	J	J	A	S	O	N
Concept development				■	■	■	■	■							
Launch and run (online)									■	■	■	■	■	■	■>
Launch (mass media)									☼						
Media exposure									--	--	--	--	--	--	--
Hits (100,000s)									1	7				11	

It was exciting to view and judge the thousands of images submitted for the *Sony Ericsson K750* competition. The winning images all had some kind of story behind them, rather than providing a one-dimensional view of the world. I think this is apparent in the shots of the row of socks, and the man dozing while holding his advertising poster. These images told us something new and fresh and almost had a punchline. (Martin Parr)

Within the first year over 20,000 registered users were uploading images to the site, which kept the site fresh and interesting for those interested in documentary photography.

Profile: shaping the site to work for the product

Research revealed that *Sony Ericsson's* niche target audience was drawn to objects with status – things that would be understood by others as being top of their range. Therefore choosing a well-known documentary photographer that had featured in the Sunday supplement magazines and prestigious galleries gave the *K750* kudos with those 'in the know'. The target audience were also known to respond to high-quality goods that had proven technology: Martin Parr's posted images demonstrated that the 2-megapixel camera was good enough for a top photographer to achieve excellent shots. The idea behind the site was therefore to demonstrate what else could be achieved. It also set a participatory challenge for *K750* users: *Could they match the efforts of a top professional?*

Creative direction

Famed for making the ordinary look extraordinary, world renowned photographer Martin Parr shows you how its done with the 2 megapixel *K750*. Then it's your turn to see if you can capture something special. (*K750* site)

Having a *brand ambassador* like Martin Parr to champion the device *pulled* viewers to the site because his particular view of everyday life through his lens provided an intriguing spectacle. By being online Parr was easily able to upload images – as other users found – and his ability to produce images without post-production made his striking shots seem achievable by other photographers.

The design of the site reiterated the spontaneity of the images. Behind each uploaded image, images of *Post-it* notes, out-takes and location notes added to the sense that viewers were looking at reportage images of the everyday, as seen through creative eyes. The appearance of the site is workmanlike, as if it were the working studio of Parr himself.

The art direction is therefore intended to make professional-quality reportage photography seem possible with the *K750*. Viewers have both the equipment and online professional studio space to upload and display their best images alongside the best in the business.

Review

A number of broadsheet newspaper articles preceded the launch, mostly explaining how the Martin Parr travelogue would operate. Details of the site were included on in-store promotions, and details came with purchases of the *K750*. The volume of traffic that the site drew propelled it up search listings for photography, and the site also featured in reviews of new online innovations.

> The site remains one of the most successful consumer participation elements in online advertising.

> (Gavin Bell, Account Director, *Dare*)

- The idea for the site developed from the campaign line, *'take your best shot'*; it was reinforced by the idea of 'shot and send' and the competition, where users could take their best shot at winning.
- The site enables amateur photographers to compare their shots with those taken by one of the world's most renowned reportage photographers. His approach to composing shots inspired many others to adopt a similar approach. The resulting quality of the shots posted served to demonstrate what could be achieved with the camera phone's technology.
- The spread of interest in the *K750's* photographic facility created a distinguished market presence for the camera phone. As research had unearthed the target market's interest in objects of status, the online buzz helped reinforce the calibre of its technology.

Martin Parr posted images daily of his adventures with the *Sony Ericsson K750* phone/camera (top and centre). The phone's users were inspired to do likewise on what became a documentary photograph network site (bottom).

Integrated mix

proportion of campaign

- ▣ Commercials
- ■ Online
- □ Public relations
- ▣ Other

Essentials

1. Building opportunities for participation around a product's features helps to highlight what distinguishes them in their market. Commissioning an expert in the field to champion a product will give its reputation a boost by association.
2. Offering users guidance on achieving good results can open up a number of opportunities to demonstrate product advantages through demonstration. It also enhanced the user experience.
3. The styling of the site remains important – here, for example, the design of the site looked like a documentary photographer's table containing work in progress.

For links see http://www.daredigital.com/creativeshowcase_june05/ and http://www. sonyericsson.com/k750/.

Dove Campaign For Real Beauty

Product:	Dove (*Unilever*) Firming Range
Target market:	women, Europe (2004), later United States (2005)
Agency/city:	*Ogilvy UK*, London
Planning/production time:	8 months
Reach:	in excess of 200 million (after unpaid-for TV exposure); over 26 million people have viewed the site
Length of customer engagement:	varied, usually between 2 and 30 minutes
	Acquired multi-network coverage
Brief:	developed
Budget:	undisclosed
Lifespan:	launched 2004
Benchmark:	cause adoption – social network sites

Rather than professional models, *Dove's* 'tick box' poster campaign featured ordinary women and formed the basis of a wider campaign that challenged media conventions about beauty. This poster aimed to drive viewers to join the debate on the campaign's website.

Project background

The *Dove* 'campaign for real beauty' is often described as a manifesto campaign because it championed a bigger cause and took on a wider remit than advertising conventionally does. The manifesto campaign stemmed from a 12-page magazine insert put out in the Netherlands and Germany, which cast 'real' women rather than agency models. The approach extended through a 'tick box' poster campaign and finally into a bigger ambition – to achieve a socially responsible campaign.

	03				04										
Timeline	S	O	N	D	J	F	M	A	M	J	J	A	S	O	N
Concept development	■	■	■	■	■										
Completed project				■	■	■	■								
Launch							✻								
Word-of-mouth/blogging							☺	☺	☺	☺	☺	☺	☺	☺	☺>
Additional promotion							◙	◙	◙	◙	◙				
Media exposure							--	--	--	--	--	--	--	--	--
Hits (100,000s)							1	5	10		20			30	

Promotional campaigns for cosmetic products often stand accused of setting the wrong ideals for women, so *Dove's* approach offered a more fundamental attitude to beauty. The campaign's agenda sought distinction by directly challenging the fashion and beauty 'norm' and deliberately set out to provoke a debate on body shapes.

Open casting sessions were held to find women who were more representative of consumers. It wasn't just how they looked but their attitude to their appearance that mattered. Footage from the auditions was issued to champion the idea of celebrating 'real beauty'. The campaign was multimedia though initially driven through posters and press. However, online activity took the brand's engagement with beauty issues a stage further with discussion boards and a 'self-esteem fund' for young girls. Within the campaign, *Dove* could claim to be empowering women to realize their own beauty rather than aiming for an unattainable ideal. The self-esteem fund and an additional support service, *Body Talk*, was set to educate young girls in schools about the dangers of beauty myths.

The strategy was fuelled with insights from a survey of 3,200 women across 10 countries. Nine per cent considered themselves attractive while fewer, 2 per cent, thought of themselves as beautiful. Eighty-two per cent of 15–64-year-olds said they would like to change something about their appearance. It seemed that the advertising industries had presented unnaturally proportioned models as role models, which made most women to feel inadequate.

Profile: cause adoption

The *call to action* was to strike a blow for women's self-esteem. Where *Dove*'s new firming range would help women make the most of their natural beauty, the campaign would help them to find confidence in their own form. The online platform played a key part in developing this proposition through an active *Dove* interest network.

While the strategy was confrontational, the imagery used was more inviting. The women cast were made to look inherently beautiful in the images by renowned photographer Rankin, and their poses conveyed their sense of self-confidence.

Creative direction

At first glance *Dove*'s website seems like a typical group interest site: it contains facts and statistics about the proportion of women dissatisfied with their bodies. However, it goes much further in setting out the case that the fashion and beauty industries advertise unrealistic ideals. There are articles, quizzes to test self-esteem and educational packs to inform and empower women. A *blog* site allows women to convey their own dilemmas, and there are consultants to advise women on how to combat doubts about their self-image. The site also presents surveys *Dove* commissioned on global attitudes to beauty, which show that beauty ideals tend to be nationally specific.

Review

The campaign and website were launched in 2004. To agitate a debate the campaign orchestrated a snowball effect in the UK. First, *The Times* was given an exclusive of *Dove*'s approach and interviewed the women featured. Then London-based paper *The Evening Standard* covered the story by questioning the idea of female celebrity role models and ideal body forms. Next, a psychologist was enlisted by *Dove* and spoke on their behalf at forums to explain why women were uneasy about the use of fashion models in beauty advertising. The perspective was also publicized through a series of (unpaid-for) magazine and press editorials and daytime television. Behind-the-scenes footage of the auditions and photo shoots was made available to television networks. In terms of column inches, PR firm *Edleman* have estimated *Dove* became the most talked-about campaign in the world between 2004 and 2007.

We researched beauty advertising, women's attitudes to their body shapes, and which celebrity role models they most admired. We found that women felt intimidated and depressed by the prevalence of 'stick-thin' models. This gave us the insight we needed to launch a campaign women can relate to, and build a story for the media.

(*Unilever* website)

Models weigh an average of twenty-three per cent less than the average woman. Twenty years ago, models weighed an average of eight percent less.

(Part of press statement at *Campaign For Real Beauty* US press launch)

The line Campaign For Real Beauty was not just the call to action; it was the advertising strapline, the URL... and it was the 'Big Ideal'.

(Malc Poynton, Executive Creative Director, O&M London)

- The 'models' chosen for the posters and website drew on key beauty issues for women; whether large or flat-chested, wrinkles or freckles were beautiful. Each woman featured seemed happy to make a virtue of what for others might have been a 'stigma'.
- The campaign's strategy makes beauty seem more attainable. There is also a sense that buying the product is effectively casting a vote 'for real beauty'.
- It has been argued that the campaign still makes women buy into the need to improve themselves – you can be curvaceous as long as your skin is firm. While the campaign advertises beauty products, it also moves into a territory where it can bring together a community of people for whom the issue is important. *Dove's social network group* can help customers move beyond advertising norms while empowering *Dove* to challenge the status quo of beauty product promotions.
- The campaign ran globally, but websites are nationally specific and address localized issues of beauty. This type of global but localized campaign is often described as *glocal*.
- *Dove's* online activity has claimed ground for its holding company, *Unilever*, by demonstrating *corporate social responsibility* in its field of operation. *Dove* now has a platform for women to debate the pressures to conform and it has empowered *Dove* to operate as a lobbying platform. It has contributed to a moral and social concern and given *Dove* an opportunity to claim an issue that is appropriate for the brand.

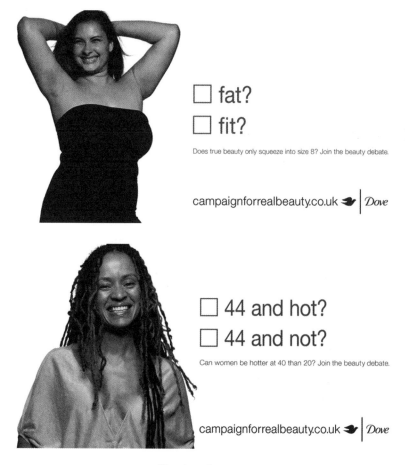

☐ fat?
☐ fit?

Does true beauty only squeeze into size 8? Join the beauty debate.

campaignforrealbeauty.co.uk 🐦 | *Dove*

☐ 44 and hot?
☐ 44 and not?

Can women be hotter at 40 than 20? Join the beauty debate.

campaignforrealbeauty.co.uk 🐦 | *Dove*

For too long,
beauty has been defined by narrow, stifling stereotypes.
You've told us it's time to change all that.
We agree.
Because we believe real beauty comes
in many shapes, sizes and ages.
It is why we started the Campaign for Real Beauty.
And why we hope you'll take part.

Welcome.

🐦 campaignforrealbeauty | *Dove*

Billboard images for *Dove's* UK *burst* campaign, which set the tone and directed viewers to *Dove's* web activities.

Integrated mix

proportion of campaign

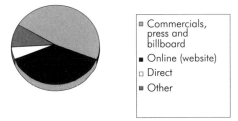

- Commercials, press and billboard
- Online (website)
- Direct
- Other

Essentials

1. Social network sites position brands at the centre of a subject. They require long-term commitment and a variety of other activities to maintain the relevance of their position.
2. Background research can be used to underpin a strategy during roll-out.
3. Advertisers need to have a qualitative understanding of their 'market community' to ensure that they are in a position to actively support an issue-led campaign.

For web links see www.campaignforrealbeauty.co.uk and www.campaignforrealbeauty.com.

PART 2

Context

7 The new media landscape

A profile of digital advertising platforms

Overview

In recent years customers have changed their viewing behaviour. Now it is the turn of marketing managers to change their promotional habits.

The advertising industry is expected to spend $1.9 billion on social networking sites in 2010, according to *eMarketer* (*Adage.com*). Presently this still represents a relatively small proportion of all future online advertising spend, but advertising through the internet is still in its early stages. This section addresses the new online advertising environment and considers what the impact of video streaming, personal web space and user-generated content will hold for advertising.

Explosion of social networking sites

Many media commentators predict advertisers will push the potential of digital communications. The most effective way of doing this so far has been either to tap into or to create online communities based around the interests of internet users. If products can appeal to people through their interests, people are likely to connect its relevance to them. Therefore effective online advertising has so far been based around making spaces on the world wide web that people *want* to see. Websites, search engines, uploads, *podcasts* and *virals* are (in 2007) the most prominent formats attracting the attention of digital advertising departments.

The objective is to *pull* interested parties into websites and get them involved with the themes, culture and ultimately the brand. Some of the first pioneering adverts of this genre are featured in chapters 5 and 6. Communication analysts believe online communities are having an incalculable impact on strategies for reaching newly empowered consumers. In the past, broadcasters could rely on guaranteed traffic – viewers and passers-by – to push information at: fixed, homogeneous audiences are no longer reachable through mainstream media on the scale that they once were. Now consumers are selectors. Through the plethora of media channels they are able to locate and indulge their own interests.

In one sense this has empowered customers. In practice it has forced successful brands to identify their core values and those of their audience to establish a range of activities around shared beliefs, reference points and social outlooks.

Broadcasting remodelled as narrow reeling

> We are dedicated to the production of new, innovative and exciting TV formats that can be replicated all over the world. It was an obvious next step for us to promote the growing market of MP3 and ringtone downloads. In order to maintain our position at the forefront of the interactive broadcasting space, we will be extending our relationship with *Opera Telecom* to incorporate mobile and telephony interactivity into future programme formats. (Morgan Holt, former Interactive Director of television production house *Endermol* and Executive Producer of the *Orange Playlist* (see chapter 3))

The medium with the biggest potential audience reach, TV broadcasting, has found that technology enabled it to develop offshoot channels to develop niche interest packages and, importantly, advertising opportunities. Offshoot programmes have the advantage of using material that would otherwise be edited out, so there is less wastage of recorded material. This is being used to offset huge declines in television audiences.

In the days of homogeneous mass television viewing, broadcasters could simply rely on millions of consumers sitting down to watch TV shows. Audiences were relatively captive. Entertainment has evolved dramatically in the past decades and the TV is just one in a long line of options available to consumers. As the introduction noted, technology has brought on a new range of digital channels via cable and satellite, the internet, multimedia mobile devices as well as PVR (personal video recorders) services such as *TiVo* (United States, Europe) and *SkyPlus* (UK, Europe) where consumers can get '*video on demand*' (VOD). The latter is having a significant impact on the TV business model as it enables viewers to skip past ads and record programmes for viewing at a later date. The waiting time that was occupied by adverts is now being fast-forwarded.

> About 7 million people watch television programmes on their PCs and laptops via broadband or on their mobile phone, up 37% since March 2006. (ICM research/UK 2006)

In 2005 a huge buzz in broadcast circles surrounded the arrival of web video technology. This has coincided with the mass roll-out of broadband in households globally. This has enabled brands from all areas of the entertainment spectrum to provide consumers with web video, not least broadcasters. As mainstream peak-time viewing has moved towards reality and consumer-created content, in much the same way broadcasters have also moved quickly to exploit digital TV. They are now moving to reach a mass of niche audiences online through the development of online channels, more often than not on a small budget. Content includes anything from complete shows to clips and extra footage that didn't make a show's original cut and a menu of programs for on-demand selection.

This has effectively rejuvenated 'free to air' terrestrial television. Many had thought that commercial television was in decline because the money underpinning its tremendous costs might desert it for new media before the mass audience does. All around the world – even in territories where digital growth has been contained by powerful media owners – advertisers have realized that the 30-second television commercial is delivering only a fraction of what it did in 2000. By reshaping formats, television programmes have managed to become multi-platform offerings: the main broadcast is the *pull* for audiences, and flow is managed to smaller niche viewing markets. Internationally franchised reality shows such as *Survivor*, *Big Brother* (both 2000) and *Pop Idol* (2001) created content that could be sliced in a number of ways to provide spin-off programmes or extensions using original viewing content for broadcast, digital and many other channels.

Extended formats and revenue opportunities in the *X-Factor* franchise

1. *X-Factor* – core TV programme: broadcast mainstream, primetime
2. Programme sponsorship
3. In-programme sponsorship (national legislation allowing)
4. *Xtra Factor* – behind-the-scenes interviews, unseen footage and replays; also sponsored
5. Phone lines (premium rate) for phone and text votes
6. Website involvement: competitions and merchandise
7. Spin-off show reviewing performances, featuring clips and extra footage
8. *X-Factor Live* performance tour (finalists also operate as brand guardians)
9. Music put out/tour merchandise
10. International *X-Factor* and other seasonal/celebrity specials.

Consumers are empowered

The vast choice of content to *snack* on – from advertising, films, TV programmes, books, magazines, music and gaming to the whole plethora of internet resources – has enabled consumers to 'cherry-pick' entertainment and information that is relevant to them, in a way and at the time that suits them. Furthermore, it empowers them to cut out what's irrelevant to them. This runs counter to perceived wisdom on advertising (Dru, 1996).

Compared to earlier writings on advertising, time is now more highly recognized as a relatively scarce and precious commodity. Attention spans are shorter, the ability to obtain immediate gratification is available and, like fast food, fast entertainment provides comfort. Even information is prioritized for brevity viewing on the most successful websites, *Google* and *Yahoo!*. Hence consumers will seek out the media that give them the best return on their time invested. Since the arrival in 2006 of *YouTube.com* – a video-sharing website that claims to stream 100 million video clips a day – broadcasters as well as other media players have realized the potential of web video to improve the consumer experience online and are investing in this area with much vigour.

Revised broadcast model

- *Adopting a multi-platform model* – traditional TV broadcasters have extended their brands into niche and narrowcast platforms. Most immediate have been digital TV, the internet and additional content put out through mobile devices (3G cellphones, video *podcasts*). Some have been more adventurous than others. For instance, UK terrestrial broadcaster *Channel 4* has extended its remit to encompass a user-generated channel (*FourDocs*) and is launching into digital radio in 2007. The *BBC* broadcast behemoth also recently announced that '360-degree multi-platform content creation' would form part of its future strategy. In the United States, in the latest round of up-front advertising selling – where broadcasters pitch to advertisers – the emphasis has shifted towards broadcasters' honed online platforms, underlining the importance of digital to the modern broadcast model. Such media might not have the reach of conventional platforms but they are capable of building stronger and longer-lasting bonds with customers.
- *Targeting niche audiences* – as a key part of digital strategies, broadcasters are launching more channels for niche audiences. This gives depth to marginal interest groups because interaction allows members to contribute their own content for specialist sites. Brand-funded niche platforms create opportunities to pool and consolidate interest groups, so brands can 'claim' the territory that they operate in by being seen to support it.
- *New broadcast competitors* – Moving into new channels brings with it new competitors:
  - There are hundreds of digital channels on cable and satellite services. Online, there is a vast raft of content seeking to 'entertain'. Search companies such as *MSN*, *Google* and *Yahoo Inc.* now buy programming and have emerged as online video destinations in their own right. Online-only broadcast brands are growing in number, often involving significant consumer input. Examples are *Current TV*, *Rocketboom.com* and *MTV Flux*.

- Newspapers and magazines are also investing heavily in audio-visual editorial content. Many now tell their stories and dispatch news bundles in a traditional pay-as-you-watch 'broadcast' way. In many cases online 'sister' publications offer rolling news to the in-depth reviews provided by published journals. Trade magazines such as *Campaign* (*Haymarket Publications*) and its digital off-shoot *Brand Republic* operate this way.
- Social networking and community sites (two examples, *YouTube* and *MySpace*, are discussed in chapter 1) have become one of the biggest threats to established information-*push* broadcasters, since they attract customers at the customers' time of choosing in their millions. US TV network *NBC* collaborated with *YouTube.com* to generate their own channel of content on the *YouTube* website. Some programme makers are leveraging their content and distributing direct to consumers. This takes online business to customer (B2C) communication a stage further as an established mass-advertising practice (see chapter 9).

- *Shift to higher quality standards* – broadcasters are raising the stakes in quality through high definition (HD) programming. Although still in its early stages, HD is starting to feature in audio-visual programming – notably in documentary features. Long term, it will be key to raising the quality of the consumer experience, standing out in a competitive environment.
- *VOD* (*video on demand*) – according to the *BBC*, on-demand represents the third age of broadcasting and the second phase of digital, giving audiences far greater control, personalization and interaction with the media they choose to view. Long term, it is seen by some as a key means of retaining customer loyalty. The art will be in maintaining relevance across a span of activity in all media, by communicating with individuals en masse.
- *Mobile TV* – trials are taking place in many countries as penetration of 3G (video-enabling) phones and video iPods increases. In 2006 most consumer research suggests that watching TV on mobile phones is not something consumers are keen on, but with better convergent portable technology, that could easily change.

Summarizing the modern broadcast model

- There are a greater number of broadcast channels available as a result of digital exploitation requiring greater volumes of video/film content.
- Consumers have different expectations and experiences with TV, mobile and the internet so content must be tailored accordingly, eg exclusive, unseen footage often posted online with programme trailers; *mobisodes* being created for mobile devices.
- Speed of content delivery has increased – the internet and VOD enable content to be accessed instantaneously and updated on a frequent basis.

Lessons

- Social network sites provide a focused target audience, who are likely to spend longer than broadcast audiences in browsing material of interest.
- Far from becoming redundant in the digital age, broadcast video production methods are in high demand for a wide range on online platforms. In effect, broadcast has been remodelled as narrow reeling.
- With broadcast media the strategy was to *push* information at audiences offline. With digital media the aim is to *pull* customers towards information online. Now push and pull methods tend to be used in conjunction through multi-media programming and advertising.
- Online there is a large volume of material seeking to entertain, because entertainment attracts large volumes of web traffic and makes sites an attractive venue for advertisers.
- Online entertainment, interest and social network sites are accessed at customers' time of choosing, so the way online advertising is received is less contained than fixed schedule broadcast advertising

Sources: Suzie Shore, Adverblog.com; paidcontent.org; Brand Republic; mad.co.uk; Interactive Advertising Bureau (iab.co.uk); Adage.com; BBC Creative Future document April 2006/Design Week; silicon.com, Shoot, Televisual.

8 The new job landscape

Job profiles

Overview

Advertising outside conventional media has led to the emergence of many new roles within the advertising profession. In the past decade, a rapid growth in digital messaging and direct marketing has led to the emergence of new advertising specialisms: the main new roles are outlined in this chapter. Also profiled are some of the more intriguing new 'jobs' within advertising, from people that make sure the right customers get to know about online advertisements to those whose job it is to be the human embodiment of products. This section maps the 'new territories' and jobs that have emerged in the 'media neutral' (multimedia) advertising industries.

At the end of the chapter there is a summary of new roles, listing the new types of advertising work and expertise required.

Data planner
Brand planner
Media planner
Customer insight specialist
Creative thinkers
Technologists
Project managers

Adweek's agency team of the future (Source: *Adweek*)

The old job landscape (in a nutshell)

Over the 70 years that advertising agencies have operated as a recognized industry, the recruitment profile has not varied greatly. The task of managing accounts has generally taken people from backgrounds in business and marketing, while creative roles have been recruited from a range of arts and classics backgrounds. In fact, it is possible to gauge the make-up of creative teams by the approaches to advertising that emerged in different periods.

Changes in approach to creative advertising

Practitioners' background:	When:	Defined by:	Example:
Military	1935–65	instructional messages, USP	*Guinness* for strength (UK, *SH Benson*)
Classics at university	1960–80	references to Greek, Latin and Classics	*Fiat Strada* Hand-built by robots (UK, *CDP*)
Art school-trained	1975–95	emphasis on visual over text	*Benson & Hedges* Pyramids (UK, *CDP*)
Advertising specialists	1990–today	emphasis on method and diversity	*KFC* Subservient Chicken (US, *CPB*)

After the Second World War many people came into advertising from the military, and the instructional tone of war posters carried across to promote brands. During the 1960s, when the roles of art director and copywriter were first established (at *DDB*, New York), creative teams often worked to balance the elements of visual and verbal persuasion. As the art developed at *DDB*, creative teams became more adept at integrating and juxtaposing copy messages with imagery, and the set-up transferred to other agencies. Advertising messages typically made definitive claims for brands – such as *beenz meanz Heinz* or *Guinness for strength* – or gave concise directions to consumers – *Go to work on an egg*. These were extensions of war-era public statements such as *Careless Talk Costs Lives* and *Dig For Victory*.

This message-driven approach endured until a wave of university graduates, most of whom had graduated from arts disciplines, discovered that their repertoire of historical and cultural references would often equate the identity of brands to levels of mythical esteem. Car and product brands such as *Allegro* and *Opera* bore references to Latin, while many popular films gave creative teams licence to tap into their audience's collective memory and evoke classics of literature in adverts for, among others, ice cream brand *Cornetto* and fizzy drinks manufacturer *Schweppes*.

From the late 1970s advertising agencies started to employ young staff with art school training because they had visual language skills. The emphasis in adverts moved from making product claims to creating visual associations. The relationship between art direction and copywriting grew as an interlocking craft, and typically consumers were presented with a visual seduction or visual challenge. The most prominent examples were campaigns for cigarette brands *Benson & Hedges* and *Silk Cut*, which were in response to tight legislation governing tobacco advertising, and a series of nostalgia-evoking campaigns for *Levi's*.

Graduates trained in creative advertising started to emerge from specialist advertising courses during the early 1990s, and characteristically applied skills synonymous with media advertising to new modes of communication as fresh media platforms emerged during the decade.

In terms of the current set-up of agencies, the wave of agencies established between the late 1950s and late 1980s tend to bear the names of the collaborative team that founded the firms. Typically this contained a combination of creative, financial director and strategist:

- Doyle (business) Dane (administration, finance, PR) Bernbach (creative)
- Crispin (business) Porter (planning) + Bogusky (creative)
- Boasse (business) Massimi (creative) Pollitt (planner)
- Bartle (planning and business) Bogle (account manager and planning) Hegarty (creative)
- Abbott (planner) Mead (business) Vickers (creative).

Account planning is said to have originated in Madison Avenue, New York, during the late 1960s and was characterized as a manipulative art (Packard, 1957) or a social science (Reeves, 1960), depending on the perspective. The role of account planner developed into a job function in London, and operates in the majority of large London advertising agencies. Stanley Pollitt (1965) is most often acknowledged as being the first to use data to underpin strategy; researchers had not previously been involved in making advertising decisions. In 1968 *J. Walter Thompson* introduced an Account Planning department, as did the newly formed *Boasse Massimi Pollitt*.

Today, with far more qualitative and qualitative data available from an increasing number of sources, account planning tends to be split into niche tasks. For instance, at *WWAV Rapp Collins* planners specialize in one of three areas: **Brand**, **Media** or **Consumer Planning**.

Why new jobs have been generated

As the case studies in this book demonstrate, the scale and range of activities encompassed by advertising have grown significantly since the late 1990s. However, the many new types of media still require the application of established advertising practices. The creative skills of art direction, copywriting, planning and creative direction are still required, as are the logistical roles of account managing and space buying for new types of on- and offline advertising. Nevertheless, as new approaches to advertising took shape, new roles emerged that filled holes in the old set of advertising processes.

It is worth noting that with so many types of media now used for advertising, campaign launches – called *burst campaigns* – tend to use a wide variety of media and a range of advertising types simultaneously to make sure that *prospects* are reached with the campaign message. In broad terms, direct advertising can address customers by name, while mass-media advertising targets by broader demographic groupings. Both methods are used still to guarantee customer awareness. This usually requires the core idea and treatment to be consistent through all aspects of the campaign, in every medium.

In visiting a modern agency therefore, you will find a mix of media-specific and cross-disciplinary roles. The working culture of each agency is mostly character-ized by the dynamics of working relationships and the personalities of employees.

New business

While planners, creative directors and 'suits' (management, such as account handlers) tend to be involved in negations before and during *pitch* processes, the position of winning new business has become a more specialist role as the compet-itive communications market has broadened.

New Business managers look for opportunities to win fresh business for their agency. They have to stay abreast of brand *rosters* and accounts put out to tender, by being actively involved in advertising networks. This involves scanning the advertising press and cold calling. New Business managers organize meetings and events to meet with prospective clients, present the agency's credentials and explore work opportunities. Therefore their work involves researching the client and spotting pitch opportunities.

While the role of New Business is not new, the functions of the New Business department have become more significant as the field of communications has expanded in recent years. The New Business department has effectively become the 'sales department' of an agency (or, advertising the advertisers). Sales in the marketing industry is not yet a concept that sits comfortably, but the more modern agencies have come to understand the importance of having a well-orchestrated approach to New Business throughout the advertising process.

The creative process: stages in multi-platform agency, from brief to final output

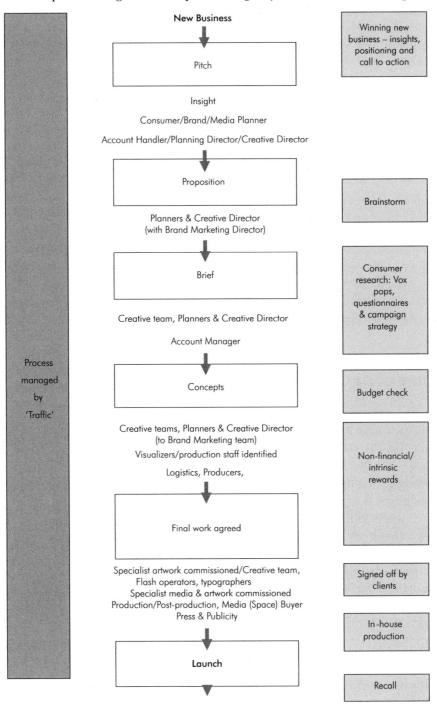

Source: Paul Springer with Ian Howorth, *WWAV Rapp Collins* and MA Advertising, *BCUC* 2006

Liz Childerley, New Business Director, *WWAV Rapp Collins*

Liz is the main liaison and initial point of contact with clients in a large multi-media advertising agency. She develops contacts with prospect companies and nurtures the through-flow of new work through the range of services offered by *WWAV Rapp Collins*. She sees her role as integral to the smooth running of the advertising process.

'The agencies that do not equip themselves with such a department suffer from the "start, stop" effect. For instance, if a situation arises when an agency has three pitches in close proximity, all their lead generation and ongoing dialogue goes out of the window – all that hard work – and they have to start over with relationship building.' Liz estimates that clients are inundated with at least 50 calls from agencies per week. Brands tell her that it is the agencies that have a genuine and consistent passion for that clients' business that get cut through – which is why the role of New Business requires specialist business-to-business relationship-building skills. 'My role is often described as being a "charming thug" – I need to build relationships, but I also have to have the tenacity and persistence that ensure my agency stays in the frame at all times. I also see my role as the custodian of the clients the agency doesn't yet have. It's just a matter of time…'

Roles that are intimate to the customer and brand

The emergence of direct marketing in the late 1970s created new opportunities for employment because direct marketing needed more precise information on customers than was used in media advertising. Many of the new roles that emerged were in managing quantitative data and turning them into qualitative analysis. As the ability to capture customer information improved with technology from the late 1980s, so data collections required expert data evaluators. As the role of data analysts developed, the link between analysing information and producing advertising strategies became seen as less of an art and more of a social science, as segmenting target markets became more critical to a company's success.

As the following headings indicate, there are now a series of new titles commonly used across the direct advertising industries that describe the different roles required for different types of campaign.

Business-to-customer (B2C)

Business-to-customer promotions is the term applied to a situation where mailers of any sort are sent on behalf of brands directly to consumers. For many years this has most commonly taken the form of direct mail, but more recently it has also encompassed *new media* such as e-mail and *SMS* text.

Tasks of the New Business director

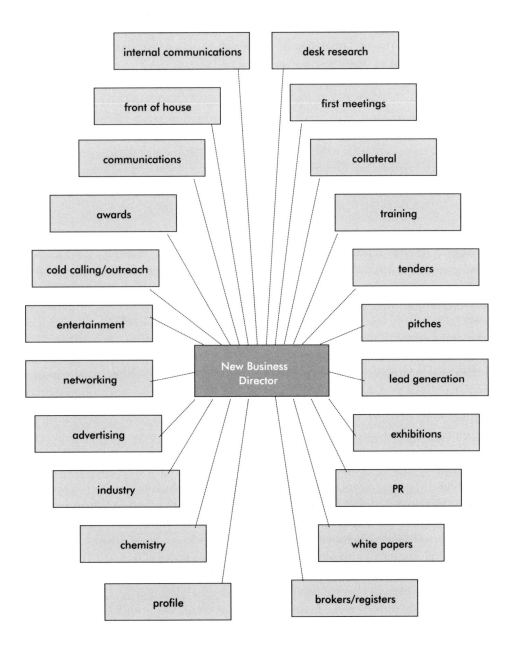

Source: Liz Childerley

Anyone texting or mailing a prospect on behalf of a brand requires briefing notes and a detailed background of both brand and target customer. Producing such material is a specialist role in itself. Similarly, an advertising planning team needs background information on *prospects* with which to plan a tactical strategy. The role of researching these customers is usually called Insight.

Insight themes at *Archibald Ingall Stretton* advertising, London (source: *AIS London*)

Insight staff research and analyse information on target markets. Information often takes the form of statistical data or lifestyle surveys. Often the work involves researchers putting themselves in the position of the consumer and locating the sort of interests they may have – websites they may visit, activities they may be involved with and issues that may raise their curiosity. The aim of the research is to pinpoint a series of unique customer insights in order to define what moves their target audience and would motivate them to respond.

Practical information and observations from the Insight team are usually passed on to a planning team who use the information as the basis for the development of a tactical strategy. This in turn is written into a design brief for the creative team to work on and put to the client for consideration. Therefore the role of Insight is to use qualitative research methods to monitor customer behaviour and provide a profile of target audiences' characteristics.

Suzie Shore, Customer Insight Manager, *Getty Images*

Getty Images is the world's leading provider of imagery, film and digital services. It creates and distributes imagery collections from contemporary creative imagery to news, sports, entertainment and archival imagery. Products can be found each day across the full range of traditional and digital media worldwide. As Customer Insight Manager at *Getty Images*, Suzie tracks trends from a plethora of global media and industry sources to identify the social, economic, technological and industry-specific factors underpinning the development of the advertising, entertainment and media landscapes.

'My role is about understanding how our customers' businesses are changing, the external issues they face within their industry and then using this knowledge to help *Getty Images* identify how we can better meet customer's imagery needs today and in the future.'

Customer-to-customer (C2C)

The role of customer-to-customer advertising has only recently developed as a fully fledged advertising tool for both direct and online media. There are many historical precedents of direct selling – most famously for *Tupperware* in the United States from the 1950s, where regional agents presented product ranges to their friends in a party gathering environment (now done successfully by lingerie distributors like *Ann Summers*).

However, C2C no longer requires gatherings but people with a bond with the brand who are willing to testify to its virtues to friends. In online advertising they aim to enlist the most influential of consumers, the *early adopters* who are quick to discover and adopt fashionable brands and the best consumer goods available. They are chosen because they are seen as taste-makers, able to influence friends and colleagues because they are regarded as filters for current tastes and trends.

> **Advertisers work on the basis that 1 person in 10 influences the tastes and choices of the others. It is assumed that late adapters tend to follow the recommendations of early adopters.**

The internet is (again) providing new opportunities for C2C selling. Many personal product experiences are recounted on *blog* and distribution sites – it is even a key feature on *Amazon* and *eBay*. More recently, *user-generated content* has brought (as yet uncontained) publicity to a number of brands such as those described in chapter 1. Customer researchers, Insight or planners are often charged with finding appropriate people for brands to adopt. Researchers tend to scan *blog* sites and web pages to find personal web spaces worth sponsoring.

Much of the creative C2C work involves providing briefing packs and defining criteria for appropriate selection of customers. In some respects this is more the work of planning departments, but creative insights can help channel the approach consumers take to representing sponsoring brands.

Business-to-business (B2B)

Creative work for B2B advertising usually involves smaller volumes of correspondence but there can be a bigger budget per head, so creative output tends to be more exclusive. Pharmaceutical goods and service contracts tend to use B2B methods. For this type of work, most of the advertising work is around devising a strategy and researching the target market. Therefore the roles of Insight and account planning tend to be heavily utilized.

> **B2B advertising usually aims to establish an ongoing dialogue with known customers and prospects.**

As the target market for B2B is tightly defined, samples or trial runs tend to be included. The aim is usually to create channels to open up opportunities for dialogue, so B2B advertising is usually designed to be layered, and is as likely to involve events organization as it is the production of printed advertising materials.

Layering communication

According to Mark Allnut of planning firm *Naked Inside*, there are four layers of communication:

> Media advertising is one-way and shouts at the consumer. Direct response attempts to generate a two-way dialogue, face to face. The third dimension is involvement, where brands take on a broader cultural role to assume ownership of their territory. The fourth dimension is brand advocacy. It relies on customers selling to other customers.

Allnut believes that digital technology is driving advertising towards diversification. It has enabled the rapid growth of more broadcast channels, internet chatrooms, *blog* sites and personal electronic mailboxes. The advertising industry has quickly learnt how to adapt these channels for commercial communication. The world wide web also allowed new modes of trading to emerge such as *eBay* and *amazon*, where customers could exercise their powers to discover more about goods on offer. The internet gave customers the ability to research products, brands and services more thoroughly. Therefore it could be argued that the role of **planning** is now more integral to the advertising process than before.

Mark Allnutt, Director and Planner, *Naked Communications*

Naked are a planning firm that map out potential media environments and traffic hot spots for advertising agencies. Rather than being part of just one agency, *Naked* work across several creative firms and offer strategic insights to creative teams.

'At *Naked* we have devised methods and promotions territories that help creatives to think beyond the message, to how it is going to be received. The target consumer's mood must be right if a promotion is to be noticed – let alone work. My work involves researching, reading and thinking around the subject to come up with fresh approaches.'

Brand consultants

Law & Kenneth is one of a breed of collectives that work as advisory agents to brands and describe themselves in broad terms as **brand strategists**. *Law & Kenneth* is run by two advertising industry luminaries, former advertising group CEOs Andy Law (ex-*St Lukes*) and Praveen Kenneth (ex-*Publicis*). In their smaller firm they have more flexibility to operate in a variety of capacities for their clients, including roles as brand strategists, project planning advisers and networkers.

Law & Kenneth has an impressive list of advisers that includes well-known businesspeople, academics and musicians. They have developed bases in Dubai, Australia, the United States, Paris, Sweden and the UK and plan to develop their base in other countries through acquisition of independent firms.

The collective experiences of the group in managing advertising processes globally, their range of contacts and their years of experience in the industry make them a valuable bank of experience to corporations. They aim to operate in eight key markets around the world by offering a full spectrum of marketing services, which include:

- global and local creative solutions;
- breakthrough brand and corporate strategy;
- modern marketing, communications and brand auditing;
- brand innovation (how to reposition to define a unique niche position);
- solutions in new media, including *ambient* and *viral* communication;
- assessment on return of ideas (determining the market potential of a concept).

Andy Law, Founder and Director, *Law & Kenneth Global*

Andy's role requires him to look at the bigger picture of advertising and consider how brands want to develop in meeting short-, mid- and long-term objectives. In a climate where the worth of a brand is in its perceived strength of identity, Andy researches the context in which brands will move to assess the risk and potential of growing in defined markets.

'When we set up *Law & Kenneth* we asked one simple question: Why are clients receiving the same creative services, in the same way, from the same organizational models as 50 years ago; why hasn't the creative communication business innovated itself like its clients have? Our clients have changed so we've modelled our operation to meet new bigger and global needs.'

The span of activities described above is similar in that they involve the management and movement of ideas. Co-founder Andy Law describes their operation loosely as a 'global creative firm': Praveen Kenneth describes the company's role as one of facilitation: 'We believe in the power of building brands and businesses by empowering local market leaders to drive their own businesses.'

In an age when there are so many avenues to communicate through but too many to get noticed by target audiences, risk management and guaranteeing a return on advertising investment are harder to predict without specialist help – which is where senior advertising experience is often sought, mostly by large corporations.

Digital advertising agencies

Every year since 2000 the amount spent by agencies developing the potential of online advertising has risen by more than 60 per cent. As a result, opportunities to specialize in digital advertising have increased, but the skills required have become significantly more specialized.

There are also a number of job titles that are commonly used across the digital advertising sector. As a platform for mass communications, digital advertising is still in its first generation; consequently digital advertising practices vary greatly between agencies. However, some specific roles have started to be commonly recognized across the advertising industry.

Ajaz Ahmed, Co-founder & Chairman, *AKQA* global interactive agency

Ajaz's advertising, marketing and design work exclusively involves digital media. *AKQA* fuse creative ideas with broad and narrowcast digital technology to create websites, *virals* and digital spaces. Their work allows brands to promote themselves and develop their identities though online activities.

'In creating effective online communications, our designers need to imagine themselves as the end users and consider what really motivates them to find out more and play with content. If the content is not intriguing, people will go off and find more interesting things online.'

In effect, the structure of digital advertising agencies tends to divide into three clear job types:

Standard groupings in a digital agency

Account services	Creative services	Technical services
programme manager	designers	Flash programmers
producers	creative directors	creative developers
account handlers	copy and content	content management

Interactive agency *AKQA's* organizational plan highlights the specific tasks required of firms whose work is based around online communications.

Digital planning

The role of online **media planning** has become significant because it helps to tailor advertising briefs directed at all media around the capabilities of digital technology. Planners for online advertising define the characteristics of a brief that can

Digital Media team structure

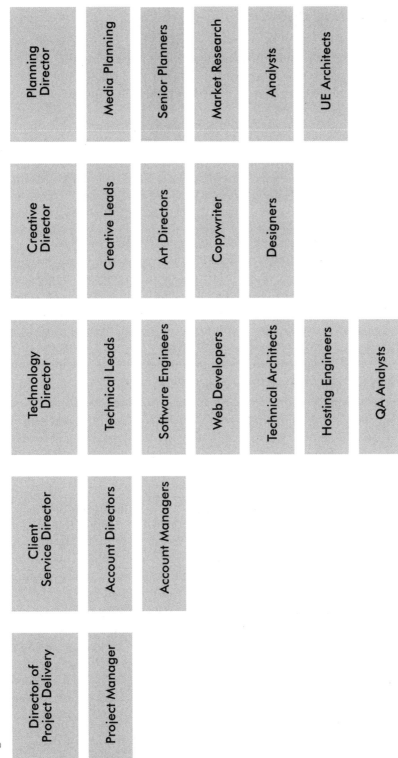

Director of Project Delivery
— Project Manager

Client Service Director
— Account Directors
— Account Managers

Technology Director
— Technical Leads
— Software Engineers
— Web Developers
— Technical Architects
— Hosting Engineers
— QA Analysts

Creative Director
— Creative Leads
— Art Directors
— Copywriter
— Designers

Planning Director
— Media Planning
— Senior Planners
— Market Research
— Analysts
— UE Architects

Source: AKQA, London

be best served digitally and need to consider how clients' needs can be best served through digital channels. Whether it involves customers discovering a brand through a website or *viral*, or whether customers are targeted through personal digital contacts via e-mail or *SMS* text, online media planners have the job of defining which digital opportunities are appropriate to circumstances presented in a brief.

Digital media planner/buyer

The right candidate will need to demonstrate excellence in strategic thinking, commercial nous, creative thinking and efficiency. Time management, prioritiza- tion, proactivity and media and budget control are also all buzzwords. You'll apply your thorough understanding of media strategy, sell strategies to internal teams and manage external third party relationships. Knowledge of all online marketing techniques is important, as are good negotiation skills. Managing the client relationship: keeping the peace and delivering the goods, is integral to this job. Personality-wise, you'll be everything a good media planner should be: a strong communicator, balanced team player and flexible under pressure. (Source: courtesy of *Brand Republic*)

Another task that requires an overview of digital operations is the role of **informa- tion architect**. Their job is to decide where information should be displayed online (which in most cases involves defining its placements on the world wide web). The role of information architect also involves putting material into the right sequence so that it is read by consumers in a logical order. In other words, the role is that of information manager and they are charged with ensuring that information is seen by the right target audience and read in the right way.

Data planners have the responsibility of breaking down and deciphering all data that have been gathered on customers, from point-of-sale listing information to questionnaire returns. Data planners construct a customer profile from all avail- able digital data to let the planning team know who the customers are. A further role of digital data planners is that they are responsible for generating data oppor- tunities around customers. They have to identify points of contact that target customers have with digital technology through day-to-day interactions and figure out how the data generated can be captured as useful research information.

Such information can be honed to reveal insights that challenge presumptions about customers. For instance, one charity in the UK assumed that one-off cash donors contributed far greater sums of money overall than regular direct-debit contributors. A simple analysis of established contribution patterns revealed a more accurate and alternative perspective: donations that were spontaneous acts of compassion were proportionately no more than the regular sums from regis- tered contributors. This information helped the charity reach a decision to adjust their campaign strategy and appeal for larger regular debit card donations rather than targeting one-off donations in retail stores.

Interactive strategist

An Interactive Strategist is required to complement a well established design & technical team. On a day-to-day basis the Interactive Strategist will contribute to the growth and strategic direction of the new media division as well as providing strategic input into all digital projects. If you can demonstrate sound business analysis, commercial thinking and can champion sound user experience and accessibility, then we'd love to hear from you! (Source: courtesy of *Brand Republic*)

Igniter   Advocate   Challenger   Activist   Explorer

Infiltrator   Alchemist   Dreamer   Provocateur

Storyteller   Deviant   Fixer   Amplifier   Champion

Connector   Oracle   Fanatic   Problem Solver

Catalyst   Architect   Initiator   Realist   Magician

Steven Walls is an Account Planning Director. On the back of his business card he lists some of the 'states of mind' that Account Planning can now incorporate.

Roles in the construction of digital advertising

Other roles that have emerged with the growth of digital advertising are more related to the production of online campaigns.

Digital technical directors (DTDs) oversee the programming of websites, *virals* and other digital communications. They have to understand new ideas that are emerging in the field of digital technology, and have a clear grasp of how the capabilities of new hardware and software might create potential for advertising, as well as how specific clients might use them.

The role of DTD involves having a detailed knowledge of current and emerging computer programs: this is essential, as often original digital communications require the joining of two types of software (called *mash-ups* in the industry). The DTD has to solve the technical problems and communicate the means of programming and using hybrid packages to the rest of the programming team. This can often involve producing a user's guide and plan for clients and account team. It often involves working with creative directors to help them produce content that performs to the strengths of software.

HTML programmers translate the creative team's artwork to operate effectively online. Often changes need to be made by negotiation, and the HTML programmer's role is to decide if artwork is technically feasible or if the approach needs to be negotiated for the program to work effectively.

The role of the HTML programmer is similar to that of a database developer. Their role also involves programming packages and establishing the interconnections between one digital communication and other related online offerings. Database developers ensure that the range of programs used across an online campaign are consistent and compatible with each other. They are also charged with devising means of capturing the number of 'hits' an advertising website or *viral* receives. In a role similar to data planners', database developers create opportunities to capture information either on consumers targeted by campaigns or on people who have themselves personally accessed online advertising platforms.

Some roles in digital advertising require staff to manage the transition of digital processes through to a project's completion. **Account handler** and **account producer** are such roles. They involve nurturing the digital process from concept phase through to a stage where the digital work is ready for release online. In some respects this fulfils many of the same responsibilities that the role of traffic encompasses in a typical large agency set-up. However, account handling and producing involves liaising and negotiating with other digital specialists to ensure that the process is managed through to launch with the right technical specifications and approvals in place. As the role requires specialist knowledge of computer packages, digital organizations and industry production contacts, the role has emerged as a separate niche discipline within digital advertising organizations.

Many other tasks require in-depth knowledge of specific computer packages. Currently the most common of these across Western digital advertising operations is the role of **Flash developer**. They use the Flash digital animation program because it is the most universally accepted online package and requires both graphic design and programming skills to make computer-generated artwork easy to operate by everyday consumers online.

Flash Ad Campaign Designer

We need an online/web designer with Flash experience to design phenomenal advertising campaigns. In addition to online work, some work would be done offline working collaboratively with other designers. Your work should include global campaigns for recognizable brands like my client's. Along with an exceptional creative ability, you should also have strong interpersonal and presentation skills – agency candidates would be ideal for this role.

Requirements: Background in a similar role with proven experience, a design-related degree, and proficiency with current packages. (Source: courtesy of *Brand Republic*)

There are similar specialist roles spanning other programs such as *Dreamweaver* and platforms such as *xhtml*: in many digital advertising agencies these tend to be grouped together and managed through the roles of digital technical directors and programmers.

Many of the roles described here have derived as a hybrid from existing advertising agency roles and positions found in specialist digital production firms. The extent to which all the roles described exist in one agency depends on the scale of digital facility. Many specialist facilities tend to be contracted in for specific tasks, although most of the roles that require the managing of processes tend to resourced in-house.

Digital creatives

Dave Bedwood and Sam Ball, Founder/Creative Directors, digital advertising team at digital agency *Lean Mean Fighting Machine*

Sam and Dave's agency specialize in producing online advertising such as banners, skyscrapers and campaign microsites. They work as an art director/ copywriter team that produce creative ideas initially as *scamps*, which are developed into storyboards before they are developed with a programming team. The process requires traditional advertising craft and writing skills and a sound understanding of digital communication possibilities.

Dave: 'The most important thing is the idea. Great writing is an overlooked skill in online advertising because everyone gets too excited by new technologies and design. The best work combines great ad writing with interactive design enhancing and dramatizing the point – you don't just want to just stream a TV ad online. Not enough creatives in the digital advertising industry actually trained in copywriting and art direction. Most creative teams on graduation still want to go into the "glamorous" world of ATL advertising. However, digital is now starting to attract this talent. Young creatives are growing up with this new medium and they are watching less TV, so knowing how to connect with consumers online is becoming second nature.'

Many creatives in the digital advertising industry originally trained in visual communication. Some may have initially aimed for media advertising because it is often perceived as being a glamorous industry. Similar art director and copywriter skills are required but there is a difference in approach to communication:

- Websites need to layer communication: the first message is usually a portal to further detailed information. Therefore they need to place themselves in the mind of the internet user and map out the processes of reading information.
- *Viral* advertisements have to be concise enough to be compressed and easily downloaded. Creatives have less control over the environment where viral ads are seen.

- Targeted digital advertisements such as e-mail or *SMS text* require a real-time unit to handle immediate responses, whereas broadcast adverts impart a one-way message to customers with the aim of provoking awareness or action.

Compared to traditional forms of advertising where the strengths and weaknesses of the media are well known, with digital advertising the emphasis is on creating to the technical strengths of digital programs. Therefore a grounded knowledge in what is possible through software packages is often required.

> It takes three-quarters of a year to train a traditional creative to work across media.
> (Bob Greenberg, CEO, *R/GA*, Cannes 2006)

Working online also requires copywriters to be skilled in maintaining a dialogue (rather than simply imparting messages) and have an ability to extrapolate campaign ideas through different types of online experiences. Digital art directors have to ensure that URL links and functional information are clear and that both the visual language on screen and movement between screens are consistent.

Training for new media creatives has only recently been distinguished from conventional advertising. Therefore the first approaches to digital advertising were little different from other adverts. Web page banners and pop-ups were an extension of media advertising where customers clicked on URL links, which typically flashed up in front of customers' intended page, and were taken to other sites with further interactive opportunities.

Today, advertising online has started to mould around established digital formats. Jobs such as **search marketing** are geared to ensure adverts get good billing on search engines and accelerate to the top of search results listings. This requires less artwork skill but greater strategic awareness and a creative ability to think laterally around formats to generate more potential points of contact with consumers. Unlike in conventional 'push' marketing, the role of search marketers is to *pull* viewers in as a campaign idea unfolds, in a manner similar to that of viral seeders (described below).

Search Specialist – Search Engine Marketing Manager

Expected to develop into an SEM expert, you'll be armed with a search background. You'll work alongside the Head of Search to develop client strategy and deliver impressive, industry leading solutions. Building solid relationships with media owners (*Google, Overture, Miva*), you'll be monitoring and maintaining daily campaign optimization and in turn, growing client spend.

(Source: courtesy of *Brand Republic*)

New advertising services

Beyond the many new roles that have been created by the expansion of advertising, new types of specialist agencies have also emerged. Many tend to operate in one medium and aim to devise ways of expanding their material across different advertising genres.

Film

Films that advertise

One such agency in the UK, *Quiet Storm Films*, describe themselves as programme makers. They operate both as a film and video production company and as an advertising agency. Their staff have expertise in film, commercial and project planning. Their output includes:

- television and cinema commercials;
- television programmes – documentaries and content advertising;
- information/demonstration films;
- advertising *virals*;
- website MPGs.

The organization operates like an advertising agency with creative teams, account handlers and planners but their creative solutions revolve around their range of media at their disposal. They also take on film work that falls outside advertising. Effectively they devise and execute their own campaigns – the whole process from advertising concept to film production is done in-house.

Quiet Storm's founder, Trevor Robinson, sees a blurring of distinction between the content of entertainment and education: 'Most of what we do is paid for by people wanting to sell things. But our aim is to arrest attention, surprise and entertain.' In other words, the company aim to make films that get noticed. In terms of their work there is no need to distinguish between commercial and educational content where the material can be *infomercials* – entertaining, informative and promoting commercial ideas (see chapter 6).

Kate Pirouet, Producer, *Quiet Storm*

Kate's role revolves around turning the film idea into reality; she has to source recording venues, sort out casting and ensure that the logistics of organizing a shoot is completed to budget.

'My role is rich and varied – no two days are the same. You need to be a good organizer and very pushy. Mistakes cost money, and in a role like this there's nowhere to hide. That's where the buzz comes from!'

Therefore *Quiet Storm* is one of a new breed of agency that operates through existing channels and new margins of mass communication.

Entertaining audiences seems to be the underlying aim of unconventional media platforms. Because most unconventional advertising relies on distracting the viewer, from the viewers' perspective the message needs to seem worthwhile if it is to be persuasive. *Quiet Storm's* method of selling through film is to create a dialogue that talks about an idea and links it to a product or service, without the viewer realizing that there is an advertising agency behind it. Robinson envisaged *Quiet Storm* as a new model of advertising agency that works in a flexible way out of necessity – 'for us to bandwagon we need to be small, lean and nimble. We can go with the flow and interlock with bigger agencies without clashing'. The problem facing specialists such as *Quiet Storm* is to make sure that the message is relevant to the target audience AND the medium. In the first instance, *Quiet Storm* needs to ensure that its target audience access the film. The content therefore has to appear relevant and arresting before it can be persuasive. Unusually for an advertisement, its pre-viewing reputation needs to be ensured before the viral is actually seen.

Digital producer

You'll work on several projects and accounts at a time, working the creative dream into a reality. You'll be responsible for taking the brief then directing internal/external creative and technical teams to ensure delivery of consistently slick, classy work on time and to budget. You'll also help to modify and improve existing production processes within the agency. Through your experience you'll have honed expertise in the technical domain and be able to demonstrate knowledge of technical hard and software. You'll have strong communication skills, exceptional organizational ability, good common sense and be able to deliver to different teams even when under pressure.

(Source: courtesy of *Brand Republic*)

Viral seeding

Placing information where interested people would find it

In making *viral* advertising popular by putting it online in the right places another new role has emerged. **Viral seeders** identify potential websites, *blog sites* and online forums to stimulate interest in their films. They often use *early adopter* channels to spread the word through their outlets. Developing a reputation through *word-of-mouth* between friends, work colleagues and family is widely recognized as the most effective way of creating demand for viral advertising and this has become the work of specialist agencies who need to be in touch with current web trends to work effectively. By being in touch, they can shape interest in media, such as films, simply by pushing them through those in the know. This approach assumes that to create demand, information about product launches, must-see films and places to go is best communicated through early adopters. They in turn spread the information through their peers, and so the message will be spread through social streams, which ensures that the information will appear to have been passed on from those close to source. E-mail and TXT networks enable this method of promotion to work quickly. Using early adopters as message carriers also makes the method of promotion seem exclusive and personal – effectively like a preview before 'official' information is released.

> **Justin Kirby, MD,** *Digital Media Communications* **(*DMC*)**
>
> Viral seeding company *DMC* ensures that adverts get noticed by being passed from person to person as entertainment. Justin makes sure that the adverts get mentioned on appropriate *blog* sites, and that what his company call 'early adopters' get first exposure of new ads, so that they can go and influence their friends.
>
>   'Forget so-called viral advertising. The future of selling products is Participation Marketing whereby companies attempt to persuade us to participate in the life of their brands.' (See also Kirby and Marsden, 2006.)

Agencies such as *DMC* that specialize in nurturing word-of-mouth channels use a mixture of public relations devices and contacts – activists and socialites – to ensure they get first news of events. In effect, they help to ensure that brands stay abreast of new cultural developments, and that advertising remains connected at the root of any innovations that may provide promotional opportunities.

Product placement

Product placement in television, radio and film also requires advertising account skills, and often involves people formerly employed at the business end of advertising to work as a conduit between brands, film producers and production houses. Product placement involves negotiating the promotional content in return for project funding, and usually operates in the form of a *third party association*. Sometimes it requires the reworking of scripts and sometimes a script or format is produced around the sponsor (a television example features in chapter 3). The job requires juggling returns on investment with the extent of coverage in programme content. The value of a production's target market to a brand is significant, and the full package of the contract requires organization between programme producers and brand marketing directors. In the UK there is still a public-funded channel – the *British Broadcasting Corporation* (*BBC*) – which is presently not allowed to receive paid-for advertising. For the most part, product placement on commercial channels involves negotiations with a number of stakeholders, including programme sponsors, brands, performers agents, broadcasters and other contracted parties.

> Marcus Vinton is an executive producer responsible for funding major multi-million-dollar Hollywood motion pictures and global TV formats in conjunction with major brands.
>
> Marcus's background was as a creative director in a traditional advertising agency before he became one of the pioneers of digital, interactive advertising and branded content.
>
> 'My company develops and fully funds the production of motion pictures targeted towards "genre" audiences and individual brand-specific consumer markets and sensibilities. We strategically integrate the brand's organization, services or product/s into the narrative structure of an entire motion picture and all of the associated marketing, DVD and other media exposure. Immersive plot structure and scenario planning can be constructed to allow the brand to assert or amplify its message, or if need be, execute radical changes in consumer perception overnight. This is not product placement, but Brand Integration Through Entertainment (or BITE).'

Brand guardian

Designers or brand managers that have worked on one brand for a long period are often given the role of **brand guardian**. They have the responsibility of making day-to-day decisions regarding the future creative and strategic development of a brand, and are given the post because they are felt to be the person closest to understanding all aspects of a brand's personality. The role exists to ensure consistency of decision making, and to manage the brand identity as if it were a person: in effect, the brand guardian *is* the brand because they are its human representative. Often the phrase *brand DNA* is used when planners are attempting to establish the very essence of a brand's persona, so having a brand guardian makes the total identity of a brand more manageable through all commercial operations.

> **Andrew Marsden, *Britvic* brand guardian**
>
> Andrew Marsden is marketing director for soft drinks manufacturer *Britvic* and as such is the brand guardian of all *Britvic* brands, including *Tango*. Andrew's role as the ultimate guardian of brand strategies include consistent messages through all channels regarding core decisions on advertising, promotions, packaging and personality of *Britvic* brands.
>
> 'As brand guardian my role is to ensure that all aspects of *Tango* marketing and promotion are consistent with the brand positioning and our strategic intent for it.'

Summary

New jobs in direct and integrated advertising

Insight	Research and analyse target markets (B2C, C2C).
Web researcher	Research niche web traffic and *early adopters* (C2C).
New Business	Discover new clients and win new business.
Media planner	Define appropriate promotional vehicles.
Brand planner	Define how brand positioning can be developed.
Consumer planner	Define niche market characteristics.
Media neutral planning	Manage big creative strategies through all media.
B2C promoter	Write briefing packs and scrip for telesales.

New jobs in online advertising

Online media planning	Shape briefs for online media.
Information architect	Define online locations.
Data planner	Research digital quantitative and qualitative customer data.
Producer	Organize generation and funding of online content.
Search marketing	Ensure advertising content is prominent on search engines.
Digital creative	Generate art, storyboards and copy for online media.
Digital technical director	Manage programming of digital work.
HTML programmer	Transfer artwork to digital formats.
Account handler/producer	Manage development of campaign processes.
Flash operator	Program online work.

New advertising services

Brand consultant	Advise firms on creative strategy.
Viral seeder	Ensure material is disseminated to target audiences online.
Product placement	Negotiate the positioning of sponsors in film content.
Film content providers	Film-making skills, for any medium that requires film content.
Brand guardian	Make decisions on behalf of a brand as its closest associate.

9 Closer

Getting closer to customers

Getting closer to customers outlines the developments in direct and online campaigns that have paved the way for 'wrapping' ads around targeted consumers. The section considers the key phases that enabled advertising to become personal and the issues that 'getting closer' provokes, and includes examples where the 'dialogue' with customers has gone wrong. This section outlines examples of best practice, including insights into attracting *early adopters* and provides a summary of key points at the end.

Overview

Benchmarks in getting closer through direct, online and experimental campaigns

1980	*Guinness* and *Marlboro* clothing lines
1989	interactive adverts in US (*Procter & Gamble*, US/*Ford*, UK)
1990	'our customer' agency research projects (*Ogilvy & Mather*, UK)
1993	niche database advertising & reward card schemes (*Land Rover*/*Tesco* and *Dunn Humby*, UK)
1994	digital *banner* advert (*hotwired.com*, US)
1995	online pay-per-view methods introduced (pornography industries internationally)
1996	rich-text advert (*Hewlett Packard*, US)
1997	branded websites
1997	*viral* adverts (*Amex*, global)
2000	branded social networks (*Nike*, UK)
2001	*advergames*
2002	interactive *virals* and spread of *advertainment*
2003	SMS text (*Cadbury Schweppes*, UK)
2004	boom in online blogs and personal web spaces
2004	*Hewlett Packard* 'Direct Smile' platform (used by *J Sainsbury*, UK)
2006	convergent advertising: text, e-mail and mass media (telecommunications firms).

Contexts for getting advertising closer

It seems that advertising has been creeping closer to individual customers in recent years. Advertising agencies have certainly adjusted their thinking about customers. The big shift since 1990 has been from demographic mapping to profiling customers based on consumption data and the online social networks they may be involved with. This has enabled advertisers to achieve more through campaigns with refocused strategies. For instance, television commercials have changed the subject of advertising from product to consumers. Where advertisements featured product shots prominently throughout a campaign, today they tend to depict the end-user experience by showing what the product will do for them. This often involves creating a mood and environment for the product which, in many cases, does not involve familiar advertising formats at all. It is worth noting that many of the world's most famous brands – *Apple*, *Nike* and *Virgin*, to name three – rarely use conventional advertising. Instead they channel their energies into closer customer-centred methods of engagement. At one point in the early 1990s, *Marlboro* in the United States and *Heinz* in the UK decided that budgets should be sunk into discount price promotions rather than advertising because it was a better way of making their product distinct and more likely to make customers switch brands. A much clearer grasp of target markets has, in some instances, even resulted in *calls to action* that are so highly detailed and targeted that they tend to ostracize people outside the niche. Excluding the non-targeted masses has in some cases had damaging consequences. For instance, a famous European yoghurt brand experienced a decline in sales following a campaign that specifically targeted women with trapped wind or digestive problems. Outside those directly affected, it caused widespread amusement.

Many cross-platform advertising agencies in the early 1990s invested in consumer research to discover triggers that made people brand-loyal. International group *Ogilvy & Mather* invested in excess of £2 million developing qualitative evidence that demonstrated that values such as brand ethos, associations and product experiences were all key factors for consumers to identify with a brand. A separate body of research noted that most children empathized with the ethos of brands to such an extent that they used them as codes of communication. Just as football shirts are an overt code of allegiance, brand identities are now commonly understood to express personal values, tastes, status and affluence.

Self-portraits by 10-year-old schoolchildren, who identify with iconic brands to the extent that they use them to convey their identity to others, 2001. (Source: author)

During the 1990s advertising strategies moved from making specific claims for products towards generic associations for brands, as they sought to become the iconic leader in their sector. *Hanson* ran a proposition that claimed a position as the ultimate Anglo-American company with their line 'a company from over here, doing rather well over there'; *Nike* moved into local sports activities on a global scale to ensure they were identified as the main sports brand; from its launch *Google* claimed to be the world's primary search engine.

New consumer journey

One could argue therefore that the agenda for advertising shifted from short-term ambition – what people bought after seeing an advertisement – to long-term objectives – what people *thought* after seeing their advertisement.

A counter-view is that advertising's methods hardly changed at all in 10 years, and to an extent this is true. Established communication skills are still required to connect with consumers. However, the strategic positioning of campaigns has developed. More often the strategy contains a more detailed plan of how and when

Brand as a generic code: territory synonymous with brands

Brand	Territory
adidas	Achievement
Amazon	Community store
Apple	Creative freedom
Audi	German engineering
British Airways	Favourite airline
BP	Environmental
Cadbury Schweppes	Break-time escapism
Dove	Natural beauty
eBay	Trading
Gillette	Best for shaving
Google	Search
Hanson	Anglo-American
Mastercard	Priceless experiences
McDonald's	Healthy youthful
MySpace	Social networking
Nike	Sport

brands should address target audiences, and a more defined route for *prospects* to respond to a *call to action*. Where previously advertisements stirred customers to go out and buy a product, advertising now calls on customers to develop dialogues and relationships with brands – as if a first-time purchase is no longer enough.

The difference now is that brand owners realize that marketing and advertising have far greater potential reach than had been realized in the mid-1990s. Advertising need no longer be just about stimulating an impulse to buy: it can now also be about shaping people's experience of a product. This is why many international pioneering brands – notably *Nike, Sony, Apple* and *Amex* – invest heavily in an advertising infrastructure to support the consumption of their products.

Making advertising an all-encompassing activity was an approach pioneered by automotive and telecommunications services – as some of the case studies in this book demonstrate. In particular, by shaping customer services with advertising techniques, brands have been able to use every bit of one-to-one customer dialogue as an opportunity to develop the user experience, which itself is an advertisement to stick with a brand. This makes for more effective returns on advertising investment.

A number of platforms have emerged as vehicles for involving customers with brands, driven in part because involvement creates opportunities to gather customer information. Interactive digital video, brand service centres and social network groups have emerged as the main platforms for customer involvement. Such platforms allow knowledge already accumulated on customers to be exercised through personalized communication.

Campaigns such as O_2's customer retention project (see chapter 4) used SMS, e-mail and call centres to enhance its relationship with existing customers for a campaign that was symptomatic of a 'second generation' approach, where brands focus on the experience of existing clients to influence others. As with many current campaigns, O_2 shaped its campaign around customers rather than the brand by using all points of customer contact at its disposal.

This ability to 'get closer' by harnessing all points of contact with customers and *prospects* has only been possible since the mid-1990s. This is because:

- Customer data are more widely accessible, with information on personal consumption and interests more readily available.
- Better means have developed for profiling and segmenting audiences. Data technology allows for easier collation and sharing of information.
- The internet has developed as an interactive visual communication tool. Not only does it make immediate mass dissemination of material to named individuals possible, it also ensures that the customer–brand dialogue can be monitored to profile individual internet habits and preferences.

Reverberations from the above are only just being felt by the communications industries. Only now is the capability of digital information gathering and message spread being realized in advertising – some of the campaigns that explore this potential are featured in chapters 1 to 6.

As I noted at the beginning of this book, it has been brands that have driven change by pushing their advertising agencies closer to target markets through digital channels, using better data. This serves the needs of advertising's clients because digital channels provide an accurate measure of advertising effectiveness. Therefore online advertising has become popular with many companies because it readily lent itself to audit processes in terms of accuracy and accountability.

> With online advertising, you've got to look at it not in terms of reaching thousands of viewers or listeners, but in terms of *effective costs per thousand* rates of return. You can track it and research it more effectively online.
>
> (Sir Martin Sorrell)

In terms of changing the advertising process, a consequence of the drive to close in on consumers has been to expand the role that research plays. There are now far more specialist research and development roles involved with larger-scale campaigns. As listing agents and brands themselves hold customer data, the tasks involved in getting market insights have rapidly developed as a pre-creative phase before and during the planning stage (some specific roles are described in chapter 8).

Closing in on customers, in four phases

There have been four distinct phases in the development of digital technology since the beginning of the 1990s which have enabled advertisers to get closer to customers.

Vehicles for getting closer to consumers, in four phases

Phase 1 *Talking to consumers*	Interactive television, *blinks* and *bumpers* Press inserts, magazine wraps and personalized mailshots Environmental wraps and *ambient* stunts Online *banners* and *pop-ups* *Defined by: broadcasting messages at viewers/listeners, pushing media possibilities*
Phase 2 *Dialogue*	E-mail text SMS Internet *virals* Rich-text links *Defined by: digital communications, addressing individuals one-to-one, direct responses*
Phase 3 *Involvement*	Interactive *virals* *Advergames* *Social network* sites *Defined by: interactive customer involvement, network sites*
Phase 4 *Advocacy*	*User-generated* video *Advertainment* *Defined by: heavy use of user-generated content, allowing consumers to adopt and co-design output, customers talking about brands*

Phase 1 – talking to consumers

Example: *Ford Mondeo* interactive commercial – see chapter 1

The first phase extended existing media channels in a more targeted way using buzz, disruption and re-framing techniques to put messages in front of consumers. Television advertising in particular was revitalized by programme sponsorship, *bumpers* and *blinks*, which were very short bits of film, usually lasting between one and three seconds, inserted during a commercial break.

Branded spaces and disruption tactics were also developed in the first 'getting close' phase, where the objective was to *push* information the customer's way. Technology placed advertising messages in personal places (such as public toilets), next to products in stores and in the urban landscape. Making an impression by making advertising an experience was one form of getting closer to customers, by filling the gap between the usual advertising channels and the moment of consumption.

Transvisual advertising screens advertising products on display in a supermarket store and strategically placed advert on a kerb next to a pub.

In the developed commercial cities during the late 1990s there was also a rapid rise in the use of direct mailers, as brands developed early forays into utilizing their customer data. *Below-the-line* agencies in particular made use of the improved access to customer data by targeting *prospects* with more expensive, better-designed mailshots than before, in the knowledge that having already registered interest to appear on the 'radar' of a database they were more likely to take note of a personalized form of address. Advertising agency *Evans Hunt Scott*'s *Tesco Clubcard*, a supermarket reward scheme in conjunction with data analysts *Dunn Humby*, was one of the most effective customer-data-fuelled approaches to emerge in the mid-1990s.

The potential of interactive television, such as *Ford Mondeo's iTV* in 1993, which transported viewers to a brand-specific television page, became feasible during this phase with satellite and cable networking. Television commercials for expensive goods – mostly audio-visual and automotive products – tended to change their *call to action* during this phase, pointing customers to a website or phone line rather than directly to showrooms. During phase one, the new formats for advertising tended to drum up awareness and guide viewers or listeners to channels where some form of dialogue could be instigated.

In the first phase of digital advertising, *banners* and *pop-ups* tagged web pages of sites that appeared relevant to brands. Entrepreneurs realized there was money to be made through high-traffic websites attracting tagged advertising, which ultimately fuelled the first 'dot com' boom. With the development of specialist interest sites, advertisers get a specific themed message in front of those searching the net for similar material. The first online banners were in GIF format during 1994 (the banner was on *hotwired.com*, according to *DoubleClick*, 2005), and not long after, many sites were designing web pages as potential revenue-earning advertising space as the first boom in internet spending took hold. For brands and advertisers such methods were an improvement on pre-phase-one advertising because revenue could be deployed more efficiently to niche audiences.

As the first real phase began to bring advertisers closer to consumers, emphasis turned to exploring the potential of the media, with a view to reaching target customers in their everyday environments, during their everyday activities.

Phase 2 – dialogue

Example: *Cadbury TXT 'n' WIN* SMS text campaign – see chapter 2

The second phase is most clearly defined by the use of digital rich-text links to generate dialogues with targeted customers. Website screens became more interactive and made responses to an advertisement a two-way interaction. In some cases it involved feeding information through a data capture system. For instance, part of an SMS text message campaign for *Cadbury Schweppes* called *TXT 'n' WIN* linked an on-pack product promotion with a central data collection bureau to capture information on new *prospects*. This gave the brand contact information on their

J Sainsbury 'Direct Smile' postcards, personalized greetings sent to *Nectar* reward card holders. *Hewlett Packard's* software could collate and segment data within a production system. This enabled interactive campaigns like *Direct Smile*, where individualized cards and appropriate gift vouchers were sent to *Nectar* card holders on their birthday. In 2006 they had the capacity to produce 300,000 individual mailers a month. In one of the most successful promotions, *Hewlett Packard's* set-up allowed *J Sainsbury* to acknowledge customers directly with personalized card and gifts to collect on their birthday.

Mass-tailoring information, business to customer

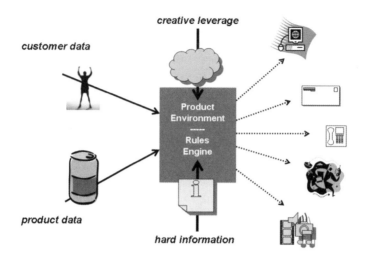

customers, for use at a later date. The potential to ensure customers were being effectively serviced by their brands did not escape the attention of banking and telecommunications service industries, which pushed formats further too, by connecting their internal working operations with their external promotion methods (see chapter 4).

As the potential of online interaction was being pushed in phase two, one of the first online objectives was to get customers to share content because it was a useful means of getting closer to target markets. Text-based e-mails were the most common form in the mid-1990s, but the sheer volume of unwanted *spam*, which managed to avoid being subject to national advertising regulation, soon led to development of sophisticated *spam* filters. When the world wide web was still in its early stages, phenomena such as the *Dancing Baby* (from 1996 by *3D Studio Max*, US), a video file of a digitally rendered baby performing animated dance moves, demonstrated how videos that people could talk about and distribute could reach a global audience. For brand marketing directors, this illustrated the potential to create and distribute commercial content online.

> With good advertising you talk to people – not shout at them.
>
> (John Hegarty, Worldwide Creative Director, *Bartle Bogle Hegarty*)

Some television commercials were finessed online to be shared as entertainment. Early examples in the UK included a short film for *John West* tinned salmon, featuring a bear fighting a fisherman karate-style for his catch. Short videos were sent as e-mail attachments or as URL links from websites.

While the *John West* commercial was typical of early TV-derived content, digital videos created for circulation online started to develop around the strengths of the new medium. Online, commercials were not subject to the same constraints as television advertising or to any one national regulatory body (see chapter 1), so digital video could be more risqué than broadcast commercials. Also, as online *virals* were downloadable, they could be manipulated by internet users. *Mastercard's Priceless* campaign inadvertently became a global phenomenon because the structure of the advert was easily adopted as the framework for many widely distributed online jokes (see chapter 5). Because online users could add their bit, the message became more personalized, and in the process helped crystallize the original advertising connection between *Mastercard* and the word *priceless*.

The impetus for 'getting closer phase two' was the development of the digital rich-text format, in which words and images could become active *click-through* links to other sites. In the first wave of rich-text formatting this took online advertising to a point where it could redirect customers from their original site of interest simply by getting them to act on impulse. Clicking on a *banner* or *pop-up* link took internet users to branded sites where the 'taster' message in the link could be fully developed. In 1996 the first version of a click-on rich-text advert was thought to have been for *Hewlett Packard* in a banner between the score reading for digital bat-and-ball game *Pong* (*DoubleClick*, 2005). Such methods were an improvement on phase one technologies because they established a traceable dialogue between customers and brands. From simple clicks of a mouse, data could be logged to acknowledge interest, and the source of information could be easily followed up by brands in campaigns.

Interactive banners that perform on a click, such as *AOL*'s by *Lean Mean Fighting Machine*, gave internet surfers an interesting proposition. Unlike commercials, if they showed interest they could instantly get more information. Their reward for enquiring would often be entertaining content.

Phase two was therefore characterized by the development of digital possibilities online. Typically the opening link of rich-text advertisements simulated personal dialogue to get a response from *prospects*, and once interest had been registered via *click-throughs*, responses on behalf of a brand could be more specific. Through this means, mass messages could be reshaped to develop an increasing degree of individual customer response.

Phase 3 – involvement

Example: *Nike Run London* – see chapter 3. See also www.jogbonita.com

Phase three of getting closer required active customer participation and involved bespoke dialogue. The potential of rich text was pushed further through more passive commercial activities than those in earlier online efforts. During the second generation of the internet, which web developers often refer to as 'Web 2.0', it was apparent that online users could expect some kind of reward for viewing commercial content – if not discounts, then 'reward' in the form of entertainment. One of the main developments was that interaction could be incorporated within digital film, where parallel narratives could potentially let viewers reshape storylines. For instance, in a 2006 online *viral* for *Danish Bacon*, 26 alternative endings were recorded for people to view and select the scenario they preferred. They could then forward their final cut to friends online. In a sense therefore, there was an element of co-creation about interactive content.

Interactive advertising had the capacity to make content more entertaining and effective because customers were engaging and discovering through primary experiences. Consumers could realize more about a product by exploring a bundle of information in their own way, rather than simply receiving transmitted information. Advertising campaigns for the automotive industry in particular took note of this. Campaigns for *Audi* and *Volvo* featured interactive elements (see chapters 5 and 6), while an online site for the *Volkswagen Passat* in 2006 went so far as to feature 120 short films to represent the 120 new designs in the *Passat* range. Each film was produced by a different artist and had its own unique style. Even the tagged information was shaped to offer choice and appeal to a range of preferences. The idea was that customers would identify with the version that most fitted them.

> By mixing digital and direct communications, it should be all about having a conversation with audiences. But where do you want the relationship to go, and what kind of relationship do you want? Is it a one-night stand, like chocolate brands that provoke a rush of blood, or a long-term monogamous relationship, like expensive car brands that can court prospects for 10 years?
>
> (Craig Elston, Senior Vice President – Account Planning, *The Integer Group*, Colorado)

In phase three, new *advergames* also provided a platform for customers to experience an advertising message through play. Film advertising championed this genre most effectively. For instance, the *Trial of Life* game, released to promote a limited-edition *Jeep/Tomb Raider* film sponsorship, allowed online gamers to go on a simulated journey in a *Jeep* over ideal terrain for the vehicle. By playing the game 'explorers' could discover how the *Jeep* negotiates a variety of off-road situations by working through the *Jeep's* unique features on screen.

To close in on customers, campaigns were often managed as a gateway to the ethos of the brand, channelled through social network groups. For instance, *Land Rover* gave customers the free spirit of the brand by organizing away-days and driving rallies. *Nike* extended the spirit of achievement evident in the organization of *Nike Stores* through to consumers by organizing 10-kilometre runs (see chapter 4). By following *Nike* training programmes online and going through the physical exertion required to complete a *Nike* 10 kilometre, customers were effectively experiencing the brand ethos.

Living to tell the tale… 10-kilometre runners, after completing their personal training journey with *Nike*, are rewarded with *Nike* medals. Runs are now staged in numerous cities, including Los Angeles (left) and London (right).

Such approaches helped brands to claim the moral high ground in the fields they operated in: *Nike* produces sports goods, so it has moved towards involvement with personal fitness. *Dove* (the Unilever beauty product brand), for example, championed the issue of female self-esteem, not only by picking non-standard models but by extending dialogue into the thorny issue of morality and beauty product advertising (see chapter 6).

	MORAL HIGH GROUND
Apple	CREATIVE
Nike	FITNESS
Dove	NATURAL BEAUTY
Amazon	COMMUNITY STORE
British Petroleum	ENVIRONMENTALLY RESPONSIBLE
McDonald's	NUTRITION
CORPORATE RESPONSIBILITY	

Corporate social responsibility – moving towards the moral high ground.

While such approaches pull together *social networks* with the brand at the heart of activities, they also work to demonstrate a brand's *corporate social responsibility*. As the ethical practices of multinationals are often closely under scrutiny, demonstrating benevolence in relevant contexts helps to make the brand part of the activity's fabric. In terms of moving closer to customers, they are able to develop within the framework of a *social network* that, in time, is likely to become synonymous with the sponsoring brand.

Another advantage of *social networks* for brands is that they draw on consumer-driven activities to constantly update the relevance of brands. Through closer engagement companies are not simply seen as large organizations but become personified by supportive sub-groups. This solves the positional problem highlighted by writer Charles Handy, where he foresaw a need for major corporations to constantly reinvent themselves through collaborations with smaller parties in order to appear personable and relevant, rather than old-school large corporate players (Handy, 2002).

Many of the approaches developed through phase three are still being refined through innovative uses on new media channels. The legacy of this phase was customer involvement, which allowed people to experience commercial messages and which in turn repositioned customers closer to the centre of brands, often in the role of brand ambassador.

Phase 4 – advocacy

Example: *Revver.com*/consumers *The Diet Coke/Mentos Experiment* digital film – see chapter 7

Phase four of getting closer moved the consumer to a position of advocate, message creator and messenger. Effectively, customers can be the advertisers, creating content in a format that promotes a brand with the consumer performing the role of both creative and distributor.

Cinema promotions have again championed developments in format to spread the word. The interaction to stimulate a buzz around release dates is often incentivized by advertising (see chapters 5 and 7). For instance, a website for the film *Snakes on a Plane* in 2006 contained a link that allowed users to match a series of profile details and send a personalized plug, voiced by the film's lead actor, Samuel L Jackson, to their friends. The hook was that the message seemed like a personal appeal by the film's star on behalf of the sender, and the approach taken ensured that follow-up customer-to-customer correspondences would have centred on the film. The strategy worked in a number of ways: the sender was rewarded for spending active time in the site, the brand was being sent to new addresses provided by consumers (generating new customer data for the company), and the brand being effectively distributed by consumers to other consumers was made prominent in the forwarded message. Such techniques proved useful in creating a buzz, but the potential of homing in on consumers during phase four is far greater when online digital and offline direct approaches are used in a convergent way. *Nike* have often championed this method through in-store activities, as a way of developing their customer database.

Nike in-store promotion for their *Festival of Air 06* challenge promotion in London's *Nike Town* invited shoppers to produce the highest jump of the week. Weekly winners received *Nike* gifts while bad jumpers like me could simply download a digitally enhanced image of their effort, with added crowd and photographic trickery to make involvement appear more impressive (designed by *AKQA* for *Nike Store*, London).

Phase four took advantage of online *snacking* as a commercial opportunity and made opportunities to involve internet users in co-developing content. Customer involvement was particularly sought within multifaceted, *convergent* propositions. *Advertainment* content started to reward participants by providing opportunities to reshape promotional content offered up by brands. For instance, the *Beatbox Mixer* was formatted to illustrate the potential of broadband for digital service provider *Verizon* and allowed site visitors to sample, mix, record and graphically style their own sound recording to keep or share over the internet (see chapters 5 and 7). Letting consumers produce and distribute content was (effectively) converting them to brand advocates as they were de facto promoting the services on offer by demonstration.

> The definition of advertising is in a state of flux at the moment... A company can do marketing and brand programming, but messages passed on from customer to customer are more powerful than advertisings. Let the customer do the advertising. (Shaun McIlrath, 'Brand Advocate')

One could argue that such a strategy is not new: its show and testify method is clearly related to the *Tupperware* distribution model of the 1950s and the door-to-door cosmetic-selling *Avon Ladies* of the 1960s. What was unique about this digital phase was that the advertising content need not be as prescriptive – users could play and send at their own free will and at their time of choosing. With *user-generated content* as an advertising model, customers could generate and upload their own video content to prime community websites such as *YouTube*, with its wide international coverage (over 65,000 video uploads a day and 20 million unique visitors a month in 2005, according to Nielson/Net Ratings). The emergence of revenue-sharing community sites for advertising-tagged new video material – discussed in chapter 7 – encouraged the creation of *user-generated content* and *mash-ups* of existing content. Marketers soon realized that customers themselves could generate and distribute advertising on their behalf, if the format allowed. All they had to do was provide an appropriate and stimulating framework.

A frame from the *Diet Coke/Mentos Experiment*, unauthorized by *Coca-Cola* and *Mentos* but posted on the *Revver* website. According to *EepyBird.com*, the video has been seen over 6 million times.

Experiments in this genre produced good and bad results: the most notorious attempt to instigate user-generated content for *Chevy Tahoe* is discussed later in this chapter. The most famous example of *user-generated content* also served to illustrate that brands do not have ultimate control of content put out by consumers. The short film titled *Diet Coke/Mentos Experiment* and circulated through public share community sites featured two men dropping *Mentos* mints into plastic bottles of *Diet Coca-Cola*. The resulting *Coke* fountain as the liquid reacts with the mint is filmed at length. Whether the footage serves to 'promote' either of the brands is open to question. It was not commissioned by either company. The manufacturer of *Mentos* was thought to be keen to feature the prank in a future mainstream advertising campaign, while *Coca-Cola's* reaction is unclear. What is evident is that both brands have been made relevant online to the profile of consumers that both brands would ordinarily be targeting. If relevance is the objective, the unlicensed customer-generated film fulfils a functional and highly effective advertising role.

User-generated content has been used within multi-platform campaigns so that individuals can involve themselves in an aspect of the promotion. This has proved to be a means of allowing customers to become evangelical advocates of their brands of choice.

The legacy of phase four in getting closer seems likely be its use of *user-generated* and distributed content. While advertisers create a branded utility platform, customers create the advertised message. This approach *pulls* customers into becoming brand advocates by adopting, co-designing and sharing the output 'advertisement'.

What can go wrong: problems with getting closer

Many groundbreaking advertising methods used in the quest to get closer to niche markets have been discovered by trial and error. I have so far concentrated on the successful benchmarks of direct and online advertising that took brands closer to consumers. However, some notable failures have produced many valuable lessons.

Too intrusive

In a measure to develop their existing customer base, a campaign for *British Telecom*'s 'Friends and Family' service in 1997 was created to demonstrate how *BT*'s services could be used more efficiently. A personalized letter was mailed to *BT* account holders. It contained four paragraphs chosen from 154 using *BT*'s customer data of personal phone usage. The letter also told customers whether they had selected the right numbers for 'friends and family' to get the best value for money, based on *BT*'s customer data.

The company received many complaints because the letters were seen to intrude on personal calls. *BT* learnt that, in their eagerness to engage technology and provide better customer support, the customer's (own sense of) privacy needed to be protected.

Too trusting

During an advertisement break during the 2006 Academy Awards ceremony in the United States, a slot for *Chevy Tahoe* offered viewers the opportunity to co-create an advert with the company by filling in the copy for recorded action footage. The reward was that customers would have the kudos of having co-created a high-profile national campaign. It was made easy to participate – people could post their entries online and distribute the advert.

Unfortunately for the *Chevy Tahoe* campaign, its attempt at instigating *user-generated content* backfired as the platform was used by many to criticize the government's policy on fuel tax, the energy consumption of 4×4 vehicles and the brand's earlier campaigns. The advertising strategy had not taken into account the fact that neither brands nor agencies can control content if the roles of editor and distributor are handed over completely to consumers.

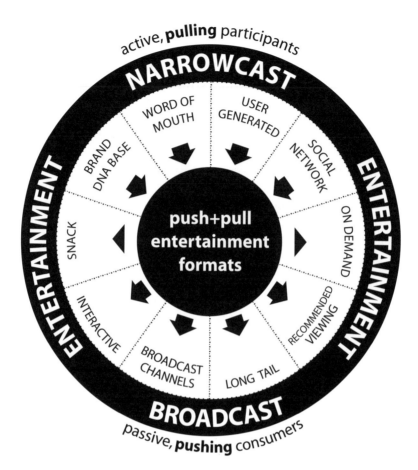

WORD OF MOUTH
virals
advergames

BRAND DNA BASE
website
offers
corporate social responsibility

SNACK
e-mails
virals
advertainment

INTERACTIVE
interactive commercials
interactive *virals*
B2C dialogue

BROADCAST CHANNELS
terrestrial, satellite, cable
specialist content channels
light entertainment
documentary programming

LONG TAIL
old and niche programming
blog
vlog > webcam

RECOMMENDED VIEWING
copy
download
URL links
'send to a friend'

USER-GENERATED
home-made
mash-ups
co-create and share

SOCIAL NETWORK
specialist interest groups
virtual worlds

ON DEMAND
audio > *podcast*
visual > *YouTube, Revver*
gaming > psp
broadcast > on-demand 'classics'

Old and new, *push* and *pull* entertainment formats.

Too big

In 2000 financial service provider *Barclays* put out a campaign to reassure customers they were a 'Big' company. Commercials featuring actors Anthony Hopkins and Robbie Coltrane emphasized that the size of the operation made the company reliable around the world.

Unfortunately, the campaign's launch collided with the bank's decision to close smaller regional branches. New stories on the plight of people in remote villages having to travel long distances to access their accounts jarred with the brave claim that the greater the size, the greater the convenience. Customers' personal experiences conflicted with the message that was being broadcast by *Barclays* in a way that made the 'Big' tag appear impersonal and uncaring. In short, the claims of the campaign did not match customers' experiences.

Too local

As a national promotion in the build-up to the 2006 football World Cup finals, confectionery brand *Mars* adjusted its packaging in the UK, replacing the word *Mars* with *believe*. This tied in with the national mood, as the England football team was expected to do well in the competition.

However, even though the campaign was limited to UK stores, news of the promotion spread and affected sales elsewhere – particularly in Scotland. *Believe* was an attempt by the American brand to be *glocal* and to locate with the national mood. The stunt attracted many press column-inches and proved to be successful throughout the summer period in England. Unfortunately for *Mars*, the migration of the news story, mostly through internet chat sites and international marketing publications, helped the word spread too far, enough to affect the brand's efforts to appear local in Europe.

Too ambitious

In 1992 in the UK, *Hoover* offered pairs of return tickets, initially to Europe, as an incentive to purchase a new vacuum cleaner or washing machine. It was assumed that the small print and *Hoover's* travel agents' efforts to sell extras as part of the package would offset costs of the promotion, and help sales increase by an estimated 20 per cent. When consumers figured that the promotion was of far greater financial worth than the vacuum cleaner on offer, there followed a rush in sales. Hoover were already in the process of extending the offer as originally planned, with flights to the United States and a television campaign that promised, '*Two return seats: Unbelievable*'.

Unfortunately, far too many viewers exploited the 'unbelievable' offer. Stock quickly sold beyond the limit of the promotion until supplies were exhausted. The over-subscribed take-up and under-valued offer meant that *Hoover* could not honour the promotion within its marketing budget. The case was pursued by angry consumers in the UK High Court, where *Hoover* was forced to reimburse consumers who took advantage of the offer. It was estimated to have cost *Hoover* in the region of £48 million – and a very public loss of face.

While the five cases above fell short in their attempts to use contemporary media effectively, they proved to be watershed moments in the development of advertising. They each tested consumer responses to advertising strategies, and the consequences of their campaigns prevented others making similar mistakes.

Feeling duped

A blog site supposedly run by a 16-year-old girl drew a wide following because it gave fresh and frank opinions on life, relationships, snack foods and religion from the perspective of a young American girl writing from her bedroom. Short video blogs from *lonelygirl15* were posted on the *YouTube* website and attracted millions of viewers in the five months before internet users started their posting their suspicions.

Inconsistencies in the narrative and the polished nature of the recordings led many to speculate that *lonelygirl15* was a fake cover for an internet viral campaign. The girl in the video, 'Bree', appeared older than 16 (her posted age) and some of her video blogs had the quality of pop videos. Eventually an anonymous '*message from the creators*' was posted thanking followers of the weblog '*for enjoying the show so far. We are amazed by the overwhelmingly positive response to our videos*'. They claimed that their actions were a 'new art form' and that *lonelygirl15* was a '*reflection of everyone. She is no more real or fictitious than the portions of our personalities that we choose to show*'. The stunt backfired because devotees did not like being fooled by something they believed was genuine. The creators tried to remain anonymous but they were traced to be a Hollywood production company. The viral campaign had been rumbled and lost the buzz of interest by being deliberately misleading.

Issues to do with getting closer

Empowerment versus branded consumers

In one sense, it could be argued that increased experimentation by advertisers online has created a fresh and varied span of new content worth exploring. In terms of branded entertainment there is now a never-ending supply for those who seek it.

The vast choice of internet content to '*snack* on' – from advertising, films, TV and radio programmes, books, magazines, music and gaming – has empowered consumers by enabling them to 'cherry-pick' the content that is relevant to them and at the time that suits them, ignoring what is irrelevant. According to the *BBC*, *video on demand* will define the next age of digital broadcasting. *VOD* gives audiences far greater scope for control, personalization and interaction with media. It may be a method of retaining a loyal audience – and brand loyalty is one of the prime objectives of online advertising for multinational brands. For advertising, *VOD* relies completely on securing viewers' interest so they don't get bypassed: already *Revver.com* and *YouTube* tag videos with adverts (see chapter 1). However, *VOD* can operate as entertainment in its own right. The models of entertainment provided by viral advertisements may prove to be the format favoured by *VOD*.

Enabling content to be accessible 7 days a week, 24 hours a day, in principle gives consumers the best return for their time, because there is less advertising infill compared to broadcast media. However, viewing is still controlled and site managers have mastered the art of providing *teaser* content as a precursor for paid-for and follow-on content.

In many respects such techniques grew out of the need in the late 1990s to create ways of attracting advertising revenue online. While the desire to advertise online has not been an issue, orchestrating channels for advertising revenue to flow through has been problematic. Some commentators anticipated a form of permission marketing, whereby it was assumed that advertisers may have to pay to get viewers to watch commercials (Godin, 1999), given that the internet was originally developed as a free information network. Most commentators correctly assumed that advertising would need to adjust approaches from disruptive methods to more inclusive and participatory approaches. In practice the advertising industry has always devised ways to negotiate technological hurdles that have emerged: advertising negotiated channel surfing with remote control handsets in the 1970s, fast-forwarding with videos in the 1980s, mass-channel networks in the 1990s and interactive digital recording methods of *TiVo* (USA) and *Sky+* (*UK*) since the millennium. Techniques around personal interest, free-to-view content were established practice within five years of the problem being diagnosed. Therefore making the internet a commercial network was simply a matter of time, trial and error.

However, the ethics of commercializing online communication is an issue. A moral argument could be made that in a commercially saturated landscape, attempting to commercialize all channels of entertainment is encroaching too far into personal territory. Branded entertainment is trying to sell goods when consumers' powers of resistance are at their lowest – when they're switched off, relaxed and having fun. They can ignore television commercial breaks, but when advertising is fused with content, messages are harder to disaggregate. Not satisfied with fully branded environments where advertising cannot be avoided in essential situations such as the risers of steps and on petrol pump handles, a fully absorbed advertising environment, where brands flavour all issues and narratives, leaves little room for neutral, free, unbranded spaces.

The argument is also often made by sociologists that consumers are conditioned to read. Advertisers have often regarded customers as brand savvy, where in fact the sheer volume of commercial messages means that few actually get noticed, and consumers have evolved means of unconsciously editing out messages. Children in particular are adept at taking on many messages at once, with very few making a lasting impression. This is largely what has driven advertisers to get closer to customers – even to the extent that telecommunications firms went to in e-mailing prospects to get them to watch their advertisements.

It seems that to get advertising noticed, brands first have to get more personal with customers than their rivals. As international legislation has run behind practices outside conventional advertising, the ethics of practice are often suspended until backlashes occur.

Experienced internet users versus novices

Often consumers are broadly divided into heavy and light information technology users. Many think the divide can be mapped onto old and young users of personal digital technology, and in many respects this is true.

Advertiser Maurice Saatchi in 2006 asserted that internet users up to the age of 25 are 'digital natives', used to multi-tasking between types of digital technology and adept at sifting more content quickly, but recalling less. Those over the age of 25 Saatchi considered to be 'digital immigrants', constantly having to catch up and learn new technologies and using one digital communication channel at once (bbc.co.uk/radio4/today accessed 21 June 2006/Cannes Advertising festival, June 2006).

> Digital natives can do a lot in 30 seconds, so the old format of television commercials needs rethinking in terms of how it attracts revenue.
>
> (Maurice Saatchi, co-founder, *M&C Saatchi*)

The extent to which consumers trust media

While advertisers are now able to address people personally, consumers are still widely resistant to the commercial messages they receive. Put simply, consumers trust the media but don't trust advertising.

Often it is the promotional methods used that repel consumers. As the volume of advertising expands through all media channels, consumers have become increasingly weary of commercial selling tools. A survey titled *What Assures Consumers?* conducted in the UK during 2006 by *Globescan* and *AccountAbility* highlighted that the trust people had for celebrity endorsements has dwindled in recent years (Whitehead, 2006). The survey found that product packaging, consumer watchdogs and advice from friends and family topped the list, while campaign groups, celebrities and leaflets delivered to consumers' homes came bottom – even below advertising.

> Advertising itself is a vaguely discredited notion. I don't trust it any more.
>
> (Shaun McIlrath, who no longer calls himself an advertiser but a *brand advocate*)

It is easy to see why people are assured by information that is independent from bodies with vested interests. Product packaging has to reveal factual information by law, while consumer watchdogs are widely regarded as being brand-neutral and on the side of customers. Friends and family naturally have an individual's interests at heart. It is of little surprise that all three channels have been used in recent years as an extension of advertising:

● Product packaging has been embellished to develop the brand's ethos through stylized information. For instance, packaging on the fruit smoothie brand *Innocent* used the product information section to reinforce the idea that their drink contains no additives: '100% pure fruit; 100% RDA of vitamin C; NO concentrates; NO added sugar; NO nasty sweeteners; NO added worms'!

● Brands often fund independent surveys in their field of practice and publicize the findings to demonstrate their corporate social responsibilities. For instance, *Dove* conducted a series of surveys with women around the world in support of their crusade to champion natural beauty (see chapter 6).

● Online advertising heavily relies on word-of-mouth recommendations from friends and family (see below).

Getting consumers to trust commercial messages still poses a problem for advertising. However, in recent drives to forge personal relationships while simultaneously growing a cultural presence in taking on social awareness issues, brands are effectively establishing their position in everyday community lives as the glue that pulls networks together. Consumers are trusting brands more because of their personal experiences as much as their developing personable reputations.

People as independents versus people as messengers

In searching for new and effective media, it is widely understood that the most powerful ways to persuade are through friends, family and colleagues. For younger heavy users of the internet with their own web pages, attracting site sponsorship is often seen as a sign that they are regarded as influential, savvy consumers (Lindstrom, 2005). Their messages tend to have relevance to the brand

The packaging on *Innocent* products (above) has been developed as an embellishment of the advertising message, that the product is high-spirited and contains no additives.

being advertised – like celebrity endorsements but more personable and connected.

> **If I have web space, I'm basically a billboard waiting to happen.**

The rise in popularity of personal web space has mostly arisen because it is free. There is competition between large media-group-owned web spaces to attract new users even though customers are not tied to contracts. Instead of charging users, money is made from placing advertisements within a site, and sites such as *myspace.com* are ideal for advertisers because they attract huge volumes of passing *traffic*.

Social network platforms such as *MySpace* (see chapter 1) earn revenue from personal *blog* spaces by managing them as separate channels with sponsorship potential, for *banners* or word-search formatted adverts.

While the number of people involved with social networks may not be as high as television viewing figures, there is a more honed understanding of user interests because of the sites they are attracted to. If they find their way to a site, they have expressed an active interest and are likely to seek out similar material. Therefore related interests – commercial or not – are more likely to appeal to the right audience at the right time.

Personal web spaces provide an opportunity for personal expression. Their space is open to interpretation by users: the subjects discussed, tone of the text, background, images and soundtrack can express the individual personalities of the user. Web communities have strength in numbers – which makes them attractive to advertisers – and are still seen as communities built by independents for the people. Like television viewing, those engaging with social networks are likely to be in the same space for upwards of 30 minutes. They are a key component in the drive towards *user-generated content* because personal websites are created, edited and put out by members of the social network community.

However, the spirit of independence running through social network platforms is at odds with conventional notions of promotion. Advertisers often want total control of the advertising environment where, as with *mash-ups* and *user-generated content* advertising, the effectiveness of a commercial placement in personal web spaces depends in large part on how a consumer 'reframes' the advert in its new context.

Independent space versus branded space

One of the ironies of advertising online is that it tries to harness the most popularly seen content, which has often achieved fame because it has the spirit of complete independence. The pornography industry was the first to establish a model of paid-for content and adspace, and it has carried through to mainstream online

The 15 most popular networking/vertical community websites in 2006, which account for 80 per cent of social network visits online (source: *wikipedia.com*)

1	MySpace	Over 127m users, nearly 7 million new members monthly. NewsCorp-owned
2	Classmates	40m users ranging from school, higher education and military
3	Bebo	22m users and was the fastest-growing site in 2006
4	hi5	50m users worldwide
5	Xanga	40m users worldwide
6	Windows Live Spaces	Over 30m users
7	Friendster	Over 29m users worldwide. *Microsoft Network*-owned
8	Orkut	Over 26m invited users. *Google*-owned
9	BlackPlanet	Over 18m users, mostly African-American worldwide
10	CyWorld	Over 15m users, centred in South Korea
11	Friends Reunited	Over 15m users, *Independent Television* (*ITV*)-owned
12	Facebook	Over 8m college-centred users in the US alone. *Yahoo*-owned
13	LiveJournal	Over 10m users, partnered by *Six Apart*
14	Flickr	Over 8m users, mostly a photo sharing site
15	Faceparty	Over 6m users, mostly British youth, partnered by *Sony BMG*

commercial entertainment. The funding of co-created commercials or *user-generated content* has had to develop a fresh income model.

Revver.com, a video content sharing site, established a 50:50 site/content provider income split model, while *Google* and *MSN* earn revenue from click-through advertising (see chapter 7). However, the methods of deriving commercial income from independent platforms remains an open market without prescribed guidelines.

One of the biggest shared digital videos around global networks featured two Chinese students lip-syncing to a song by *The Back Street Boys*, '*I want it that way*'. It was seen by millions globally and featured on all the major video sharing platforms. Eventually the film became the basis of an independent website featuring follow-up mimes and copycat films posted from around the world. The site did not allow advertisements, and maintained its sense of ad-hoc, easily created independence. However, *adidas* benefited from unpaid-for *borrowed interest* in that the boys wore *adidas*-branded clothing in the promotion, and as the fame of the self-styled *Back Dormitory Boys* snowballed, they embarked on a sponsored tour in China. Eventually they re-created the stunt for a television commercial to capitalize on their fame.

Independent spaces such as unique stand-alone websites, digital video and *mash-ups* such as the *Diet Coke/Mentos Experiment* are not straightforward commercial platforms in that there is no overriding control for brands of how they will be portrayed, beyond basic association with the platform and message carrier. Yet this is often enough to be effective. As advertiser Patrick Collister remarked, '60 per cent of impact isn't what said but how you reach them'.

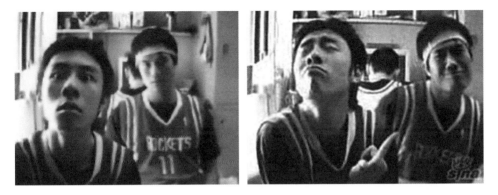

The Back Dormitory Boys from China, miming to a *Back Street Boys* song that earned them in excess of 100 million online viewers worldwide. Yet the platform was not sponsored.

With established service providers, advertising is becoming more of a science as the number of hits and profile of audiences can be clearly gauged. Unlike independent spaces, branded internet space can be assured of appropriate traffic, but is less likely to become an online icon.

The ideal: why it's good to get closer

There are many reasons why the convergence of communications channels is ideal, but perhaps the most significant is that all aspects of a multi-channel campaign can be managed centrally and 'wrapped' around target customers. When design, production and marketing strategies are integrated within a larger advertising solution, all consumer touch-points can be linked. This means that messages can be made relevant to a receptive audience, not repeated and can be received at a time appropriate to customers rather than advertisers. As Jean-Marie Dru, President and CEO of *TBWA*, noted, through digital means customers can now get closer to brands than before by interacting and experiencing brands directly, and they can gain immediate benefits on a customized basis (Dru, 2002). With person-to-person dialogues, messages can be read in real time and acted upon impulsively, rather than being diluted by the 'lag time' expected between seeing a commercial and being in a position to act on the message.

Using personalized communication will prove cost-effective. The shift to online advertising is in large part due to lower overall costs compared to media advertising. It is also where customers are tending to spend more time.

With the enhanced digital technologies available now, the linkage between advertising–branding–customer-experiences can be seamless. Many firms now operate outside their original domain by extending their range of services, distribution methods and events to involve customers. They have chosen not to adopt a predetermined 'roll-out' campaign, but allowing the brand–customer conversation to develop. Promotional strategies need to be fused with development strategies and remain not just media neutral but 'strategy flexible'. The role of advertising has increasingly become that of facilitator – no longer simply the bearer of messages.

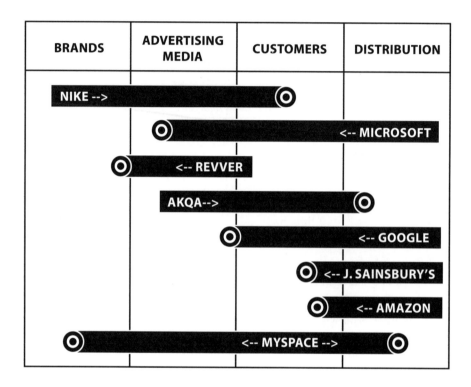

Where superbrands are moving to: the strategic direction of leading brands.

Summary

- More accurate customer profiling has created the possibility for advertising to get much closer to identified consumers.

- Major brands have attempted to make themselves synonymous with their areas of operation.

- Improvements in personal technology have created new and more accurate channels for advertisers to communicate, but effective strategies for communicating are still being defined.

- Since 1990, technology has helped advertisers reach customers in four phases:
  - phase 1: *talking to customers* through interactive broadcast, in-store, direct and online channels;
  - phase 2: stimulating *dialogue* through personal digital channels, SMS text and online virals;
  - phase 3: customer *involvement* through advergames and social interest groups by demonstrating corporate social responsibilities;
  - phase 4: brand *advocacy* through advertainment, customer-generated content and social networks.

- Using personal communication channels to reach customers can backfire if advertising methods are too intrusive, leave scope for misuse, are too big or too localized or if the response has not been anticipated correctly.

- Whether the capability of more information channels empowers customers or makes them more vulnerable is open to question.

- Even though advertisers can approach consumers personally, messages are mistrusted because it is still advertising. This is why brands have started to advertise through many different guises.

- The free-to-use ethos of personal web space is at odds with the aims of advertising.

10 Where advertising stops... and marketing begins

> **Wu Xiaobo (China)**: 'In China, advertising is part of marketing. We don't separate these two things. The "advertising" here means traditional advertising (TVC, magazine, newspaper, radio, etc.) and the "marketing" means new advertising methods and media (events, internet, MMS).'
>
> **David Droga (United States)**: 'Distraction and disruption is no longer an acceptable advertising model. Today to stay relevant brands need to connect with consumers on mutually beneficial terms.'
>
> **John Bartle (UK)**: 'What's changed is the definition of advertising. Marketing hasn't changed. But there's now a blur between advertising and communication – the terms are interchangeable. Advertising has encroached on other areas.'

This chapter maps out the perspectives of current advertising against the 'bigger picture' of modern communication.

Almost all books on advertising in the past decade have failed to address the rapid emergence of niche *ambient* methods, notably ambient or the somewhat dated term 'new media' advertising, meaning digital. This chapter takes a long view of the past decade to assess why advertisers and ad agencies are now equipped to take on chunks of promotion work that used to fall within the remit of marketing, public relations and clients' own boardrooms.

To do this, one first needs to consider changes in 'advertising work' and the organization of advertising practices. This has been the most significant shift in recent years.

Then and now: the 10 big shifts in advertising

	1987 'advertising's heyday'	1997 'industry in transition'	2007 'communications mix'
1	media advertisers McCann Erickson	above/below the line & integrated HHCL+ Partners	consultancies and specialist shops AKQA, @radical media
2	boom & bust	direct marketing & data boom	digital boom (+76% in 2005–8)
3	above or below the line work	media leads, direct marketing follows	integrated multimedia campaigns
4	commercial breaks (push)	mailers and events (push and pull)	niche and exclusive (pull)
5	awareness (broadcast)	dialogue (integrated channels)	involvement (multi-platform)
6	fear = recession & buyouts	fear = speed of change	fear = adapt or fold
7	consumer (demographics)	selector (by purchasing profile)	evangelist (by interest)
8	emotive selling proposition	niche selling proposition	personal interest
9	brand names, product-centred	brand symbols (*Nike, Sony*), brand and service-centred	branded interest groups, involvement
10	linear (pre-determined) narrative	hyper- (multiple) narratives	user-generated (unfixed) narratives

From agencies to consultancies (and other big shifts)

Perhaps the single biggest change in advertising has been to the way agencies have shaped to take on new work. In the mid-1990s advertising's trade press was filled with stories of takeovers and mergers, in which conglomerates took on a wider range of advertising hot shops, and established agencies bought up small specialist units – mostly direct marketing and specialist production units.

The new dynamic is for smaller specialist operations to drive their advertising work through one body of expertise – usually digital. They use customer insight to gauge how to reach customers and can consult with firms to assess how far their skills will benefit the particular requirements of a company. Because they have been founded on a more recent footing, the advantages they have over established agency set-ups include:

- flexible ways of working that integrate the clients in the process;
- being receptive to other aspects of a campaign – tapping into other media as campaigns progress;

- accountability – impact is easy to measure in terms of exact 'hits';
- a rolling workforce – bringing in freelance specialists as and when required means fewer fixed overheads;
- no need to maintain a wide base of production equipment – like the workforce, specialist kit need only be hired for specific tasks.

Therefore the past years have seen a challenge to the established 'agency' model. More of the smaller agencies are now capable of winning large advertising accounts, as the case studies in this book illustrate, with brands such as *Nike*, *Apple*, *BMW* and *Sega* using specialist single-media creative houses to drive launches.

Such a situation seemed unlikely in the years leading up to 2000, when production and service industries had been moving to bring strategic planning and creative work in-house. At one point brands such as *Heinz* in the UK and *Marlboro* in the United States drove their promotional budget through price promotion activities rather than advertising (*Marlboro Friday* discussed in Klein, 2000) while *Coca-Cola* employed a media consultant to deploy different promotional tasks to agencies rather than push most work to their main advertising agent.

With the rapid growth of new media, large advertising agencies have acknowledged that they need specialist programmers to construct campaigns and also specialist communicators to get the most from new media. Although larger agencies are attempting to embrace integrated and interactive work, putting the changes into practice is proving a challenge because it involves a fundamental change in their structure and personnel.

An overview of key changes

From awareness to involvement

The objective of television commercials is to raise awareness, where effectiveness has been measured in an audience's ability to recall specific advertisements. Direct marketing manages to go further. Reward card schemes in particular draw on data marketing activities to establish a dialogue with customers. The ability to profile individual customers through point of purchase and internet activity data has helped brands identify precisely the characteristics of their customers (see chapter 9). By advertising through the internet, data analysts can precisely monitor the visits a website receives and record the length of engagement. The potential has enabled advertisers to develop ever closer relationships with customers based on information for (on- and offline) consumption and online movement. As a consequence, online interest groups have developed into a main area of attention for advertisers because they require a personal level of interest and participation from individuals which is recordable through online data capture services. Advertisers use this information to develop an involved dialogue with their online customer base. A significant change in the function of advertising has been seen, from making customers aware to getting them involved in campaigns.

From product propositions on television to personal propositions and media convergence

Improved customer research has had a significant impact on the way advertising is carried out. For instance, most established creatives in advertising would have been trained to devise *unique selling propositions* (*USPs*). This involved shaping campaigns around distinguishing characteristics of the goods and services on offer and had been the prominent approach since the 1950s. In television commercials *USPs* often took the form of product testimonies or appeared in scenarios where the product was the star.

Commercial advertising appeared more sophisticated by the 1980s, when advertisers were often praised for their visual persuasion skills rather than rational advertising propositions. In an era that saw a boom in film and video techniques and the rapid growth of the pop video industry, emotive selling propositions emerged as a powerful selling tool. ESP placed emphasis on art direction, and its chief formats were print and broadcast television media. Both formats worked because the media could rely on being seen by big audiences.

One consequence of dwindling television audiences is that advertisers can no longer rely on a mass of viewers seeing one message at the same moment. This reduces the prospect of commercials being talked about. To overcome this, advertisers have devised what are often termed *convergent* means. This is where several formats are used at once and where the sequential order in which information is put out requires *convergent* programming. Formats tend to be selected around the researched habits of target audiences. If research shows targeted customers to be commuters, adverts might appear on their route to work, and if they are heavy internet users, online formats will be used.

The change in formats has also driven a change in the style of communication. Commercials had sometimes appeared like mini television programmes, with serial storylines and established characters developing over several years – the *OXO* family, *Nescafé* couple and *Barclaycard's* secret service man were famous examples in the UK. With converging cross-media campaigns the lifespan of a single approach tends to be shorter. There are now often several narratives running simultaneously through a campaign which are viewed in the order that consumers find them. The way commercials are constructed and the way they are read has therefore been one of the key shifts in advertising.

Another notable change has been in the way advertising strategies are devised. From the early 1990s advertisers have been able to shape promotional strategies around defined niche markets. Consumer planning, Insight research (see Chapter

8) and customer databases have enabled creatives to reconstruct more authentic representations of their intended consumers and scenarios for consumption. This has not stopped image-led agencies from continuing with more generalized product-based approaches: media agencies coined the term ISP in the late 1990s to mean *Irrational* Selling Propositions, where apparently unconnected but provocative juxtapositions drew attention. The *Levi's 501* campaign featuring *Flat Eric* was symptomatic of this 'off the wall' approach. Meanwhile data marketing and direct advertising agencies took *ISP* to mean *Individual* Selling Propositions. Supermarket reward scheme *Tesco Clubcard* is the most celebrated of this genre (see Humby, Hunt and Phillips, 2003).

Individual propositions embraced the idea of people being brand loyal, and online communications have allowed this approach to develop by creating more opportunities to engage (Schmitt, 1999). This has emerged with the development of niche interest websites, where engagement has taken the form of entertainment.

The fear factor in advertising: from mergers to the need to adapt

The factors driving change have also changed in recent years. During the 1980s, advertising industries in late-capitalist countries went through a period of rapid expansion, for which many agencies expanded their staff in response to a buoyant economy. The stock market collapse in 1987 led to a series of 'boom and bust' years. Some agencies went into liquidation, while others changed their operational model by cutting numbers of permanent staff and recruiting on sessional project contracts. There was a shift in emphasis in the 1990s, when mergers and takeovers dominated trade press headlines. Agencies feared being swallowed by larger groups and attempted to meet a diversifying communications market by buying smaller specialist (direct) advertising units. The fear that drove change in the 1990s was therefore the speed of technological change and need to stay relevant.

The speed of change is still driving agencies, although the technological development is faster than before and the potential of online digital interaction has emerged as the main threat to the status quo.

Now agencies risk losing clients that feel value for money is better achieved through one of the many options increasingly available. Agencies risk losing out to specialist shops, and some of advertising's biggest-spending clients have demonstrated in recent years that they are willing to split budgets and offer larger proportions of marketing budgets to small specialist advertising firms.

Rethinking customers: from consumers to selectors

As advertising has been able to observe its prospects more closely, there has been a shift from the broad notion of consumers as a homogeneous demographic mass.

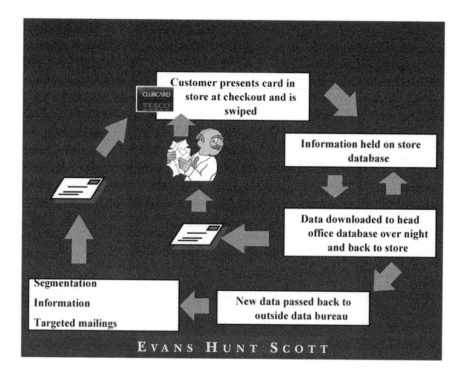

ISPs of the 1990s: mass media's *Irrational* Selling promotion (Flat Eric, part of the *Levi's Sta-Prest* campaign, 1999) and direct advertising's *Individual* Selling Proposition (*Tesco Clubcard*, 1993)

Many direct and online advertising agencies prefer the term *selector* because it more accurately describes people willing to exercise choice.

Customers are more empowered than ever before to shop around and choose from a plethora of products and services. A (mostly) deregulated online market aids this. Clients have to acknowledge this difference and, in turn, this puts more pressure on agencies to create a distinct market presence for their clients. The smarter agencies have homed in on what motivates customers: purchasing profiles can be formed to tap into personal interests as a means to get people involved. More often, however, people are drawn to promotional offers by getting customers to participate in competitions and 'added value' events such as those described in chapter 3, where there is more scope to involve customers and turn prospects into brand evangelists.

Phases in advertising, as characterized in the UK

	Incremental	Radical	Fundamental
Message	Beanz Meanz Heinz Heinz (Y&R 1967)	Labour Isn't Working Conservative Party (S&S 1979)	Your Country Needs You (War Office 1914)
Product	Iguana Benson & Hedges (CDP 1978)	I'd like to teach the world... Coca-Cola (McCann Erickson 1979)	Think Small Volkswagen Beetle (DDB 1965)
Brand	Slap Britvic Tango (HHCL 1992)	Swoosh Nike (various 1992)	iMac Apple (Chiat Day/ various 1999)
Service	Adventures Land Rover (WCRS/CJ 1993)	That'll be the Daewoo Daewoo (DFGW 1994)	Clubcard Tesco (EHS 1993)
Involvement	Subservient Chicken Burger King (CP+B 2004)	Run London Nike (AKQA 2001)	Mentos/Diet Coke Experiment User-generated (Revver 2006)

Convergence – all that is selling melts into advertising

> Advertising used to come under communication, which came under marketing.
> That's not the case any more – the terms are interchangeable.
>
> (John Bartle, co-founder, *Bartle Bogle Hegarty*)

Does advertising absorb all communications?

Throughout this book I have reasoned that *guerrilla* (*ambient*, stunts, stealth marketing), digital (new media, online) and direct methods (*direct* or *relationship marketing*) are in fact advertising. This is because they use techniques that are familiar to advertising practices and have been produced for the most part by advertisers. Even multi-channel advertising campaigns tend to converge through one uniting advertising idea, blurring approaches that were previously considered as separate *above-the-line*, *below-the-line* and *thru-the-line* projects.

There are many that would claim the examples in this book fall into sub-sections of marketing. Indeed, some texts have claimed that marketing and PR have become all-encompassing as advertising has dwindled (Godin, 1999; Ries and Ries, 2002; Zyman, 2002).

However, by *advertising* they tend to mean television, billboard and press advertising – and the drop in revenue for each over the years has been greatly exaggerated. Most books of this type have been written for the large, established marketing book category. Advertising books tend to be 'best of' anthologies or models of classic campaigns. With the convergence of practices, marketing texts already occupy much of the ground that I would argue advertising has moved into. It is therefore easier to map creative campaigns into pre-existing categories than review it for what it is – *advertising*. Most recent marketing texts have assumed that the rise of alternative platforms must detract from the established advertising systems. Rather, new platforms have clarified the purpose of older media channels. With online advertising, some film-based advertising shops have found new opportunities for their output.

Therefore my position stands: where a big advertising idea distils ideas into a single tangible message, the message carriers in their various media *are* versions of advertising. Whether people creating promotional content for whatever media have *brand consultant*, *marketing* or *communications* on their business cards, they are effectively advertisers.

> **Don't tell mum I'm in advertising. She thinks I play piano in a whore house.**
>
> **(Anon., widely quoted, thought to be French)**
> **(advertising quotes: www.advertising.utexas.edu/ research/quotes/q100.html)**

Part of the problem with using the title 'advertising' has been that it became a reviled term in the boom-and-bust years from the late 1980s.

It was during this time that brands started to challenge media commission levels and effectiveness of advertising, at a time when the advertising industries had elevated creative craft to the realms of an art form. One commercial for *Dunlop*, directed by star commercial film maker Tony Kaye, was lauded by the international advertising press as excellent advertising craft for its beauty rather than its ability to sell tyres. Like the *Dunlop* commercial, prominent campaigns for cars, computer games and fizzy drinks even made it into the collections of art galleries, where their purpose and funding were supposed to be geared to selling products. Understandably, marketing directors wanted to 'push the pound' and get better returns on their advertising investments. Hence new platforms such as direct advertising became more widely used as cheaper, more targeted but effective (if less celebrated) approaches.

The rapid establishment and success of direct advertising agencies dispelled the idea that advertising was simply a commercial art. With the use of customer databases, persuasive communication became repositioned in publications of the day as both a social and marketing science.

The dialogue around campaigns increasingly emphasized value for money and relationships with niche markets. However, *creative* ideas continued to underpin the strategies that drove successful campaigns.

At one point in the late 1990s *advertising* was inextricably linked with the term *branding* – which became a buzz word in the way that *design* did in the 1980s. In politics too, advertising has been seen as the answer to re-engaging voters. Before New Labour won the 1997 General Election, some of the country's leading lights were asked to contribute to communication strategies to an extent that was new to the UK. This approach may not be new in the United States – famously the American advertiser Rosser Reeves helped the Republican Party develop communication strategies in the 1970s. The nurturing of communication channels by 'communications specialists' in politics helped to make the management of information as newsworthy as the messages being communicated. To some extent this has made advertising appear more interconnected with all forms of mass message communication.

However, the image of advertising was also pigeonholed as an expensive luxury. Whereas data analysts could define the motivational sources in target markets, advertising was regarded as being obsessed with fame over message, image over sales, style over substance.

> **Advertising design, in persuading people to buy things they don't need, with money they don't have, to impress others who don't care, is probably the phoniest field in existence today.**
>
> **(Victor Papanek's famous tirade against advertising, in the 1984 book Design for the Real World)**

Two developments have revitalized the use of advertising skills in recent years:

1. The development of digital production technologies has meant that recording and editing can be done quickly. Some advertisements have been known to be conceived, produced and put out within a day, compared to an average of a month in the making in 1990.
2. The rise in popularity of pop promos and video channels has pushed the envelope of visual communication.

To create a fluid 'dialogue' of communication, as fast-moving as the pace of modern communications, *people* skills were needed as much as *technological* know-how. Advertising could 'speak' through popular media in a style and visual/written language that resonated with people. Therefore the speed of production and fashionability of fast visuals – two phenomena of the era – have had a rejuvenating effect on advertising.

How advertising has changed since the 1990s

Rather than choosing which route to take – advertising or marketing? – communication strategies have tended to integrate expertise and marketing/advertising platforms in campaigns. As the examples in this book demonstrate, one idea tends to run simultaneously across all media. *LynxJet*, a campaign in 2006 for *Axe Lynx* products in Australia, used as many as 25 different types of media in one promotion, ranging from commercials and stunts to websites and online games.

> **Art of advertising + science of data = integrated communication**

This is where the science and art of communication have come together: the *science* of data analysis can pinpoint niche audiences and provide information on motivational 'hotspots', but *creative* interpretation is still needed to use this information effectively. Put simply, people – not technologies – sell well because the appeal still involves tapping into human emotions.

However, while advertising skills are fundamental in current multi-platform communications, there has been a significant shift in approach. Strategies are moving from the '*push*' of information through broadcast and published messaging to the '*pull*' of networking, which involves drawing customers into websites, online services and membership schemes.

From the push of broadcasting to the pull of networking

This is because media that pull viewers in can appeal on a one-to-one basis, communicating through honed channels of interest relative to the targeted consumer. For instance, *pulling* techniques found on an online web page have a good chance of persuasion because customers have already had to engage by clicking their way to finding promotional content. Consumers are already in a click-and-find frame of mind. Broadcasting, which is perhaps the most famous *push* medium, has the ability to affect public attitudes towards brands and make them famous and relevant, but it does not have the penetration to distinguish consumers by anything other than broad demographics. When a broadcast advertisement is on air it disrupts viewers by pushing ideas at them. This has annoyed viewers to the extent that technological devices have been developed to cut out unwanted advertising interruptions (this is discussed in chapter 9). In a nutshell, pushing ideas is not as effective as pulling people in to find out more. Where the emphasis was previously on raising awareness, it is now moving to engagement.

Absorb	**Push media: *broadcasting, billboards, ambient***
Click & find	**Pull media: *narrowcasting, books, virals, blogs, mobile downloads, online sites, blogs***

Some of the biggest brands are moving their advertising spend towards pulling techniques. For instance, *Nike* does not use paid-for television space much. Instead it mixes channels to connect with its audience. It has built an online community site for football enthusiasts (www.nikefootball.com) and for runners (jogabonita.com; see also *Nike Run London*, chapter 4).

How far advertising will extend

> The client said yes.
> The building's management said no.
> The building's owners said no.
> The police department said no.
> The fire department said no.
> The public safety authorities said no.
> The advertising regulatory body said no.
> The ward office said no.
> The metropolitan government said no.
> The insurance companies said no.
> No, no, no, we said.
> Impossible is Nothing.
>
> (Shintaro Hashimoto, Hirofumi Nakajima, John Merrifield, *TBWA\Tokyo*)

The poem above summed up the difficulties staff at *TBWA\Tokyo* had in constructing the multi-award-winning *Gold on Gold: The Impossible Sprint*. The stunt featured a 100-metre vertical sprint tournament up two running tracks fixed on the side of skyscrapers in Tokyo and Osaka during the 2004 Olympics. It featured a sprint tournament. The event, in conjunction with *adidas*'s *Impossible is Nothing* campaign, attracted huge audiences in both cities. However, getting clearance for the event caused logistical problems on a number of levels – as the project's Creative Executive Officer John Merrifield remarked at the time,

The Impossible Sprint: a vertical sprint tournament staged by *adidas* up skyscrapers in Japan, held to coincide with the 2004 Olympics.

'Coming up with the idea and selling it to the client was a cinch. Making it happen aged me by about three years!'

Moving the boundaries of advertising is undoubtedly hard work and requires negotiation skills in bringing all stakeholders together and getting them to agree. The benefits are that such moves capture people's imagination in a way that usual media platforms no longer can.

The moon, the countryside, people and even imaginary spaces have at some time been used as advertising media by becoming re-appropriated spaces to project brands. However, while they may have drawn attention as alternative billboards they were not necessarily effective as advertising media.

As this book has highlighted, many big-budget campaigns now use a variety of media rooted together in conjunction with one core advertising message. Advertisers now speak of multimedia campaigns as *360 degree advertising*, where creative ideas can reach the target audience through any number of formats. This has had a major effect on the deployment of work within advertising agencies. While overall global advertising budgets are not increasing significantly, costs have become more widely spread so that a message will reach the target market through any number of avenues. Potentially, advertising platforms can be anything as long as they resonate with the target audience.

Now, in 2007, there is a variety of experimentation taking place with non-traditional (and often unconventional) spaces, services and personnel involved. The objective is to devise fresh and innovative ways to connect with the potential consumer. The thinking is that if the idea connects with the viewer, it will motivate them into *pulling* for more information. Rather than awareness, the aim is to instigate a dialogue to make people believe (and buy into) a brand.

Online advertising, discussed in chapters 5 and 6, is providing the main platform for the pursuit of interactive customer engagement.

The scope for advertising to grow

I have argued throughout this book that advertising now works best when it extends into new territories. The examples in chapters 1–6 show where advertising has managed to be absorbed within forms of popular entertainment. In many cases this has been driven in response to customers' mature advertising avoidance skills. The broadening of approach has given rise to a number of hybrid advertising–marketing techniques and roles such as *product placement*, branded *content* and *brand ambassadors* (see glossary).

While reliable sources such as *ZenithOptimedia* forecast a 6 per cent growth in global advertising spend during 2006, much of the rapid growth is expected in advertising on the internet (*ZenithOptimedia* predict a growth of 76 per cent between 2005 and 2008).

The platforms for advertising described in this book frequently benefit by not being immediately recognizable as advertisements. In other words, their advantage has been that their message has been understood before the messenger has

Formats that will expand advertising's thresholds, online and offline (see chapter 7)

Integrated campaigns:	one idea executed across multiple media
Branded entertainment:	television programmes, online *virals* and upload sites such as *YouTube*
Brand-based communities:	integrating within *social network channels*
Experiential marketing –	events, *advertainment* and new opportunities for customer involvement
Gaming:	*in-gaming, pre-gaming* and *advergaming*
Podcasting:	narrowcast audio and video streaming
Viral:	online and offline
User-generated content:	getting customers to enhance, add to or create advertising on an interactive platform
Cellphone:	*SMS text*, branded services and a variety of voice messaging methods
Digital brand platforms:	building awareness by devising unique presence online
Search platforms:	recognized search engines and social channels are establishing their own advertising formats, notably *Google, MSN* and *Yahoo*

Where advertising merges into culture

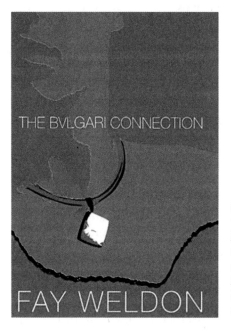

Sponsored fiction: in 2001 best-selling author Fay Weldon was sponsored by Italian jewellery firm *Bulgari* on the basis that in her next book the company's products receive no fewer than a dozen mentions. In the resulting book, *The Bulgari Connection*, scenes are set in *Bulgari's* London store and at one point one of its necklaces is described in lavish detail.

been revealed. Advertising therefore seems to be far more effective when it moves away from media that it has long been associated with. As long as the content is engaging and relevant to the interests of the target audience, it seems that advertising will be readily received as an adjunct to entertainment and information. As with broadcast advertising, if it is poor it will simply not register with people.

The new advertising landscape, where ads become icons

In the introduction I described an 'advertising colonized metropolis': how the Hong Kong metro system's pillars, escalators, steps, rails and trains became wrapped in advertising messages. Such visual noise serves only to increase people's resistance to the communicated world around them. Things that jump out are the contrasts – quiet spaces, natural, uncluttered and un-colonized by commercial communication. Paul Du Gay, *The Production of Cultures/Cultures of Production* (Du Gay, 2000), made a compelling case that advertising is so ingrained within the public consciousness that it has become an intrinsic part of popular culture (in this sense, *popular* means *mass*). Most people now assume that unsolicited messages they receive are selling something. Postal mail marked *urgent* often contains a 'last-minute exclusive offer', while mainstream TV entertainment in the West is 'brought to you, courtesy of' a sponsoring body. All forms of popular mass entertainment in the West are now moulded by advertising because entertainments are a powerful way of getting products seen in the right way – and films, music and sport are reliant on the funds sponsorship brings. In many respects entertainments are now more shaped as sponsorship opportunities than ever before. In particular, TV show formats have been designed to promote the viewing of advertisements in commercial breaks, while rap music actively adopts brands and seeks sponsorship in return for name checks in music lyrics.

MY ADIDAS
Artist: Run DMC
My *adidas*…
My *adidas*…
My *adidas*…
Now the *adidas* I possess for one man is rare/ myself homeboy got 50 pair
got blue and black cos I like the chill/ and yellow and green when its time to get ill
got a pair that I wear when I'm playin ball/ with the heal inside make me ten feet tall
my *adidas* only bring good news/ they're black and white, white with black stripe
the ones that I wear when I rock the mic…

GIN AND JUICE
Artist: Snoop Doggy Dogg
My homey Dr Dre came through with a gang of *Tanqueray*… (Source: *www.hiphopcity.com*)

One of the most successful placement platforms has proved to be music. While films have placed and name-checked brands for years, East and West Coast rap from the 1980s looped in brand promotions to such an extent that brands figure in glossaries of 'rap' terms.

Charles Leadbeater in *Living on Thin Air* (Leadbeater, 1999) remarked that the movement of ideas in online communications had become the new global economy. However, the problem he outlined was that fiscal systems are geared to measuring *gross national product* in terms of physical distribution – bricks rather than clicks. Many of Leadbeater's concerns have been resolved as the major online powers – high-volume-traffic sites such as *Google, eBay, Amazon* and *MySpace* – have devised secure purchasing systems and revenue flows. Once the masses gained confidence in online financial services, the 'new economy' had a scale of trade to give it global commercial credence.

The advertising industries have a huge role to play in the development of the internet as a communication tool, which is why, according to the *Financial Times* (UK), the amount advertisers spend on online advertising will overtake that spent on national newspapers in 2007.

Where culture merges into advertising

With the growth of the *user-generated content* phenomenon, it is becoming increasingly hard to distinguish between advertising and everyday unusual happenings. Formats familiar to advertising are often being used to make little more than cleverly engineered moments of interest. Similarly, many people have realized that creating new media platforms can be a way of earning quick money, as long as they figure out a way of getting lots of people to take notice.

Here are just a few 'happenings' that have helped to blur the boundaries between advertising and everyday life:

- *Lobbying*: When an agency decided they could raise greater awareness for the plight of London's homeless by making an event rather than advertising, they circulated a message through homeless communities to head for a billboard site near the city centre on a particular date. At the site, they were provided with free soup and clothing. As word spread, many homeless people made their way to the site, news agencies sent photographers and the event helped to illustrate the scale of the problem in a single image. Photographs of the stunt proved to be a useful graphic tool for lobbyists.

- *Platform*: Adam Tims, a student from Nottingham University, offered every pixel on what he described as his $1 million website for sponsorship. In the event he generated his $1 million and because the concept was so unique, he attracted enough press coverage to make sponsorship worth while.

- *Art:* Artist Simon Poulter sent out promotional flyers and approached press and television companies to promote a forthcoming financial scheme, *UK: Ltd*, which offered shares in the ancient British monument Stonehenge. The campaign made national headlines and caused much indignation until it was revealed as a spoof, designed to show how such outrageous schemes could seem plausible today.

- *Message*: A frustrated housewife, known only as 'Emily', hired a billboard on Hollywood's Sunset Boulevard to announce to 'Steven' that 'I know all about her, you dirty, sneaky, immoral, unfaithful, poorly-endowed slimeball. Everything's caught on tape. Your (soon to be-ex) Wife'. She succeeded in letting the world know: the 'divorce billboard' made news as far as London, China and Australia. The end line read 'P.S. I paid for this billboard from OUR joint bank account'. It later transpired that the same billboard appeared in Brooklyn and Chicago and bore an uncanny similarity to the synopsis of a show on *Court TV* in the United States.

- *Prank*: A marketing designer known by his eBay user name, *Twinklydog*, entered a bogus ad on the trading site. In the 560-word seller's description he offered two wedding invitations, which included 'a sit-down meal in a four-star restaurant and an evening of serious boozing' to the highest bidder and described the bride and her mother in rather unflattering terms. While the bids reached into many thousands of pounds, it was assumed that the bidders, like the advert, were fake. Having attracted international press coverage, the 'sale' was withdrawn with another made-up press story – it was claimed that *Twinklydog* was still in love with the bride-to-be.

All of the above succeeded in arresting attention and all could – and should – be thought of as a form of advertising in the same way as big-budget campaigns. Their success in creating jarring juxtapositions of media and message has led many marketing directors to consider how best to reposition their advertising outside familiar frames.

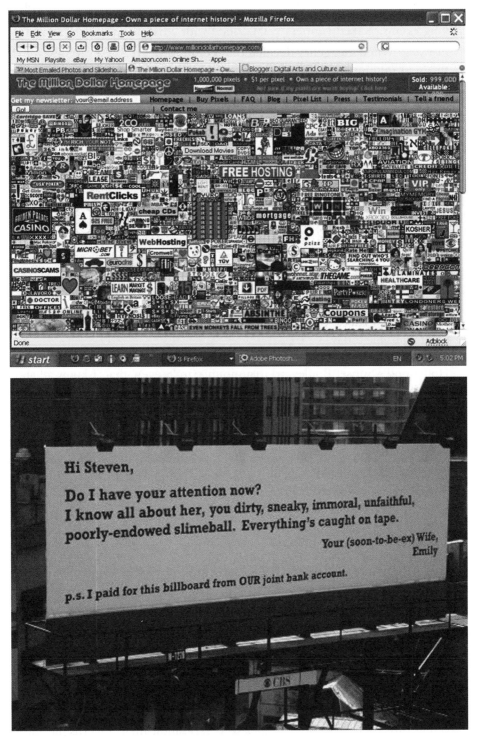

Top: the $1m website, Nottingham 2005. Bottom: wife announcing pending divorce to husband on a billboard, California 2006.

However, opportunist 'advertising' has become a near regular feature at major sporting events. Naked runners emblazoned with advertising slogans and brand caricatures in sporting crowds strategically positioned in camera shot may make television cameras for a split second – enough to be noticed. However, the success of novel approaches tends to work only once.

The late marketing guru Mark McCormack, founder of *IMC* and agent of many sporting superstars, famously jumped on stage after his client Arnold Palmer had won a golfing tournament to turn the label of the winner's bottle of champagne away from camera: Palmer was not receiving revenue from the champagne sponsors. As advertisements become icons and grow out of their old advertising spaces, the battle for who owns viewing spaces and places will intensify – online and offline. Therefore one can comfortably claim that advertising has become so deep-rooted in popular culture that one must accept it as 'given'.

Where ads are our icons, all space is adspace.

Summary

- As advertising techniques have become increasingly essential to most commercial communication platforms, the remit of advertising has extended into marketing and public relations activities.

- Effective multimedia advertising fuses the science of defining markets with the art of advertising communication.

- Advertising has moved on greatly since the 1990s because it uses a far wider variety of advertising channels.

- Advertising is shifting in its approach from *pushing* messages to *pulling* customers towards information.

- Following the development of digital technologies, the dynamic generated by convergence of skills has generated a fresh range of original creative solutions.

- Digital media are becoming the places where advertising formats are developing the quickest.

- The most effective advertising tends not to look like adverts.

- Advertising is blurring into forms of entertainment and information, while the style and language of advertising is finding its way into everyday communication.

- Stunts generally have only one life before they cease to be effective.

- New advertising spaces, whether online or offline, will be actively pursued to re-engage an increasingly resistant, ad-conditioned customer.

- There will be fierce competition for new advertising spaces.

Glossary of terms

advergame An online bespoke game that has incorporated a brand or product within its content. This sometimes takes the form of *in-game* or *pre-game advertising*.
advergaming Usually part of a broader advertising campaign.
advertainment A promotional technique where an advert is packaged as entertainment. Usually associated with online or branded *content* programming.
advertorials Magazine or television programmes where the content contains a promotion for goods or services.
adware Software downloaded onto computers that displays ads based on the user's computing activities. Some software collects customer data based on computer habits. Often called 'spyware'.
ambient Branded spaces and artefacts used to promote in everyday environments. They usually use surprise tactics and use their space as a context to work effectively. Also called *stealth* advertising.

banners The masts on a web page, often used as a platform for an ad message. The horizontal equivalent of *skyscrapers*.
below-the-line Advertising work that fell below the 15.5 per cent commission level in the 1990s. Now a term used to describe direct mail and other non-mass-media advertising.
blinks Small bits of film, lasting between one and two seconds, slotted into an advert break. Most commonly used to promote forthcoming television shows.
blipverts See *opticals*: television or computer adverts that flash up unannounced, then vanish. They are usually short 'bumper ads' (promotional spots), approx 1 second long, that usually fall outside conventional commercials and after programme *idents*. They are most commonly used to plug programmes.
blog Personal online diaries often on personal websites, social network space and internet chatroom sites, often used for online discussions. Such sites usually draw like-minded internet users.

bluecasting   An electronic billboard picks up signals from Bluetooth telephones, and switches on when you are in range. The medium aims to target digital technology users and *early adopters* (stemmed from the Netherlands).

borrowed interest   A promotion that uses the existing popularity or reputation of other advertising: a campaign that draws on capital created by another campaign.

brand ambassadors   Celebrities, company representatives or assistants that have been briefed/trained to represent a brand. They are designated spokespeople for the product/production company.

brand DNA   The essence of a brand, from which all aspects of a brand's identity can be developed.

brand equity   The existing value, worth or establishment of a product, service or company.

brand evangelists   Customers that choose to be loyal to a brand and are happy to speak up on its behalf. Also called *brand champions* or *brand advocates*.

brand extension   Stretching an existing ad campaign or identity into another field or product range. Where a theme is developed in a different medium.

brand salient   A campaign strategy that aims to enhance the reputation and standing of a brand, usually by organizing a campaign around existing customers.

brown or black goods   Audio/visual electrical or digital goods such as stereos, televisions and radios.

bumpers   Short ads, or *idents*, that bracket a programme with ad product or brand promotion, resulting from programme sponsorship. Sometimes called *buffers*.

burst   A launch campaign that aims to maximize awareness of the new product or brand advertised.

buzz marketing   Information disseminated by *word-of-mouth* as 'must see' content, usually online.

C2C   Customer to customer, word-of-mouth *peer-to-peer*.

call to action   The aspect within an advert that explains what its purpose is. It tells the advertiser what their advertising proposition is, and in an advert it tells the viewer what they should do.

character migration   Brand caricatures or personalities designed for adverts that have a lease of life outside a campaign. When a brand icon – usually a person or cartoon – becomes popular it can represent the brand beyond the frame of an advert.

click-throughs   Name given to online consumers who click on key-word advertising URL links.

communications mix   A collection of different types of advertising media coordinated to work in a campaign. Also called multimedia advertising.

content snacking   A term used to describe browsing internet users dipping in and out of websites and other online spaces.

convergence   A term commonly used to describe the mixed use of above-the-line, *below-the-line*, broadcast, narrowcast, online and offline advertising techniques.

conversions The term given to customers who *click-through* advertising links then follow up on advertising messages.

corporate social responsibility A requirement of firms to demonstrate that they are accountable for, and active in, the fields in which they operate.

direct advertising Materials that target the customer at home, usually by name. The most common forms are money-off vouchers, offer letters, magazine inserts and flyers.

disruptive advertising Commercials that involve a break in the viewer's choice of listening or viewing, usually incorporated in mass media. TV and radio broadcast ads are the most common formats.

early adopters Label given to consumers that are quick to find out about, and buy into, new goods and services. They feed their knowledge and experiences through to their friends, the 'mid-' and 'late-adopters'.

endline The punchline at the end of a commercial which usually contains the advert's central message. Also called a 'strapline'.

experiential Opportunities for customers to interact, thereby getting first-hand experience of a product, service or brand. The term was coined by Bernd H Schmitt in his book *Experiential Marketing* (1999).

fast-moving consumer goods (FMCG) Often used to describe goods that have a quick turnover or short shelf-life, such as confectionery.

filter advertising Public activities designed to get noticed and channel attention to a product, service or brand.

flash ads Also called 'pop-ups'. Adverts that pop up in front of a selected web page.

flash stores Stores for exclusive brand ranges that open in rented spaces, usually in urban capitals, for a very brief time then disappear before they become mainstream. The device is often used by exclusive fashion brands. See also *guerrilla stores*.

footfall The increased amount of people going into a store as a result of a campaign, used as a measure if the client is retail.

full service agency An advertising group offering a complete range of advertising mass media, *direct* and digital advertising approaches.

gaming Electronic games, which are often generated as *viral* ads, or carry adverts within their content.

glocal A global campaign tailored to local (or national) markets.

guerrilla advertising Another term for stunt or ambient advertising that uses shock tactics, usually in a live event, to make an impression on consumers.

guerrilla stores Similar in concept to *flash stores*, they aim to be exclusive (term sometimes used is 'massclusive') and aim for an *early-adopter*-only following. They tend to close down before reaching the mainstream.

hatched brand   Placement of brands or products in television programmes or film.
hooks   Content in advertising designed to motivate the target audience.

idents   Mini-advert programme sponsorships that are placed between television programmes and an ad break. They brand the programme content.
in-game   An online game that has a brand integrated or name-checked within its content. For instance, an advert that appears within the set of the game.
infomercial   Programme content where the editorial provides consumer information containing a brand or product promotion. Usually associated with online or brand content advertising.
Information Age   A broad term used to describe the revolution in internet, mobile communications, e-commerce activity. The term is often used to describe what cultural commentators call the Post-Industrial Age.
interactive TV   Cable and satellite TV services allow viewers to respond to programme content or commercials by using the buttons on a remote control.

junk mail   Unwanted leaflets and letters, received via the mail service or through door drops. Often referred to as *direct advertising* or direct mail.

mash-ups   1. Internet users making their own video content or reusing existing versions and uploading them to websites. 2. A term referring to the fusion of existing programs with new software to design new interactive features.
media advertising   Television, cinema and radio commercials, billboards and print adverts in the popular press and magazines. The most established.
MMS   Multimedia (digital) messaging.
multichannel   Refers to a mix of new and old media formats, on- and offline.

narrowcasting   Communications – mostly radio or internet – transmitted to a small span of recipients, usually defined by specialist content.
new media   A term usually taken to mean digital advertising, but often describes any new platform for communication that does not use *traditional media*.

one-to-one   Direct dialogue with targeted consumers, person-to-person messaging, usually practised by *direct advertising* firms to address consumers directly. Also used to describe 'company-to-individual' approaches.
online advertising   A term that is used to describe a range of advertising that uses the world wide web. It includes websites, *virals*, e-mail messages, banners and pop-ups.
online community   Social networks of interest groups and personal *blog* sites that correspond over the internet.
opticals   See *blipverts*: programme brand frames, usually aired for one second, slotted between programme content, *bumpers* and a commercial break. In the United States and UK they tend to be used to remind viewers of forthcoming programmes.

P-marketing   'Permission marketing', where customers receive benefits for receiving commercial messages. Coined in Seth Godin's *Permission Marketing* (1999).

peer-to-peer   Passing information on from person to person, *c2c*, word-of-mouth, usually by way of product endorsement.

pitch   The process most agencies go through to win new advertising business. Strategies and suggestions are presented at pitch stage in a bid to win the account from other agencies.

platform   A space or artefact that is used as an advertising medium.

podcast   Narrowcast audio transmissions from networks or individuals, in a similar form to that of radio stations. Transmissions can be live-streamed or uploaded online.

pop-ups   See *flash ads*.

pre-game   An advert that appears before a digital game starts, as the game is downloading.

product placement   A technique where a brand, product or service is positioned or mentioned within a non-advertising medium – usually a film, broadcast or book.

product testimony   Word-of-mouth recommendation about a product/service, best delivered by someone whose opinion you trust and respect. Regarded as one of the best forms of advertising communication.

promiscuous consumers/consumption   Customers who vary their buying habits and seek the best deals by playing competing brands off against each other. Usually motivated by special offers.

prospects   Potential customers targeted because previous consumption habits suggest they are likely to be interested in the goods advertised.

pull   Media that draw in consumers to find out more information. Includes digital and personal modes of communication. A term used to describe the opposite to *push* tactics.

push   Media that send out or broadcast information to push the consumer. Includes broadcast (TV, cinema and radio), billboards and some *guerrilla advertising* activity. A term used to describe the opposite to *pull* tactics.

reality advertising   Promotional content in a way that is not re-created but drawn from everyday footage, often live and in real time, to communicate in an advert.

relationship marketing   Advertising through personal address, establishing a dialogue between advertiser/product and consumer.

repertoire buying   Consumers' habitual choice of brand from a range of products competing in the same market. Decisions that people automatically make at the point of purchase.

ROI   'Return on investment': the conversion rate of viewers to customers.

roll-out   The plan of action for a campaign designed to unravel over a period of time. Sometimes used to denote the campaign start date.

roster   List of agencies working on different aspects of a brand or product's overall campaign.

sample mounts   Free music CDs or film/programme DVDs that are used to promote other products, usually newspapers or magazine (mostly UK).

scamps   Rough drawings on layout sheets that creative teams use to present their concepts during the early creative stages of an ad campaign. This is the preferred mode of initial presentation by most advertising agencies.

search marketing   A skill of using search engines as an advertising tool. Search engines are the first point of contact for brands online, so finding listed links is itself an advertising opportunity.

selectors   Often used to describe advertising-conscious, promiscuous customers, because the term 'consumer' is deemed to be too passive.

self-liquidating promotion   A campaign that has a built-in obsolescence; a project that contains its own end point.

skyscrapers   Paid-for adverts that run up along the side of content on websites. The vertical equivalent of *banners*.

SMS text   Short Messaging Service, word-based communications sent via mobile phone. Advertisers tend to add links to text messages which make replying easier.

snacking   Views online habits of surfing the internet, flitting through content and sampling short bits of interest. This is often assumed to take place on work breaks.

social network channels   Web chatrooms or specialist sites where people with similar interests can share views.

social network spaces   Media platforms designed for web users to create their own communication spaces. Such sites attract huge volumes of *traffic* and are therefore an attractive proposition for advertisers.

spam filter   Unsolicited e-mails containing adverts filtered as junk mail away from inboxes.

spamdexing   Creating the impression in search engines that a website generates more hits than it actually does. Devices used to dupe consumers into thinking sites are more popular than they are because they appear towards the top of internet searches.

strap line   The final line in a commercial, the core copy and idea holding an advertising campaign together. Also called an *endline*.

sub-brand   A marque or product identity that is promoted separately from its parent brand: a follow-on product range marketed independently.

subcultural capital   Term used to describe the aim of promotions at dance, club and festival events targeting alternative and counter-cultures. Coined by Sarah Thornton in *Club Cultures* (1995).

subviral   distributed digital video of uncertain origin; footage that conceals if it is authorized messaging.

tagging   A term used when adverts are hooked to the end of digital videos. This has become a means of online advertising, via *virals* and *advertainment*.

teaser   A pre-promotion stunt or piece of publicity put out to stoke interest in the imminent launch of a product or campaign. Often called a 'taster'.

ten-minute break-time   The supposed work-break time during a day when people habitually surf the net and check out, tag, play and send online entertainment.

third party association   Two existing brands joining forces to create a joint promotion. This method is usually used when the brands share fields but are not competing products, such as fizzy drinks and food products in leisure environments.

three hundred and sixty degree promotion   A campaign that fuses broadcast and narrowcast techniques in a multimedia approach to advertising.

through-the-line   A neutral approach to advertising that can use mass media and direct advertising approaches.

traditional media   A term used to describe established media advertising platforms, notably television and cinema commercials, radio, press and billboard adverts.

traffic   The name given to someone with the role of managing the advertising process at an agency. They time-manage stages of a campaign and ensure that work is delivered on time. Also a term used to describe the volume of information moving through a communication channel.

transvisuals   Large screens carrying silent films or commercials. Usually found in transport stations or mounted onto buildings in major cities (mostly United States, China, UK).

user-generated content   1. Material generated by internet users. 2. Web space that allows people to engage others with similar interests, which currently includes *podcasts*, *blogs* and digital video.

video advertising   Commercials filmed and compressed into various formats for use through a variety of channels, including online and mass media.

video on demand (VOD)   Online adverts, *QuickTime* movies or *Mpegs* that can be uploaded at the time of viewer's choosing. Videos are put on website browsers for people to see at leisure.

virals   Branded internet commercials or games that are shared on the internet.

webisode   A term that has developed for online programmes put out exclusively on branded websites. Instalments are designed to encourage people to register and log on.

white goods   Domestic appliances such as fridges, washing machines and dishwashers.

wobblers   Advertising signage found in shops and supermarkets, usually suspended on shelves and ceilings.

word-of-mouth   Messages passed on from person to person by way of recommendation. Such *buzz* techniques are often used to make messages relevant across niche markets.

Bibliography

Introduction

Aitchison, J (1999) *Cutting Edge Advertising*, Prentice Hall, London

Bannister, L (26 August 2005) *Why TV Advertising Will Never Die*, Campaign, Haymarket Press, London

Butterfield, Leslie, ed (1999) *Excellence in Advertising*, Butterworth-Heinemann, Oxford/Institute of Practitioners in Advertising

Hallberg, G (1995) *All Consumers Are Not Created Equal: The differential marketing strategy for brand loyalty and profits*, J Wiley, New York

Mendoza, M (1 July 2005) MPG managing partner in Campaign, Haymarket Press, London

Smith, PR and Taylor, Jonathan (1993) *Marketing Communications: An integrated approach*, Kogan Page, London

Chapter 1

Aho Williamson, D (2006) Report: *Social Network Marketing: Carving out some MySpace*, emarketer (online), New York [emarketer.com] (accessed August 2006)

Anon. How to boost your AdSense revenue www.associateprograms.com/search/adsense.shtml (accessed August 2006)

Arango, T (23 July 2006) *$ky's the limit; Sun Valley Buzz boosts YouTube toward $1bn*, New York Post online edition, NYP Holdings, New York (accessed August 2006)

Battelle, John (2005) *The Search: How Google and its rivals rewrote the rules of business and transformed our culture*, Nicholas Brealey, London

Chan, K and McNeal, JU (November 2003) *Regulation of Children's Advertising in China*, Dunedin, New Zealand

Handy, C (2001) *The Elephant and the Flea*, Hutchinson, London

Heath, J and Potter, A (2005) *The Rebel Sell: How the counterculture became consumer culture*, Capstone, Sussex

Japan Advertising Review Organization (JARO) *The History and Current Activities of the Japan Advertising Review Organization Inc.* www.jaro.or.jp (accessed July 2004)

Leonardi, D (April 2004) *Self-regulation and the Broadcast Media: Availability of mechanisms for self-regulation in the broadcasting sector in countries of the EU* www.selfregulation.info/iapcoda/0405-broadcast-report-dl.pdf

Lindstrom, M (2005) *Brand Sense: How to build powerful brands through touch, taste, smell, sight and sound*, Kogan Page, London

Reuters, New York (11 July 2006) MySpace *gains top ranking of US Web sites* (accessed August 2006)

Saatchi, M (June 2006) Single word branding, paper delivered to Cannes Advertising Festival, Cannes. Summary presented on www.onewordequity.com (accessed September 2006)

Sweney, M (23 May 2006) MySpace searches for revenue, Guardian.co.uk

Swift, A (23 June 2006) http://www.crikey.com.au/articles/2006/06/23-1547-3275.html (accessed August 2006)

Vise, DA (2005) *The Google Story*, Bantam Dell, New York

Chapter 2

Bond, J and Kirchenbaum, R (1998) *Under the Radar: Talking to today's cynical consumers*, J Wiley, New York

Bull, M (2002) The seduction of sound in consumer culture, *Journal of Consumer Culture*, **2**, pp. 81–101

Charlick, S, London Underground Technical Specialist Manager, quoted on www.london-underground.blogspot.com (accessed June 2006)

Lindstrom, M (2005) *Brand Sense: How to build powerful brands through touch, taste, smell, sight and sound*, Kogan Page, London

Ries, A and Ries, L (2002) *The Fall of Advertising and the Rise of PR*, HarperCollins, New York

Schmitt, BH (1999) *Experiential Marketing*, Free Press, New York

Smith, PR and Taylor, J (1993) *Marketing Communications: An integrated approach*, Kogan Page, London

Steinbock, D (July/August 2005) How marketers can exploit new mobile services, *Admap*, World Advertising Research Center, New York

Chapter 3

Design & Art Direction (2001) *Creativity Works: Irreverent Britart.com*, D&AD in association with Royal Mail and The Design Council, supported by the Institute of Practitioners in Advertising, London

Dru, JM (1996) *Disruption: Overturning conventions and shaking up the marketplace*, J Wiley, New York

Suggested further reading

Godin, S (2006) *Small is the New Big: And 193 other riffs, rants, and remarkable business ideas*, Penguin, New York

Kaden, RJ (2006) *Guerrilla Marketing Research*, Kogan Page, London

Mikunda, C (2006) *Brand Lands, Hot Spots and Cool Places*, Kogan Page, London

Chapter 4

Brown, S (1998) *Postmodern Marketing 2: Telling tales*, Routledge, London

Dru, JM (2002) *Beyond Disruption*, J Wiley, New York

Julier, G (2000) *The Culture of Design*, Sage, London

Chapter 5

Anon (17 June 2005) *The Art behind The Art of the H3ist*, Motor Trend, Primedia, US online http://www.motortrend.com/features/auto_news/112_news050617audi/ (accessed July 2006)

Gladwell, M (2005) *Blink: The power of thinking without thinking*, Little, Brown, New York

Kirby, J and Marsden, P, ed (2006) *Connected Marketing*, Butterworth-Heinemann, Oxford

Lucas, G and Dorrian, M (2006) *Guerrilla Marketing: Unconventional brand communication*, Laurence King, London

Martina/Permalink (1 February 2006) *Integrated Marketing: 5 seconds of fame*, *adverblog.com*, online: http://www.adverblog.com/archives/cat_integrated_marketing.htm (accessed August 2006)

Peters, S (26 June 2005) *'Art of the H3ist' Finale Set for Wednesday*, Alternative Reality Gaming Network, La Broquerie, MB, Canada online, http://www.argn.com/archive/000284art_of_the_h3ist_finale_ set_for_wednesday.php (accessed July 2006)

Ward, C (30 June 2005) *The Art of the H3ist Wrap-up and Review*, Alternative Reality Gaming Network, La Broquerie, MB, Canada online: http://www.argn.com/archive/000285the_art_of_the_h3ist_wrap-up_and_ review.php (accessed July 2006)

Wong Bryan, N (26 January 2004) *More and More, Marketers Got Game*, iMedia Communications Inc, USA online: http://www.imediaconnection.com/content/2699.asp (accessed August 2006)

Chapter 6

Gladwell, M (2000) *The Tipping Point: How little things can make a difference*, Little, Brown, New York

Leadbeater, C (1999) *Living on Thin Air: The new economy with a blueprint for the 21st century*, Viking, London

Lindstrom, M (2003) *Brand Child*, Kogan Page, London

Chapter 7
Sources cited at end of chapter 7.

Chapter 8
Brierley, S (1995) *The Advertising Handbook*, Routledge, London

Kirby, J and Marsden, P (ed 2006) *Connected Marketing*, Butterworth-Heinemann, Oxford

Packard, V (1957) *The Hidden Persuaders*, David McKay, New York

Reeves, R (1961) *Reality in Advertising*, Alfred A Knopf, New York

Chapter 9
Anon (12 May 2004) *Hoover's free flights fiasco recalled*, published on UK White Goods Ltd, online http://www.ukwhitegoods.co.uk/modules.php?name= News&file=article&sid=70 (accessed September 2006)

DoubleClick Report 'The Decade in Online Advertising 1994–2004' available at Doubleclick.com (knowledge central section, accessed May 2006)

Dru, JM (1996) *Disruption: Overturning conventions and shaking up the marketplace*, Wiley, New York

Glaister, D (9 September 2006) Cult blog a fake, admit 'lonelygirl' creators, *The Guardian*, The Guardian Newspapers Ltd, London

Godin, S (1999) *Permission Marketing*, Simon & Schuster, New York

Handy, C (2002) *The Elephant and the Flea: Looking backwards to the future*, Arrow/ Random House, London

Humby, C, Hunt, T and Phillips, T (2003) *Scoring Points: How Tesco is winning customer loyalty*, Kogan Page, London

Lindstrom, M (2005) *Brand Sense: How to build powerful brands through touch, taste, smell, sight and sound*, Kogan Page, London

Schmitt, BH (1999) *Experiential Marketing*, Free Press, New York

Thornton, S (1995) *Club Cultures: Music, media and subcultural capital*, Polity, Cambridge

Whitehead, J (19 July 2006) *A-list celeb endorsements not trusted, survey finds*, Brand Republic, Haymarket Press, London

Chapter 10
Godin, S (1999) *Permission Marketing*, Simon & Schuster, New York

Grande, C (29 May 2006) Net ad spend poised to overtake national press, Financial Times, Financial Times Ltd, online www.us.ft.com/ftgateway/super-page.ft? news_id=fto052920061706070914 (accessed August 2006)

Humby, C, Hunt, T and Phillips, T (2003) *Scoring Points: How Tesco is winning customer loyalty*, Kogan Page, London

Klein, N (2000) *No Logo*, Flamingo, London

Leadbeater, C (1999) *Living on Thin Air: The new economy with a blueprint for the 21st century*, Viking, London

Ries, A and Ries, A (2002) *The Fall of Advertising and the Rise of PR*, HarperCollins, New York

Schmitt, BH (1999) *Experiential Marketing*, Free Press, New York

Zyman, S (2002) *The End of Advertising as We Know It*, J Wiley, New York

Recommended websites

www.adverblog.com

www.ambient-planet.com

www.artifact.ac.uk

www.brandrepublic.com

www.cunningwork.com

www.creativeclub.co.uk

www.eatmail.tv (viaCakemedia.com, 2 August 2006)

www.ifyourmindwasaroom.net

www.proquest.com

www.superbrands.org

www.thereel.net

www.bandt.net

www.tbtrade.com

www.detnews.com

www.asa.org.uk

www.r&y.com

www.adweek.com   best spots of September 2004

www.craikjones.com

www.carpages.co.uk/land_rover

www.bestdmever.com

www.glamslamentertainments.com/shotgirls.htm

www.statistics.gov.uk

www.smirnoffexperience.com

www.myvillage.co.uk/pages/health-nike-run.htm

www.reports.mintel.comMintel Group Ltd. '2002 Vision Tomorrow's Consumer', March 02; 'Effectiveness of Advertising and Promotion in Financial Services', April 04

www.tescolegalstore.comwww.tesco.com

www.vma.ac.uk/vastatic/microsites/brandnew_site/flashframe

Index